Great Western Railway

ANDREW RODEN is a railway journalist and campaigner now based in Cornwall. He has worked on a range of railway magazines over the past 10 years from *Rail* to *Hornby Magazine* and the prestigious *International Railway Journal*. In 2005 he led the campaign to save the 'Night Riviera' sleeper train to Cornwall from closure. His previous books *Flying Scotsman* and *The Duchesses* (both published by Aurum) were highly acclaimed, and he is a regular writer and broadcaster on transport matters across the South West.

www.andrewroden.com

D1340865

520 733 29 X

This book is dedicated to George Behrend, 1922–2010, that Great Writer of Railways who cast a spell over me and many thousands of others with that marvellous evocation of a long gone age, Gone With Regret. *I was lucky enough to meet George some years ago shortly after the campaign to save the 'Night Riviera' had been won. His expertise, wide-ranging knowledge and crystal-clear memories provided all of us present with an unforgettable afternoon. He will be missed very greatly by all who knew him.*

GREAT WESTERN RAILWAY

RAILWAY

A History

ANDREW RODEN

First published 2010 by
Aurum Press Limited
7 Greenland Street
London NW1 0ND
www.aurumpress.co.uk

This paperback edition first published in 2012 by Aurum Press Ltd.

A catalogue record for this book is available from the British Library.

ISBN 978 1 78131 015 1

10 9 8 7 6 5 4 3 2 1
2017 2106 2015 2014 2013 2012

Typeset by SX Composing DTP, Rayleigh, Essex
Printed and bound in Great Britain by CPI Group (UK) Ltd., Croydon, CR0 4YY

Contents

Rules

Employees MUST —

  (i) *see that the safety of the public is their chief care under all circumstances.*

 (ii) *be prompt, civil and obliging, afford every proper facility for the Company's business, give correct information, and, when asked, give their names or numbers without hesitation.*

(iii) *when on duty be neat in appearance, and, where supplied, wear uniform, number and badge.*

(iv) *if required, make good any article provided by the Company when damaged by improper use on their part.*

The Company may at any time —

  (i) *dismiss without notice, or*

 (ii) *suspend from duty and, after enquiry, dismiss without notice, or*

(iii) *suspend from duty as a disciplinary measure an employee of the Company for any one or more of the following offences, viz.:*

    (a) *drunkenness,*

    (b) *disobedience of orders,*

    (c) *misconduct or negligence,*

    (d) *absence from duty without leave.*

Great Western Railway Rule Book, Rules 2 & 4

Preface

At Platform 1 of London Paddington station next to the statue of Isambard Kingdom Brunel sits a train. It is painted in the same mauve livery as most of those that rest there in the daytime but, for those who board it, the differences are vast. The windows are the giveaway. Smaller and more numerous than on other coaches, they hint of cosy compartments, and curious onlookers who find one with a raised blind can gaze into a kind of mini hotel room with a bed, sink and coat hangers. This is no ordinary train: this is the overnight sleeper to Penzance.

For well over a century, a unique ritual has taken place at London Paddington station. As evening turns to night, this great building — which sometimes seems more like a cathedral than a railway station — takes on a completely different character to the hustle and bustle of the daytime. From around 22:30 when the train's dedicated stewards and stewardesses open the doors, the train comes alive. Soft Cornish burrs mingle with clipped London voices, sailors rub shoulders with business people, politicians with churchmen, and tourists with the Cornish on their way home. The atmosphere is friendly and relaxed. Regular travellers know the train crews by name and are greeted like old friends, while those travelling for the first time are welcomed warmly and with pride. Some passengers head to their berths, shown there by a steward on call throughout the night. Others go to the lounge car where they can relax with a warming drink of cocoa, or something stronger if they prefer. Whatever their choice, the lounge car of the Cornish sleeper is a meeting place par excellence. Lone passengers soon talk to those nearby, finding common ground in the simple fact that they are travelling on what today is the only all-English sleeper train left. The locomotives, coaches — even the timings of the train and its route itself – have all changed vastly, but even so, it wasn't all that different nearly a hundred years ago . . .

Two major differences would immediately strike you about the scene in 1902. The first is the smell of coal smoke mingling with that of the warm, thick, black cylinder oil of the steam locomotives. The best Welsh steam coal the Great Western Railway prefers emits a pungent smell, but the coal itself is second to none for its ability to burn cleanly and without clogging the fire grate of the locomotive. The second surprise is that Paddington is not the pristine station of 2010, complete with polished floors. The Paddington of 1902 is a much grimier affair despite the best efforts of an army of cleaners – there are simply too many steam locomotives emitting too much smoke to keep pace, and London's dirty air doesn't help either. At the front of the sleeper train is one of the GWR's express passenger 4-4-0 steam locomotives. (The '4-4-0' refers to the wheel arrangement of steam locomotives under the 'Whyte Notation' system; the first number refers to the number of wheels that support the front end, the second to the number of driving wheels and the third to the number of trailing wheels at the rear of the locomotive.) The 4-4-0s are curious hybrids of the old fashioned and modern – old fashioned because of their outside frames which hide most of the wheels, but with a modern and free-steaming boiler unrivalled in Britain. Its safety-valve bonnet is of polished brass, and at the top of the chimney is a burnished band of copper, complementing the rich and extravagantly decorated green paintwork. It might all be for show, but what a show it is, even late at night!

Inside the chocolate-brown-and-cream-liveried coaches of the 1902 sleeper, the berths are panelled and with pictures showing tourist attractions on the company's routes. They are pleasantly decorated rather like a small hotel room and to complete the ensemble, a narrow mattress is covered with a blanket emblazoned with the GWR's intricately intertwined lettering. Blinds on the door to the coach's corridor allow passengers to sleep with a degree of privacy.

On the guard's whistle, the train eases out of Paddington gently, trying not to disturb those passengers already asleep. The train has to follow the so-called Great Way Round via Bristol rather than the much shorter route via Newbury it will eventually follow in later years and so it continues straight on at Reading rather than taking the left turn to the Berks & Hants line. It scurries past the shed at Didcot and then on past Swindon, where the GWR's gigantic engineering works that build many of the company's most famous locomotives and the bulk of its carriages are approaching their heyday. Swindon is not just renowned all over the world for its works — the GWR also built one of the first factory villages in the world there, and has gone to great lengths to provide a degree of social security for its staff at the works which won't reach most of the country until almost fifty years hence.

From Swindon the sleeper continues west, most of its passengers now slumbering. The value of the sleeper service at the start of the twentieth century is immense, allowing Cornwall to punch its weight in business and politics, and to avoid being regarded as helplessly peripheral to the country's interests. It is Cornwall's umbilical cord — the one service that even if all others were axed, would allow the county to link to the outside world effectively and in timely fashion. The sleeper may not have the capacity of a daytime express but its value is out of all proportion to the numbers of passengers it carries.

Perhaps some restless passengers notice the steep descent to the 1.83 mile Box Tunnel, engineered, like the rest of the largely flat route to Bristol, by Isambard Kingdom Brunel. It is said that the sun shines through the tunnel on Brunel's birthday, but the tunnel itself was a marvel when it was built — easily the most challenging engineering project of its day. At Georgian Bath, the railway threads neatly through the classical gentrified town and then on towards Bristol Temple Meads. Brunel's original train shed is still in use but the station was dramatically expanded in the late nineteenth century to cope with increasing traffic. Even so, in daytime the station strains at its limits to cope, with many trains coming through the Severn Tunnel (still the longest in Britain at the time) from Wales. At Bristol the sleeper turns south west over the Somerset levels and, if there are any railway enthusiasts on the train, now would be a good time to wake up. At

Taunton, passengers on later trains can connect with the scenic secondary lines to Minehead and Barnstaple. The sleeper train then heads onto Exeter St David's. At Exeter the London & South Western Railway's rival route to Cornwall from Waterloo joins at the station's west end and leaves at the east before looping over the northern side of Dartmoor.

Now the GWR route skirts the south of Dartmoor, and for a few glorious miles skims the sea between Exminster and Teignmouth on one of the most wonderful stretches of railway anywhere in the world. With dawn now breaking, perhaps some passengers raise their blinds to enjoy the Sea Wall section; others might even get up so they can sit in comfort and watch the beautiful scenery from the lounge car before the train pauses for an engine change at Newton Abbot. From Newton Abbot to Plymouth are a series of vicious steep banks, the legacy of Brunel's failed attempt at providing an alternative to the steam locomotive in the 1840s. In 1902, the fast express engines that power the train from Paddington have to be replaced by slower but more sure-footed locomotives to take the sleeper over the Devon Banks to Plymouth – an operational headache that will not finally be resolved until the 1960s.

Plymouth is served by another sleeper service from London, reflecting the town's importance as a naval and merchant port (it didn't become a city until the 1920s): the Cornish sleeper simply cannot cope with demand so although it pauses there it won't have done much business. Shortly after leaving Plymouth, the sleeper crosses another Brunel masterpiece, the Royal Albert Bridge over the River Tamar at Saltash. Built in 1859 it provided the first railway link into the county and a memorial to its designer, who died only months after it was completed.

Through east Cornwall the sleeper passes drowsy stations on the main line as far as Liskeard, where the switchback branch to Looe departs at right angles to the main line. Then it is onwards west, passing Lostwithiel and entering the china clay country of Par and St Austell before reaching prosperous and industrialised Truro, whose cathedral is still being built. At Truro the railway to the deep-water port of Falmouth diverges, but the sleeper train heads on the main line, through the mining towns of Camborne and Redruth, and through St Erth where the picturesque branch line to St Ives (the last broad gauge railway opened in Britain) curves away.

Soon its speed slackens, the platforms of Penzance station are sliding alongside the train, and at last we are drawing to a halt: the end of the line in every sense. West lies Land's End, the sea and beyond that the Isles of Scilly, where some of the passengers are doubtless travelling to, ambling from the station to the docks for their boat. Others perhaps take the opportunity for a stroll along the seafront, and breakfast in one of the hotels in this fast-developing resort. The railway goes no further, and from here onwards in 1902 at least, travel will be by foot or horse-drawn carriage.

Everyone who used the sleeper then did so in order to make the very best use of their time – and they do the same today – it is still the umbilical cord. Rather than taking the best part of three days and two overnight stays to spend a day in the capital (or, in the other direction, in Cornwall), the sleeper allows people to do a day's work, travel overnight, do business for a whole day away from their main work-place, and travel overnight on their return should they wish, arriving in time for another day at the office.

Even in its heyday the Cornish sleeper was never a great moneymaker, but to the Great Western Railway that wasn't the point. Even though the company had an effective monopoly across large tracts of south-west England, it regarded services like this as an important part of the whole – a reason to travel by rail in general, and a reason to travel by the Great Western in particular. In a sense, it was a service provided as a public service to Cornwall by a company which was starting to regain its reputation for approaching things in a distinct and to today's eyes, remarkably fair and decent way.

The 'Night Riviera', as the service is now branded, now leaves Paddington at 23:45, calls at stations from Taunton through Devon and on to Plymouth, from where today it serves a dual role as the first westbound commuter train of the day through Cornwall. It arrives in Penzance just before 08:00, in time for passengers to enjoy breakfast, take a stroll, or connect onwards to the Scilly Isles. In the opposite direction, it leaves Penzance at 21:45, arrives in London at 05:40, and provides a dizzying range of connections to destinations in Britain – and beyond, for passengers travelling to London St Pancras and Heathrow Airport. There may be flights from Cornwall to London that can get passengers into the city before 09:00, and passengers can do almost a full day's work before flying back – but while the flights are frequently cancelled or delayed due to bad weather at Newquay Airport, the 'Night Riviera' virtually always runs. Whatever happens, the sleeper invariably gets through.

For most of my life I have lived on or near the Great Western Railway's routes. I've been reading about it since I was a small child, I've visited the heritage railways and absorbed the lore surrounding this remarkable company, which was nationalised in 1948 but still exerts a curious pull on our national consciousness today. After a decade writing about the trials and tribulations of the present day railway at home and abroad I wanted to see if the Great Western would stand up to objective scrutiny. Do the many legends have any basis in fact – does that imagined account of the 1902 sleeper bear any relation to how things really were – or was the reality of the Great Western often perhaps rather less polished than the glistening brass safety-valve bonnets which adorned its locomotives? It would prove a fascinating journey of discovery, and one that began not in Penzance, or even London, because the Great Western Railway had its roots in Bristol.

Chapter 1
Small Beginnings

By 1833 Bristol was rapidly losing its pre-eminence as England's second city. It was still second only to London but its status was waning as foreign produce was increasingly delivered to ports nearer their markets. The centre of business gravity was rapidly moving north – and to make matters worse, inland communications from Bristol were poor, relying on dangerous roads and unreliable river and canal navigation.

Since Richard Trevithick's invention of the steam locomotive in 1804, the technology had been developed from novelty into a practical and powerful if unreliable form of transport and in 1824, a year before the opening of the world's first steam railway – the Stockton & Darlington – the first bid was made to improve Bristol's communication problems. The London & Bristol Rail-Road Company was set up with John Loudon McAdam as its engineer. McAdam was a road builder par excellence and this ensured his selection to survey the railway. He chose the flattest possible route, running from Bristol via the Vale of the White Horse, through the Berkshire Downs and Wantage, to Wallingford where running to London – either via Reading to Brentford on the southern bank of the River Thames or on the north side – would have resulted in a railway shorter than any current road between Bristol and London. In 1825, the directors approved McAdam's plans but even though the share capital was apparently taken up, no application was made to Parliament. The first attempt to build a railway was stillborn.

The second attempt in 1830 failed too but the need for a railway was becoming ever more pressing and in autumn 1832, four businessmen formed a committee to push forward a third attempt to link Bristol and London by rail. They were George Jones and John Harford, both successful merchants and directors of the Bristol & Gloucestershire Railway (a horse-drawn tramway connecting a coal pit 10 miles north of Bristol with the harbour), along with sugar refiner Thomas Guppy and William Tothill, a manufacturing chemist, Quaker and Liberal Free Trader. Where other schemes had failed to win over enough of Bristol's powerful business community, these four men's ideas succeeded and by the end of the year had won support from Bristol Corporation, the Society of Merchant Venturers, Bristol Dock Company and the city's chamber of commerce. With such heavyweight backing, this scheme had a much more realistic chance of success.

The group's proposals were not a mere flight of fancy. They looked at the expected costs of construction and the risks involved very carefully before reporting that a railway appeared feasible. It was initially to be known as the Bristol & London Railroad and a sub-committee was formed to start the process of surveying and building the railway as well as choosing the engineer responsible for designing and building it. The choice of engineer was amongst the most important decisions of all. Railways were still very much in their infancy in the 1830s, with any number of theories about how best to build and operate them. Other than George and Robert Stephenson of Stockton & Darlington and Liverpool & Manchester fame, and Joseph Locke, there were few proven railway engineers, so the field was wide open for anyone with sufficient confidence and brio to try and persuade the promoters of new routes to take them on. It was at this point that a bold young engineer called Isambard Kingdom Brunel arrived on the scene.

Isambard was born in 1806, the son of Marc Brunel, who was himself possibly the finest mechanical engineer of his generation. Brunel senior fled his native France during the revolutionary fervour of the late 1700s as his Royalist sympathies placed him in danger. He went to the United States to work as an architect and civil engineer before travelling to Britain in 1799, where his plans to make ship's rigging pulleys mechanically were accepted by the Royal Navy in time for its decisive battles of the Napoleonic wars. This was one of the first examples of

100 per cent mechanical production and it heralded a genuine revolution.

Isambard inherited his father's talent for mechanical engineering. After trying but failing to gain entry to the prestigious Ecole Polytechnique in Paris (the only technical college in the world at the time), young Brunel worked with Marc on construction of the Thames Tunnel in London where his father had developed the world's first tunnelling shield, a technique which remains in use today. The younger Brunel's nature was daring and impetuous; where his father was calm and easy-going, Isambard loved danger and risk. Above all though, he wanted to be given the recognition and glory he felt his father deserved but never really got. As Adrian Vaughan so succinctly put it in *Brunel: An Engineering Biography*:

> He did want to become rich and famous but only by means of creating great and vital works of engineering. When there was a choice between money and 'The Work' – he would choose the latter and work without pay in order to achieve his end. He wanted most of all to be 'the first Engineer' and example to all others.

Isambard's bravery was proven beyond doubt on 24 June 1827 when he and William Gravatt attempted to save the life of a man drowning in the Thames Tunnel, then under construction. Later on in the same project, on 11 January 1828, Brunel himself was almost drowned. Rocks thrown into the river to seal a hole in the riverbed had fallen into the tunnel through the tunnelling shield on 2 January. Prudence demanded that work stop while the breach was sealed but Brunel opted to press on regardless. A week later, the inevitable happened and the roof gave way, the flood sweeping Brunel off the shield. He tried to help two men with him but became trapped under a platform. He struggled free but was knocked unconscious and carried up the shaft by the deluge. His assistant Richard Beamish grabbed him and dragged him outside. It was as close and as lucky an escape as it could be.

Brunel was keen to break into the railway business and applied for the engineer's position on the Newcastle & Carlisle Railway in 1829 but this was rejected: perhaps he was regarded as too young and unknown at the time. This rejection, however, brought him to Bristol for the competition to build a bridge spanning the Avon Gorge at Clifton. Isambard and Marc's design was rejected but the father and son team provided such a compelling critique of Thomas Telford's winning entry that the competition was reopened the following year. In 1831, his design for a lengthy suspension bridge over the Avon Gorge (developed with significant help from his father) was accepted and Isambard was appointed engineer.

This appointment introduced him to the great and good of Bristol, including Thomas Guppy of the Bristol & London Railroad. In 1832, young Brunel was consulted about improvements to the Bristol Dock Company's floating harbour, which after much deliberation were accepted with great success. His potential was clear to the promoters of the Bristol & London Railroad and they approached him about building their railway.

The committee investigating the railway decided to hedge its bets, however, and Brunel was asked to submit his proposals for the route in conjunction with W.H. Townsend, a local landowner and surveyor of the Bristol & Gloucestershire Railway. Brunel wasn't convinced of Townsend's ability: Townsend's timekeeping was poor and just finding him in Bristol was always a challenge as Townsend was rather peripatetic. At the end of February, Brunel wrote to the committee outlining his plan to survey a route in as much detail as possible in order to provide a solid basis for the application for an Act of Parliament but still the committee wanted to hold a competition to select the best engineer. At the start of March Brunel wrote again, arguing that a competition to decide the surveyor was unnecessary: 'It is quite obvious that the man who has either least reputation at stake or who has more to gain by temporary success and least to lose by the consequences of disappointment must be the winner in such a race.'

Brunel's impulsiveness almost got the better of him. Vaughan describes his letter as 'a Brunellian bombardment with "facts", slightly incoherent, or hysterical in places, hammering the Committee into submission with words.'

It says much of the committee's tolerance that it didn't reject Brunel there and then, and Brunel was in the right place at the right time to enter the railway business on a truly epic scale. On 7 March 1833, Isambard Kingdom Brunel was appointed engineer for what would become known as the Great Western Railway. His appointment was passed by just one vote.

Two days later, Brunel and Townsend – late as usual – set off from Bristol to begin their survey. From 11 March Brunel worked like a dervish, scouting territory east of Bath to Claverton, 3½ miles distant, on foot. Returning to Bristol in order to dissuade the committee from issuing prospectuses before a route had even been decided, he then surveyed the entire route between Bristol and London at breakneck speed on horseback, staying in suitable inns overnight. Working twenty-hour days for nine weeks, Townsend was evidently unable to keep up as Brunel quickly appointed local surveyors to take levels and provide detailed annotations to the Ordnance Survey maps. Brunel worked these men hard, often following them as they did their work and always wanting – needing – to be in complete control.

The route he chose was remarkable. Brunel ignored ancient coaching towns like Devizes and Hungerford in favour of a much more direct route between Bristol and London. It ran from London to Reading along the Thames Valley, then headed north via Didcot, skirting Chippenham and onwards to Bath from where the route would follow the Avon Valley to Bristol. Whereas most engineers would have tried to serve as many traffic centres as possible, Brunel believed that doing so would create a long winding route with steep gradients that the steam locomotives of the time would have been hard-pushed to haul themselves over, never mind a worthwhile trailing load.

So Brunel's Bristol to London railway was a very flat route indeed. For the first 50 miles from London to just past Cholsey, the average gradient is 1-in-1,320 – a vertical rise of just 4ft a mile – and from there to Bristol it is no steeper than 1-in-500 except for two short stretches of 1-in-100: it was a route designed from the outset for very high speeds or heavy loads. There were still some important details to be settled on – how to exit Bristol, negotiate Bath and where to site the station in London, for example – but the broad outline was complete. The cost of the 120-odd mile railway was estimated at just over £2.8 million: a fortune, but with projected revenues of almost £750,000 a year, one that would be recouped quickly.

Brunel presented his proposals at a public meeting held in Bristol on 30 July 1833. The committee rubber-stamped the plans and decided to form a company to build the railway. Two groups of directors, one in Bristol and the other in London, would be selected to form a management board. Prominent businessmen in Bristol had been working their contacts in the capital and a committee had been formed there to further the railway's cause in London.

This committee was to be an integral part of the railway in its early days but its most important decision – perhaps the most important of all in the history of the Great Western Railway – was to hire Charles Saunders, the man who proved more influential than any other in making the Great Western Railway a success. Of Scottish descent, Saunders was born in Kent in December 1796. Becoming a government clerk in 1814 after attending Winchester College, he pursued a business career that took him as far afield as Mauritius. When he became secretary of the London committee he was 36.

The first joint meeting of the Bristol and London committees took place on 19 or 27 August 1833 (MacDermot's account suggests the former; other more recent histories suggest the latter) and it was then that the title 'Great Western Railway' was formally adopted, superseding the Bristol & London Railroad. It is uncertain exactly who coined the name but it does seem to have a touch of Brunel about it. Whoever came up with it had a moment of outright genius: 'Great Western' had an almost tangible sense of grandeur and ambition from the very start. All they had to do now was raise the money and get the GWR its own Act of Parliament.

In October 1833, Saunders was tasked with raising the funds needed to build the Great Western Railway as, in order to obtain an Act of Parliament, half the capital had to be subscribed before the bill could move forward. Saunders may not have been blessed with Brunel's manic energy but his extensive business experience led him to travel all over England to win support for the railway. He travelled far and wide rallying support and won over many Members of Parliament as well as some peers. Given that the prospectus was only issued in August, he did well to raise a quarter of the capital by the end of October 1833. He was going well but the arrival of a competitor meant the GWR needed to get its Act in quickly.

The London & Windsor Railway wanted to use some of the ground near London that the GWR had earmarked for its route and this could only be opposed if the GWR Act was in motion. The GWR directors acted quickly and decisively: they decided that the railway would not initially run all the way between Bristol and London – it would run from Bristol to Bath and London to Reading with a proposed branch to Windsor.

Brunel meanwhile was beavering away turning the GWR from a roughly surveyed line on a map into a detailed railway. He leased 53 Parliament Street in London and swiftly hired a full-time staff to help him. He also commissioned a Britzka – a fast two-horse coach with enough room to house a bed and mobile office – so he could negotiate with landowners and direct his staff on the ground. The decision to split the route meant he was forced initially to lay-off the surveyors between Bath and Reading, only to reinstate them when he persuaded the Board that the full survey should be completed because they would inevitably wish to use it later.

Brunel continued the frantic pace he set in the initial survey of the route, racing round the countryside in his Britzka overseeing the surveyors and trying to placate as many landowners as possible. A typical day started at 0500 for a meeting before breakfast; another meeting at 0800; travelling to leave messages for other surveyors and then on this particular occasion to the Thames at Streatley where he tried to find an alternative to crossing the Thames at Goring (there wasn't); then returning to Reading for yet more meetings before returning to London by mail coach. Even the most energetic surveyor would be pushed to do that today with a four-wheel-drive car: Brunel truly was a human dynamo.

Wealthy landowners posed particular problems, wanting either money in recompense or major engineering to hide the railway out of sight – and sometimes just opposing the railway outright. One such landowner was Reading MP Robert Palmer, for whom the GWR originally offered to build a tunnel of more than a mile long even though Palmer didn't actually occupy the affected property! Palmer opposed the railway on principle it seemed, and in the end the GWR drove a massive cutting through at Sonning instead. Eton College proved an implacable opponent of the Windsor branch, arguing that 'no possible good could come of the railway' and that it would 'pollute the minds' of its dedicated scholars.

These were just some of the large-scale difficulties Brunel and the surveyors had: everywhere they went they would have been greeted with scepticism and sometimes outright suspicion and hostility – how would you feel if some surveyors appeared in your back garden planning a motorway? The poor, of course, had little say in things: their houses would have been demolished during the railway's construction without compensation but the landowners on whose property the houses stood *were* compensated.

Finally, Brunel settled on routes out of Bristol, past Bath and into London where he proposed to turn south east around Hanwell towards Kensington, passing the Royal Chelsea Hospital and into a terminus on the site of the gasworks at Vauxhall Bridge. Ever the strategist, Brunel was determined to have a connection with the River Thames to maximise the traffic potential. After all this effort, the bill was deposited in November 1833. By any measure it was quick work.

Initially things looked good. The bill passed its second reading in the Commons on 10 March 1834 having won high-profile support and it was referred to a committee where evidence to prove its public advantages was heard. Amongst the supporters was George Stephenson, who had bought £3,000 of GWR shares.

From the traffic point of view, the benefits of faster journey times for passengers were fairly clear. For freight, the weaknesses of the existing waterways – the River Avon from Bristol to Bath, the Kennet & Avon Canal and the River Thames – were also great, with low water levels in summer and winter floods on the rivers holding up passage for weeks at times. On paper the arguments looked good.

Ranged against the railway were a host of vested interests from Eton College to the Corporation of Maidenhead, which was set to lose toll revenue from its bridge over the Thames; farmers near London who feared lower prices for their produce; the Earl of Cadogan and Duke of Westminster because the GWR would cut through recent developments of theirs; and finally the London & Southampton Railway (which was seeking its own Act of Incorporation) arguing that the west of England could be served by a branch from its own route.

Brunel was cross-examined for eleven days after giving his engineering evidence and many of the questions seem to have been proposed by a Dr Dionysius Lardner, whom we will come across later. Brunel dealt with it all expertly and patiently, supported by the eminent railway engineers George Stephenson and Joseph Locke who both spoke in his favour. In view of the hostility to the proposed terminus at Vauxhall Bridge by prominent landowning MPs, it was agreed to amend the plans to terminate at Brompton.

Brunel's efforts appeared to have won the day when the committee gave its approval after fifty-seven days of hearings, followed by the House of Commons. Despite this, their Lordships were not to be denied. The second reading in the House of Lords was rejected on 25 July by a vote of 47 to 30.

After that result, the remainder of the year saw the GWR committees make preparations for a second bill, this time for the full route, and the directors invited subscriptions for 10,000 additional shares which they believed, when combined with the same number already subscribed, would allow them to get the bill through

Parliament. The cost was confidently estimated at £2.5 million — £305,000 less than the original forecast, thanks to Brunel 'having now sufficient data to calculate the cost with accuracy; in the absence of which data on the former occasion the Directors preferred stating a sum which should exceed rather than fall short of the greatest probable cost.'

This time, the London terminus wasn't specified — the Directors had learned their lesson about upsetting landowners — but they were also negotiating with the London & Birmingham Railway to share its terminus at Euston. The prospectus was issued in November 1834, suggesting a line 114 miles long.

Saunders came into his own, drumming up support, and a series of public meetings held at towns on the route showed there was widespread public approval of the GWR and disapproval of the Lords. Petitions in support of the railway were arranged across the West Country and to places as far away as Truro and even the County of Tipperary in Ireland, which depended heavily on Bristol as a main port for exported agricultural produce.

To garner support as far as Ireland may sound surprising but no stone was left unturned. In a letter of 14 December 1834, Charles Saunders wrote to his chief, Thomas Merriman Ward, confident of selling 3,000 shares in Ireland, South Wales and Gloucestershire and another 5,000 in Bristol, with the remaining 2,000 to existing shareholders and their friends and families. Saunders later described the process of selling the shares as 'sad harassing work' but by the end of February 1835 the whole lot had been sold, providing a capital of £2 million: more than enough to be getting on with.

The GWR's revised bill was submitted in February 1835 and was read without opposition on 9 March, going again to a Commons committee. Because the landowners had been compensated or had simply just given up hope of defeating the railway, the only major opposition came, yet again, from Eton College and the London & Southampton, who proposed an alternative route via Basingstoke and Bath. The opposition was spiked by the London Committee's chairman, Charles Russell, who directed that no further evidence on the advantages or otherwise of the GWR was to be taken in light of the previous year's exhaustive examinations. The London & Southampton was forced to admit that its gradients would be steeper than those of the Great Western but asserted they balanced each other out, rendering the line practically level. Russell, who became Chairman of the GWR in 1839, argued that by the same logic the Highlands of Scotland would be just as suitable for a railway!

Despite the controversial evidence presented against the GWR, and after a proposal that no trains should run on Sundays was heavily defeated, the bill received and passed its third reading in the House of Commons on 26 May. It then went to the House of Lords where it was passed at its second reading, this time by 46 votes to 34, on 10 June. Despite this, the bill was referred to another committee chaired by Lord Wharncliffe and again there was no debate about the need for a railway between London and Bristol, effectively making the hearings a contest between the GWR and the London & Southampton's plans.

One bone of contention was the proposed 1 mile 1,452 yards (2.9km) Box Tunnel between Bath and Chippenham. The London & Southampton wheeled out Dr Lardner, a Professor of Natural Philosophy and Astronomy at London University. Lardner was one of those people who feel the need to have an opinion on anything and everything – untrammelled by evidence yet proved by 'mathematical' logic. In one of his more outrageous assertions Lardner believed that a train with no brakes would emerge from Box Tunnel at 120mph with passengers suffocating because of the speed! Brunel, however, had tested Lardner's theory in another tunnel and found it sadly wanting, with friction and air resistance limiting even a runaway train to 56mph. Lardner was denied.

Throughout the forty-day committee hearing, Brunel was at his brilliant, imperious best. Where exact answers were called for he gave them; when irrelevant or plain daft questions were asked – such as whether a viaduct had more arches than in the first plan because it now crossed a wider valley (it did) – he answered politely and with patience.

Brunel also drew the Committee's attention to a statement circulated by the opposition just before the second reading of the bill, which according to MacDermot contained several 'gross falsehoods', the discovery of which fatally undermined the London & Southampton's case. Finally, as August drew to a close, the Committee approved the bill for a third reading in the House of Lords by 33 to 21 and despite the opposition of the Duke of Cumberland it was passed by 49 to 27. It was given Royal Assent by King William IV on 31 August 1835.

The Great Western Railway would at last *be* a railway and it would be very different from anything else in the world because Brunel had been doing some thinking in between bills that would stoke controversy to the present day.

Chapter 2
Gauging Opinion

Brunel had travelled on the world's first inter-city railway, the Liverpool & Manchester, in 1831 and he wasn't impressed with the smoothness of the ride at all. In wobbly handwriting, he wrote in his diary: 'I record this specimen of the shaking on the Manchester Railway. The time is not far off when we shall be able to take our coffee and write while going noiselessly and smoothly at 45mph. Let me try.'

Brunel believed he could provide much better ride and stability for the Great Western and put his mind to solving the Liverpool & Manchester's problems. The shaky ride was down to George and Robert Stephenson's practice of supporting the rails on hefty stones laid in the ballast. This gave a hard ride and the stones were prone to both vertical and horizontal movement, which meant that keeping the track straight, level and with the rails the correct distance apart was a maintenance nightmare.

He had his own thoughts on how to improve the track but far more contentious was his belief that the gauge itself – the distance between the inner faces of the rails – was also to blame for the poor riding of those early trains. When George Stephenson engineered the Stockton & Darlington railway, he chose a gauge of 4ft 8in (1422mm) as that was the gauge used at the colliery railways in the North-East with which he was involved. Legend suggests that horse-drawn carts used by the Romans had their wheels a similar distance apart – evidenced by ruts found in ancient roads – but suggestions that the Romans consciously chose a particular set gauge have never been proved. If there were such a thing as a gauge in those ancient times, it would have almost certainly been determined by the width of a horse's bottom! Whatever the origins of the gauge, however, the Stephensons wisely stuck to what they knew and were comfortable with (rarely a bad engineering practice) and, as collieries and other industries sought to connect with the Stockton & Darlington and Liverpool & Manchester railways, it was natural they would adopt a similar gauge.

By the mid 1830s, as the author Christopher Awdry notes in *Brunel's Broad Gauge Railway*, there was still no such thing as a 'standard' gauge, so early railway builders were free to choose whatever they liked. In practice though, a consensus was gradually emerging from railways already built and planned that a gauge of between 4 and 5ft wide would become the norm.

Brunel blamed the 4ft 8in gauge for the poor stability of many early trains and thought a much wider gauge would improve things. The effect would, in Brunel's mind, be the railway equivalent of standing with your legs further apart on a moving vehicle to prevent yourself falling over. The 4ft 8in gauge became the standard gauge used today across most of the world and for the sake of clarity, I'll refer to this as 'standard gauge' although the term did not come into widespread use until later.

Having rejected standard gauge, there was little point in making the difference a small one; however, a gauge of 6ft (the next step up) would have been almost identical to the distance between two tracks: a train could derail from one line and run in the gap between the tracks – an obvious safety hazard. With 6ft rejected, the next mark was something around 7ft. Brunel must have discussed his thinking on the matter of gauge with Saunders because unusually he persuaded Lord Shaftesbury, the Chairman of Committees in the House of Lords, to allow the GWR to omit a clause specifying the gauge on the basis that a wider gauge could be better. Even at the time, most railway bills specified the gauge so this was very much an exception to the rule.

Brunel waited until 15 September 1835 before he outlined his thoughts to the directors – twelve days *after* setting Townsend to start on preliminary construction works on 3 September. In a detailed letter he outlined why he believed a wider gauge than 4ft 8in would be superior. Brunel's arguments were that by making the gauge wider, carriages and wagons could be larger than their standard gauge counterparts; by allowing larger wheels there would be less friction from the bearings; and placing the locomotive and carriage bodies between the wheels would lower the centre of gravity, improving stability. He wrote:

> I should propose 6 feet 10 inches to 7 feet as the width of the rails, which would, I think admit of sufficient width of carriages for all purposes. I am not by any means prepared at present to recommend any particular size of wheel or even any great increase of the present dimensions. I believe they will be materially increased, but my great object would be in every possible way to render each part capable of improvement, and to remove what appears to be an obstacle to any great progress in such a very important point as the diameter of the wheels, upon which the resistance, which governs the cost of transport and the speed that may be obtained, so materially depends.

Against these benefits, Brunel acknowledged that the cuttings, embankments and tunnels would need to be wider, that there would be greater friction in curves, extra weight for the rolling stock, and problems when meeting the London & Birmingham Railway, with which, at the time, it was proposed to share the company's planned station at Euston Square. The first three arguments he believed would pose few problems, but the latter he considered 'to be the only real obstacle to the adoption of the plan'. While extra rails could be laid to allow dual running, as Brunel acknowledged: 'undoubtedly the London & Birmingham Railway Company may object to it, and in that case I see no remedy, the plan must be abandoned.'

Brunel eventually arrived at a gauge of 7ft ¼in, half as wide again as standard gauge, a figure that wouldn't have escaped his notice. For a romantic such as Brunel, that his conclusions worked out so neatly would have been irresistible.

The board considered Brunel's proposals carefully, being well aware of the potential problems such a wildly different gauge could pose. On

29 October 1835 it sanctioned the use of Brunel's gauge but didn't officially publish this until August the following year, by which time the proposals were well known. The broad gauge was classic Brunel thinking. It was a mixture of careful analysis and bold vision and, when negotiations to share the LBR's terminus at Euston collapsed in December 1835, the last conceptual obstacle to his dream of the grandest railway in the land was removed.

Yet for all his calculations, vision and analysis, Brunel's broad gauge was ultimately found wanting. It is astonishing that he of all people failed to appreciate that the railways being built in various parts of the country would inevitably connect to form a national network, and equally incredible that the board of directors didn't either. Could Brunel really not see that there would be problems for passengers travelling long distances – that they would have to change trains when the broad gauge gave way to standard gauge – and that the problems for goods traffic would be magnified further? Did Brunel imagine that other railways would fall into line and adopt his gauge, or did he simply not realise there would be problems?

His diary entry of 19 October 1827 may provide a clue as to his motivation: 'My self-conceit and love of glory vie with each other which shall govern me. My self-conceit renders me domineering, intolerant – even quarrelsome with those who do not flatter.'

When it comes to the broad gauge, it is difficult to decide whether Brunel was guilty of naivety, hubris or even arrogance in ignoring the huge benefits of simplifying connections with other railways. If he had first engineered the Liverpool & Manchester or Stockton & Darlington railways with the broad gauge, things could have been very different as it would have been him who established the norm. The decision to adopt the broad gauge would prove an expensive and time-consuming mistake that would take fifty-seven years to correct.

*

Though Brunel's broad gauge inevitably dominates the early years of the Great Western, it had little effect on the actual construction of the railway, which was largely a civil-engineering exercise. Work started concurrently at both the Bristol and London ends of the route, the London terminus being sited at Bishop's Road, just outside the current Paddington station.

Then, as now, contractors undertook the actual construction and Brunel was, as ever, at the heart of things, designing almost every aspect of the railway – from the earthworks the track was laid on to the various structures and stations along the route. The route from London to Bristol was split into five sections: London itself, then Reading, Swindon, Chippenham and finally Bristol. Once the contracts were let, the route was pegged out, property fenced and then construction proper would begin.

It was at the London end where construction made most early progress. The first contract was signed on 26 November 1835 for a viaduct across the Brent Valley near Hanwell, around seven miles from Paddington. This viaduct was 300 yards long and 65ft high, running on eight 70-ft-wide arches. It was by far the most challenging engineering feature on the route between London and the River Thames at Maidenhead, which would be the first part of the Great Western to open. The contract was awarded to Messrs Grissell & Peto and they lost no time in beginning work. Construction facilities including a brickyard and carpentry workshops were set up in January 1836 with work beginning on 1 February that year.

The contracts were demanding in the extreme: contractors were liable for all mistakes – whether their own or Brunel's – and Brunel would resolve any disputes. If Brunel wanted other work done on the site, the contractors would have to do that too. As Vaughan so succinctly puts it in *Brunel: An Engineering Biography*: 'It is remarkable – to a layman at any rate – that anyone ever became a contractor'.

If life was demanding for the contractors it was infinitely more so for the men charged with building the line, the navvies. Deriving their name from the 'navigators' who built the canal network in the eighteenth century, the navvies have passed into legend as an anarchic, hard-drinking, hard-fighting and above all, hard-working tribe. The dangers they faced were real and lethal: the Great Western, like all railways until the end of the nineteenth century, was built with pick and shovel, gunpowder and sweat.

The navvies lived in camps near to wherever they were working, often in appalling conditions when they couldn't lodge in villages. They were paid monthly at best and on pay day often drank all their wages in what became known as a 'randy'. When the money ran out they depended on tickets from the contractor which they could exchange for the bare essentials at inflated prices, and when the food ran out they fought – the Irish against the Scots, the English amongst themselves – according to Terry Coleman in *The Railway Navvies*. It's little wonder that locals already bewildered by the railway regarded the navvies with fear and not a little loathing. Accidents were frequent too. They were often caused by men working drunk, and more often still by carelessness – and while there is little evidence of widespread disaster on this first section of the Great Western from London to Maidenhead, death and serious injury were part of everyday life for these men.

Later in 1836, the first contracts were let at the Bristol end for the five miles to Keynsham, just west of Bath. This contract included a bridge over the River Avon at Bristol and three tunnels on the route out of Bristol. In Bristol itself, the terminus at Temple Meads was to be built on arches 15ft above ground, leading on to bridges over the Floating Harbour and a canal as well as the Avon. It was some of the most demanding engineering of all on the route.

With work underway on sites along the route, by the end of 1836 Brunel was everywhere. He was always suspicious that his contractors would try to pass off shoddy workmanship and skimp on work. His mania for perfection meant he lashed out regularly at even those who worked diligently and in one case demanded the removal of one of Peto's foremen for disobeying his orders. Brunel was a tyrant but gradually his vision began to take shape.

At Maidenhead, where the railway crosses the Thames, Brunel faced a particularly difficult problem as in order to maintain the level of the railway the bridge would be low over the water. The need to provide navigation meant that using conventional arches was impossible but Brunel wasn't deterred. He designed a bridge with two flat, graceful elliptical arches supported in construction by wooden centrings as carefully designed as the bridge itself. Sceptics said that the bridge would fall down but they were wrong. In response to their fears, Brunel left the centrings in place but there was no effective contact between them and the arches. When the centrings were blown away in a gale, Brunel then revealed they had not actually been supporting the bridge anyway, and the doubts disappeared.

Maidenhead Bridge is the most visible of Brunel's works on the route but the most challenging, by far, was Box Tunnel. Preliminary work on this daunting project started in early 1836 with the sinking of exploratory shafts to determine the nature of the ground. Construction of six permanent and two temporary shafts from the top of Box Hill to the eventual rail level were let in November 1836 and by autumn 1837 these had been sunk. The shafts varied in depth from 70ft to 300ft and each represented significant engineering feats in themselves. Brunel advertised for contractors to drive the tunnel itself in August 1837 but such was his treatment of contractors that only two offered to undertake the work. In February 1838, Lewis & Brewer – quarry owners from Corsham – took on half a mile at the eastern end of the tunnel, with George Burge undertaking to complete the remaining 1¼ miles from the west. He was tasked with completing his contract in just thirty months and if he failed to meet monthly targets, would be penalised financially.

Not only was Box Tunnel perhaps the most complex and dangerous civil-engineering project in the world at the time: it was also perilous financially for the contractors. They had to contend with floods – one of the shafts flooded to a height of 56ft – as well as the inherent dangers of blasting in confined spaces with gunpowder using candlelight. Work went on twenty-four hours a day and Burge employed around 1,100 men throughout the course of the work. It would take six years to complete this mammoth engineering work and on Brunel's birthday,

9 April, the sun would shine through the tunnel – an unlikely coincidence given that this was his crowning achievement so far.

And yet, despite all of this construction work taking place, Brunel also went to great lengths to ensure that the railway enhanced the landscape rather than ravaging it in the way motorways and dual carriageways can do today. Structures were built to look as if they were meant to be there, and that meant a lot of architectural detail that today might be regarded as extravagant. Tunnel portals were given decorative mouths, often with crenellations to make them look like parts of old castles; stations were designed in elegant, often Italianate, fashion; and bridges and viaducts in sensitive areas such as Maidenhead and Bath were designed to blend in to the landscape. Nowhere is this approach more noticeable than at Bath where the railway runs into town from the east through cuttings and tunnels, then alongside Sydney Gardens in a cutting (one of the all-time great railway photographic locations), onto an elegant viaduct to the station and then out to the west. Nowhere does the railway's presence jar in this most gentrified of towns. Though construction of the railway through Bath was fraught with difficulty it is one of Brunel's greatest achievements.

Brunel was running himself ragged resolving major and minor problems along the whole length of route. There were delays caused by unexpected conditions and by poor workmanship of the contractors. In December 1837 he wrote to Charles Saunders, exasperated by what he considered a constant need for attention on the part of the contractors:

In my endeavour to introduce a few – really, but a few – improvements in the principal part of the whole I have involved myself in a mass of novelties.

I can compare it to nothing but the sudden adoption of a language, familiar enough to the speaker, and, in itself, simple enough, but unfortunately understood by nobody about him; every word has to be translated. And so it is with my work – one alteration has involved another and no one part can be copied from what others have done.

I have thus cut myself off from the help usually received from assistants. No one can fill up the details. I am obliged to do all myself, and the quantity of writing, in instructions alone, takes four or five hours a day, and an invention is something like a spring of water – limited. I fear I sometimes pump myself dry and remain for an hour or so utterly stupid . . .

. . . If I ever go mad I shall have the ghost of the opening of the railway walking before me, or rather standing in front of me, holding out its hand, and when it steps forward, a little swarm of devils in the shape of leavy pickle-tanks, uncut timber, half-finished station houses, sinking embankments, broken screws, absent guard plates, unfinished drawings and sketches, will, quietly and quite as a matter of course and as if I ought to have expected it, lift up my ghost and put him a little further off than before.

Given his workload – which by then also included the Bristol & Exeter Railway, which had received its Act of Parliament in 1836, and the giant steam ship *Great Western* – it was little surprise that Brunel thought he was going mad at times.

The pressure on Brunel mounted in 1837 when, with work progressing well on the London to Maidenhead section, the board of directors announced that the civil engineering would be completed in October and that once tracklaying had been completed, services would begin in November that year.

The tracklaying gave Brunel the opportunity to correct another of the defects he perceived of the Liverpool & Manchester Railway – the track itself. Not for Brunel the Stephensons' practice of supporting the rail on stone blocks: he wanted the rails to be continuously supported on lengths of pine with cross-members every 15ft. These cross-members were bolted to piles that were driven deep into the trackbed. The result was certainly rigid but it was complicated to assemble and the weight of the locomotives pressing on the piles would drive them deeper into the trackbed, unfortunately ensuring the sort of subsidence he was trying to avoid! As with the broad gauge, if Brunel had engineered the first railways this would have been excusable but as far back as 1831, Joseph Locke had understood that the track needed to be slightly flexible and that laying transverse sleepers at regular intervals not only provided that flexibility but also ensured the rails kept to gauge. In addition, the sleepers could be levered up one at a time and packing inserted underneath in order to keep the track level. Locke took over the engineering of the Grand Junction Railway in 1834 and the directors of the Liverpool & Manchester recognised his track's superiority so they readily agreed to entirely re-lay Stephenson's track with Locke's sleepered equivalent in 1837. So good was Locke's solution that it is the basis of almost every railway in the world today. Needless to say, Brunel ignored Locke's invention: he was never one to use somebody else's ideas if he had his own.

By November 1837 the directors realised that the line was never going to open that year. Delivery of timbers and rails for the track had been delayed so badly that only half the quantity of wood due to be delivered in the summer had arrived even by November that year, while the precision needed to lay Brunel's 'baulk road' – as his design of track became known – needed a great deal of attention in supervision.

In London, much work was still to be completed on the Acton to Bishop's Road section, including several bridges. Brunel's proposed grand terminus at Paddington was postponed in favour of a timber structure at Bishop's Road Bridge. When the railway did open from Paddington to Maidenhead it would not at first be the grand venture Brunel initially had in mind.

*

With the start of passenger services in some form expected in late 1837 or early 1838, Brunel turned his attention to the locomotives that would haul the trains. At the time, if you wanted a new steam locomotive, you had to buy one from an outside contractor because the expertise was specialised and concentrated in just a handful of firms. Brunel had invited companies to submit designs as early as June 1836 but had imposed stringent specifications on certain technical aspects which were to prove tremendous handicaps.

Among his stipulations were that 30mph was to be considered the standard speed and piston speeds should be no greater than 280ft per minute, boiler pressure should not exceed 50 pounds per square inch (psi); in addition, locomotives should exert a tractive effort of 800lbs on the level and should not weigh more than 10½ tons and, if they did weigh more than 8 tons, should be carried on six wheels rather than four.

The combined effect of these edicts was that locomotive builders were forced to compromise their designs horribly in order to comply. The speed Brunel specified was 15mph less than the 45mph he had so boldly envisaged in 1831, while Robert Stephenson's *Northumbrian* of 1830 had a tractive effort of 1,300lbs and, in the six years to 1837, the size and power of standard gauge locomotives had increased massively. Piston speeds of 504ft per minute were starting to become common and locomotive weights had risen to 14 tons and more. Brunel's extreme caution in specifying the locomotives meant that the first few to be delivered to the Great Western would be obsolete and underpowered before the first train even ran.

This was the situation that the man who would without doubt become Brunel's finest appointee found himself in when he was appointed as Locomotive Engineer in August 1837. Daniel Gooch was just twenty-one when he wrote to Brunel seeking employment. He was born on 24 August 1816 in Bedlington, Northumberland, where his father worked in the local ironworks. He seems to have been a particularly fearless and inquisitive child: in his diaries he writes of spending Saturdays driving the trucks at a local pit called the Glebe and like so many boys then, inherited his father's love of mechanics.

At the age of twelve, Daniel was bought a lathe and a box of tools and this prompted him to read extensively about engineering and science. In 1831, his family moved to Tredegar Ironworks in Monmouthshire, Wales and there Gooch began his engineering career, starting in the moulding department but also being called on to help repair the steam engines used to drive the blowers. While this gave him a good grounding in steam engines, on one occasion it almost cost him his life when after finishing some work in the cylinder the engine was restarted with Gooch and a colleague inside. The piston's first movement was upwards and this gave Gooch time to crouch in the valve box at the bottom of the cylinder. The piston moved down, stopping within an inch of Gooch's head before moving upwards and the engine was finally stopped. Despite this dramatic incident, when he compiled his diaries late in life, Gooch wrote: 'I look back upon the time spent at Tredegar as by far the most important years of my life.'

In 1834 he next went to work at Vulcan Foundry, Newton-le-Willows, near Warrington, which had recently started building steam locomotives, before moving to Dundee to be a draughtsman. There he met Archibald Sturrock, a man who would become very important to the Great Western Railway in the future by helping to set up the company's principal engineering works at Swindon. Gooch left Dundee in January 1836, returning to his native North East to work at Robert Stephenson's famous works in Newcastle. During his time in the drawing office there he helped design some 6ft gauge locomotives for Russia and this prompted him to advocate a wider gauge than 4ft 8½ins even before Brunel's views had been made public.

In late 1836, Gooch tried to meet Brunel in Bristol to secure a locomotive order for Robert Stephenson but Brunel was absent. It was Gooch's first connection with the Great Western Railway and in July 1837 he heard of Brunel's search for a locomotive engineer. At the time, Gooch was working for the Manchester & Leeds Railway, so he wrote to Brunel seeking the job and on 9 August passed an interview and was hired immediately. His starting salary was to be £330 per year until the line opened, when it would rise to £550. Although the directors almost certainly questioned the wisdom of appointing a mere twenty-one-year-old, Brunel (himself only thirty-one), recognised the younger man's talent and on 18 August 1837, six days before his twenty-first birthday, Gooch took the reins as Locomotive Superintendent.

Nineteen locomotives had already been requisitioned from a variety of firms, and on delivery Gooch was not impressed with any of them: 'I was not much pleased with the design of engines ordered,' he wrote, 'They had very small boilers and cylinders and very large wheels. . . . I felt very uneasy about the working of these machines, feeling sure they would have enough to do to drive themselves along the road.'

Nevertheless, the first two locomotives arrived on 25 November 1837, delivered first by sea to London Docks and then by canal to West Drayton, where Gooch lived and had built an engine shed in anticipation of the first services running from there. One engine, *Premier*, was from Mather, Dixon & Co of Liverpool, and the other, *Vulcan*, was from Vulcan Foundry.

Vulcan made the first movements by a steam locomotive on the Great Western Railway on 28 December 1839, but to little acclaim, it would seem. One might imagine that there would have been cause for celebration, but of course the reality was that the railway was still very much a work in progress and the directors, chastened by their over-optimistic predictions of the railway's opening, would almost certainly have wanted to keep things under wraps until they were sure everything would work as planned – especially the locomotives. The initial trials would have been carefully scrutinised and very quickly two important considerations may have become apparent: that the first two locomotives would struggle in service, and that Brunel's baulk road was going to be desperately vulnerable when the frozen ground thawed – the only thing supporting it before too long would be the piles.

Nonetheless, on 9 January 1838, *Vulcan* and *Premier* were rolled out for a trial in the presence of the directors. One, G.H. Gibbs, reported difficulties in raising steam in the locomotives and multiple derailments as they exited the locomotive shed at West Drayton because of a particularly tight turnout (a track component which allows trains to be switched from one line to another). Once they had finally accessed the main line, however, Gibbs reported that they performed 'beautifully'. Presumably Gibbs accepted the derailments as a matter of course.

The directors must have been relieved to see anything at all moving on the line and before long, frequent tests were made from West Drayton. In recognition of the start of testing a grand dinner was held at West Drayton on 16 January. According to Gooch, 'Some Irish gentlemen took more wine than was good for them and amused themselves by dancing an Irish war dance on our hats, which happened to be piled up in a corner of the room. I was rather disgusted with the termination of our dinner, and resolved never to have anything to do with another.'

At Maidenhead, the other end of the initial section, a much more successful locomotive was waiting its first turns of duty. Because Gooch had anticipated that Brunel's initial locomotives would prove unsuccessful, he had persuaded him to buy a locomotive originally built by Robert Stephenson for the 5ft 6in gauge New Orleans & Carrollton Railroad in the United States. This had not been paid for and was sat at the works awaiting a customer. Although this locomotive was far heavier than Brunel's specification, weighing 19 tons, its axles were extended to fit the broad gauge and its 6ft 6in diameter driving wheels (the wheels which the pistons connect to and provide the traction) were replaced by a pair of 7ft diameter in order to bring the piston speed more in line with Brunel's requirements.

Named *North Star*, the locomotive was delivered in January 1838 by barge to Maidenhead, where it would effectively be marooned until the rails reached there. Brunel supervised its unloading but the crane collapsed, killing a man and narrowly missing Brunel.

Testing continued throughout the winter and early spring but track-laying continued to be painfully slow: according to Gibbs (in MacDermot, *History of GWR*), just 5⅔ miles had been laid by 12 April. Progress from then on must have been much more rapid, as on 22 May the directors were able to travel the 11 miles from Hayes to Maidenhead station, which at the time was a wooden structure about ¼ mile east of the river. Soon after this the railway was complete enough for a trip to be made from Bishop's Road to Maidenhead. Gibbs was one of the directors on board the train on 31 May, and MacDermot quotes from his diary:

May 31st. This being the day appointed for the opening of our Railway, the Directors and the Company invited met at the Depot [West Drayton] before 11:00. A very pretty sight it was. At 11:30 we entered the carriages of the first train, and proceeding at a moderate pace reached Maidenhead station in 49 minutes, or at about 28 miles an hour. After visiting the works we returned to Salt Hill, where a cold luncheon for about 300 people was laid under a tent. After the usual complement of toasts we returned to the line and reached Paddington (19 miles) in 34 minutes, or 33½ miles an hour.

This milestone train trip was hauled by *North Star*, the only locomotive Gooch had any real confidence in, and the return after luncheon saw a director from Bristol, a Mr Guppy (who had taken full advantage of the hospitality on offer), walk along the top of the carriages from end to end while the train was travelling at full speed. It was a good job there were no low bridges in the way!

With the route proved, the public opening date was set for 4 June 1838. Although he had suffered a very bad fall on the steam ship *Great Western* on 1 April, Brunel had still attended the directors' preview and was, inevitably, there on 4 June.

One of the only eye-witness accounts of the official opening was left by Lisa Frere, the sister of a Resident Engineer. Although she was shocked by Brunel's frailty after his accident she was thrilled by the spectacle of the train:

The warning shriek was given when it [the engine] first moved and again when it was fixed to its burden, and we saw it approach again and rush on with gradually increasing speed past us, the steam giving a hoarse coughing sound at regular intervals as it puffed forth from the chimney, which was echoed with a short roaring sound when the carriages passed under the arches, growing fainter and fainter in the distance till it died away. The clouds of steam were beautiful in themselves with the morning sun shining upon them as they rose on the further side of the several bridges.

With the service up and running, trains would call at West Drayton, Slough and Maidenhead on their way from Paddington, with hourly trains from 08:00 until 12:00 and then hourly again from 1600 to 1900 on weekdays. Six trains per day ran on Sundays too. The cheapest second-class fares in an open carriage from Paddington to Maidenhead cost 3s 6d, while those wealthy enough to afford the luxury of Brunel's Posting Carriage would have to stump up 6s 6d.

Calling at Slough posed something of a problem as, thanks to Eton College's constant opposition to the railway, no station was actually allowed there. However, the directors had promised that trains *would* call at Slough, and apologised profusely to passengers for having no station and their having to clamber off the train on to the track. Although Eton predictably appealed against the decision to stop trains in the vicinity of Slough, the Lord Chancellor ruled that because the clause preventing a station was forced on the GWR it was entitled to do anything 'not expressly forbidden by it': so while there could be no station at Slough, there was nothing preventing trains stopping in the neighbourhood. Luckily, by the end of June 1838, Eton College's attitude had however changed so much that they requested a special train to take its scholars to London for Queen Victoria's coronation on the 28 June. Slough would finally get its own station two years later, in 1840.

Thus, after all the pain, disruption and struggles, the Great Western Railway – or at least, a small but significant part of it – was open for business.

Chapter 3
Raising Steam

From the start the locomotives had caused Daniel Gooch grief: 'The *North Star* and the six from the Vulcan Foundry Company were the only ones I could at all depend on,' he wrote. Long nights were spent in the workshops rectifying failures and trying to get enough engines ready for the following day's service, whilst things went wrong in the day too. Gooch also described the practice of sending a locomotive out from the shed to look for a late train and reversing when it had been spotted – it was a miracle there were no fatal accidents in those very early days!

These failures should not have come as a surprise really. Brunel's odd specifications notwithstanding, steam locomotives represented the cutting edge of an immature technology that pushed existing knowledge to the limit. They were hand-built bespoke machines, and no two were exactly the same. It was inevitable they would fail and that they would do so often, just like the early aeroplanes.

If life was tough for Gooch, spare a thought for the passengers. There were three classes of travel and the best, the Posting Carriages, were fitted with cushioned seats and a table but had little ventilation and no lighting. Another Brunel innovation that wouldn't become common currency on the railways until the 1960s – rubber air bag suspension – was also tried unsuccessfully in these carriages. Second-class conditions were far less savoury – for 4 shillings from Paddington to Maidenhead, passengers were given the luxury of a roof but little else: not even full-height doors to prevent them falling out. Those opting for the cheapest form of travel, open coaches, had nothing to shield them from the wind, the elements – and above all, the shower of cinders issuing from the locomotive's chimney. Even so, it was little worse for these passengers than the alternatives, which were riding on the outside of a stagecoach or walking.

However, whatever class one took, the Great Western Railway was not a comfortable ride. As predicted, the baulk road proved to be intolerably hard with carriages jolted backwards and forwards thanks to the rudimentary couplings, which were little more than chains between the vehicles. Today, a low-speed ride on the Great Western Society's demonstration track at Didcot shows us just how firm and jolting the ride really was. Still, then as now, time was money for many people. In the first week of service a whopping 10,360 passengers were carried, with takings of £1,552. It was by any measure a promising start – but it wouldn't last.

By today's standards the railways of the time, GWR included, were not particularly safe. Trains were kept from hitting each other by the time interval system. Sentries based at regular intervals manually set the disc and crossbar signals Brunel had designed to their danger position when a train passed. Then, after sufficient time was thought to have allowed the train to pass to the next sentry, the signal was cleared.

Brunel's signals worked by simply turning a circular disc to face oncoming traffic, indicating danger. Crossbars provided an indication of whether a train had passed within five minutes, ten minutes or longer and then the disc was turned alongside the track, making it invisible to the driver. When set at danger it provided an indication that the line was blocked but the great weakness of the time interval system was that it couldn't *prove* the line was clear ahead. A train could break down around the corner, the signal then be set at clear and there would be nothing indicating the danger – or to stop following trains colliding with the failed train.

Incredibly there were no serious accidents in the first couple of weeks' operation but, as word of the hard and jolting ride spread, concern about the railway's safety and viability mounted rapidly amongst the directors and shareholders. Director G.H. Gibbs, who was Brunel's biggest supporter, acknowledged disappointment about speed and comfort, not to mention the share price, which had fallen significantly since the railway's opening. Concern was also mounting about Maidenhead Bridge, which was still under construction and which sceptics were sure would collapse under its own weight thanks to its flat arches.

A report was hastily commissioned which blamed the position of the axles under the carriage bodies and poor springs on some of them for the roughness of the ride; it also promised action to insert packing under the particularly poor stretches of track to firm up the baulk road. This, however, wasn't enough for a body of shareholders based in Liverpool who believed their investment was being jeopardised by Brunel's broad gauge and baulk road. Although none of them were on the GWR board they formed a body known as the Liverpool Proprietors and collectively they held 4.9 per cent of the shares. They were able to exert enough pressure on the board of directors to examine the whole issue of the broad gauge.

Recognising the severity of this potential revolt, Brunel suggested that other railway engineers should report independently on the railway. Some directors called for Brunel's resignation – and he offered to do so – but enough retained their faith in him to reject this. The stage was set for the first of the battles for the broad gauge.

The importance of the battle between the Liverpool Proprietors and Brunel over the future of the broad gauge is often given short shrift by railway historians but it established the Great Western Railway's policy in the short term and helped create a mindset that with only a handful of aberrations was to set the railway apart for another 110 years.

In July 1838 the directors decided to go along with Brunel's idea of commissioning independent studies from leading engineers. They invited Robert Stephenson, James Walker the Institution of Civil Engineers President, and Nicholas Wood (an independent engineer) to examine the track, the gauge, and the rolling stock. Stephenson and Walker declined the invitation on the grounds of partiality leaving Wood to conduct a study alone.

Wood's investigations could not take place until September that year, which gave Brunel a chance to defend his methods at the Half-Yearly meeting on 15 August after being asked to prepare his own report. He took comfort from a Royal Commission decision to adopt a gauge of 6ft 2in for railways in Ireland (though in the end, Irish standard gauge became 5ft 3in!) and referred at length to this fact. His report was uncharacteristically rambling – so much so, in fact, that Brunel seemed to argue that the correct gauge would vary from one railway to another: 'The gauge which is well adapted to the one, is not well adapted to the other, unless, indeed, some mysterious cause exists which has never yet been explained for the empirical law which would fix the gauge under all circumstances,' Brunel wrote. He apparently wasn't thinking as clearly as normal.

Furthermore, in his defence of the broad gauge, rather than arguing that a much bigger loading gauge (the maximum width and height to which locomotives, carriages and wagons can be built) was possible with his gauge, he pointed out the *similarities* between the GWR and the London & Birmingham Railway's loading gauges. He admitted the track was below par but blamed that on inadequate packing of the timbers between the supporting piles, ignoring the fact that it was the piles which were causing many of the problems, and that his accident on *Great Western* in April had prevented proper supervision of the track works. He did agree to abandon the use of the supporting piles, but only on the grounds that they required 'perhaps too great a perfection in the whole work'. Brunel was trying to defend the indefensible and doing a particularly poor job of it.

At the Half-Yearly meeting all seemed civil and polite but the Liverpool Proprietors pushed for a resolution that another engineer should be appointed alongside Brunel – effectively forcing him out. They also demanded representation on the board, and would probably have found a majority in favour had they the conviction to force a vote. One other key fact passed with little comment – surprising given that the whole aim of the Liverpool Proprietors was to preserve their investment – which was that the predicted cost of the entire route from London to Bristol had risen to £4,568,928 from £2.5 million.

Opposition mounted and in August the engineer of the Manchester & Leeds Railway, John Hawkshaw, was called in to study the Great Western and other lines alongside Nicholas Wood. Wood himself called on the services of Dr Dionysius Lardner – who does seem to have become a peculiar thorn in Brunel's side – to assist him. Calls for another engineer to work alongside Brunel and for a place on the board gathered pace too. Such was the force of the opposition that divisions broke out on the board of directors. The Chairman, Charles Russell, was ready to accede. Gibbs and the other faction were willing to agree to a consulting engineer but not to the appointment of the Liverpool Proprietors to the board. Until the reports were received from Wood and Hawkshaw, the leadership of the Great Western was paralysed by indecision.

Brunel was shattered: Gibbs wrote of Brunel being 'almost broken hearted' on 17 September and pushed for gentle treatment of the diminutive engineer, arguing that Brunel would be 'an invaluable servant' in the future.

Hawkshaw's report arrived first and it attacked Brunel's track and locomotives, which were without question the weakest links in the Great Western Railway. Hawkshaw concluded that adopting the standard gauge immediately and re-laying the existing broad gauge track would save more than £30,000, even after scrapping the existing locomotives and coaches. His rationale was that the railway had been promoted to make a profit and as he saw it, continuing with the broad gauge would limit those opportunities. He also took issue with some of Brunel's technical assertions on the broad gauge but his ultimate argument against it was the sensible one: that being incompatible with other railways would eventually cause huge difficulties.

Gibbs was scathing about Hawkshaw's report and although the directors showed it to a group of Liverpool shareholders, they withheld it from the majority until Wood's report was completed. It took until 12 December and when the report did arrive it was rather an odd creation. Wood disagreed with Hawkshaw on the question of gauge, arguing that because the Great Western Railway was self-contained there would be little impact on it, although connecting branches might be affected. Most surprising of all though was that Wood relied on Lardner for practical experiments. Lardner, remember, believed trains would run out of control in Box Tunnel and that passengers would suffocate at high speeds! Wood did agree, however, that the piles used in the track hindered rather than helped it and recommended that the piles should be abandoned and the rest of the track strengthened accordingly.

Lardner undertook experiments with *North Star* and concluded that the atmospheric resistance of the larger coaches was limiting speed and increasing coke consumption to unsustainable levels on the loco-motives. Even though many of Lardner's theories had been categorically proved incorrect – he even argued with Brunel about the practicality of the steamship *Great Western* – Wood recommended that 35mph was the practical limit for passenger trains.

Both reports were remarkably inconclusive when it came to deciding one way or another on the technical merits of the broad gauge but the combined weight of opinion gently advising against it on practical or (somewhat spurious) technical grounds shook the management of the railway to the core. Saunders and Gibbs even considered replacing Brunel.

The Chairman, Charles Russell, went to see Brunel on 14 December and director G.H. Gibbs wrote in his diary:

He [Brunel] in a very modest way said that the evidence which was accumulating against him appeared to be too great to be resisted without injury to the Company, and therefore he was prepared to give way. . . .

If it were necessary to yield, he had no objection to it being said that he had been defeated for he felt confident in the correctness of his views and was sure that he should have opportunities of proving it . . . if it was proposed to connect another engineer with him, he could not see how such a scheme could possibly work, for which he gave his reasons, nor could he understand the meaning of a consulting engineer.

He gave us clearly to understand that he could not and would not submit to either of these alternatives, but that he would resign his situation as engineer whenever we pleased.

The London Committee proposed that an engineer should be appointed to investigate any new ideas of Brunel's but the two reports really seem to have spooked the Bristol Committee, which was ready to give in to the Liverpool Proprietors' demands. The Company's Deputy Chairman, Mr Bright (who also chaired the Bristol Committee), suggested a compromise measure which would see any decisions postponed until a Special Meeting which had been delayed from 20 December 1838 to 9 January 1839 thanks to the late arrival of Wood's report.

Brunel and Gooch, having had time to study Wood's report, were convinced they could disprove the one definite conclusion presented – that 35mph was the practical maximum speed – and set out to do so. When Gibbs visited him on 14 December Brunel said of Wood's report that he was convinced that 'a great fallacy pervades it,' and promised to prove this. Wood's delay in delivering the report gave Brunel and Gooch the opportunity they needed to prove Lardner wrong once and for all.

They took *North Star*, the best of the company's locomotives, and examined it carefully to discover why such a theoretically powerful machine was capable of so little. The problem lay with its blastpipe. The blastpipe is to the steam locomotive what the exhaust is to the car – an outlet for used steam from the cylinders. If the pipe is too narrow, the locomotive's power is strangled. If too wide, the steam doesn't leave the blastpipe with enough force to rise up the chimney, meaning that it doesn't suck up hot gases from the firebox with it, limiting the temperature of the fire and thus the amount of steam generated. *North Star* had been delivered with a 3¼in blastpipe but for some reason it had been narrowed to 2⅝in. Furthermore, whoever had changed the blastpipe (and it wasn't Gooch) hadn't aligned it with the chimney properly. It was no wonder the locomotive's performance was strangled.

Brunel wanted to try a cross-shaped blastpipe and as there was no point in Gooch trying to dissuade him they spent most of Christmas Day 1838 building just such a device. They tried it but a simple circular blastpipe worked best, and indeed they had previously worked the locomotive up to 40mph just before Christmas and found that the revised blastpipe used only a third of the coke.

On 29 December a similar experiment was made, this time with the directors on board, – with a load of 43 tons, *North Star* consumed 0.9lbs of coke per ton per mile compared with 2.8lbs when Wood tried in September. Wood's – or rather – Lardner's arguments about atmospheric resistance had been demolished by Brunel, who wasted no opportunity on casting doubt on the good Doctor's other experiments too.

Also by this time, the other locomotives were proving highly unreliable and Gooch came under pressure as few were available for service. Even Gibbs was questioning the young man's appointment. The directors gave Gooch a stay of execution until after the Special Meeting, where after long discussion the directors won a decisive victory against the Liverpool Proprietors' ambitions to unseat Brunel.

In light of subsequent events it is tempting to wonder what might have happened if the GWR had converted to standard gauge in 1838. It would certainly have proved a cheaper option than retaining the broad gauge, but it seems unlikely Brunel or Gooch would have remained with the company. The victory over the Liverpool Proprietors meant that the Great Western was consciously distancing itself from the wider railway system but while this mindset of being above (or more accurately, apart) from other railways would more often hinder the Great Western, it would also help to ensure that it outlived all of its rivals.

As 1838 drew to a close, the way was finally clear for the broad gauge to run all the way from London to Bristol, though it would be more than a year before the railway extended further west than Maidenhead, and by then the bare bones of a broad gauge network were starting to take shape.

*

If the Liverpool & Manchester Railway was the world's first inter-city railway then the Great Western Main Line from London to Bristol was the world's first dedicated high-speed line, set out for speed and ease of running rather than the shortest distance. It had taken six long years to develop Brunel's concepts but by the start of 1839 the broad gauge had been proved technically and (at the time) operationally feasible. The early opposition to its propagation had been defeated.

With this veritable speedway under construction between London and Bristol, it was little surprise that minds soon turned to connecting other towns and cities to it. In 1836, two Acts of Parliament had been passed for broad gauge railways connecting with the Great Western. The Bristol & Exeter (B&E) and Cheltenham & Great Western Union Railways (CGWUR) would be engineered by Brunel (though not, admittedly, to the cripplingly expensive standards of the London–Bristol line) and the Great Western would run its trains over their metals, providing a raft of new services. It made a lot of sense for the promoters of these routes to connect with an existing line rather than attempt to build their own route into the capital, and indeed, the Bristol & Exeter trains would initially be provided by the Great Western to avoid the costs of acquiring and maintaining locomotives and rolling stock. When the first trains ran between London and Maidenhead in 1838, the prospect was always of trains running at least as far as Exeter from Paddington rather than just to Bristol as envisaged originally.

Construction of these railways was underway by the time the first trains ran on the Great Western proper, and very early in 1839 services were extended over Maidenhead Bridge to Twyford. They started operation on 1 July that year. Between Twyford and Reading, work on the gigantic cutting through Sonning Hill was underway too. At almost two miles long and 60ft deep this was an engineering work almost on the scale of Box Tunnel. The original contractor, William Ranger, was unable to complete the works in the specified timescale and the railway took matters out of his hands, stripping him of the contract and splitting the job into three portions in order to get it done. It would take until the end of the year to complete but one of the biggest jobs of all on the railway was complete.

By any reckoning, the 12 miles from Bristol to Bath were the toughest of all to build, requiring extensive bridges over Bristol's floating harbour, followed by numerous cuttings, tunnels and embankments. There were difficulties in acquiring land near Bath and to add to it all, the contractor for the Bristol section, William Ranger (who was also responsible for Sonning Cutting) was again sacked for lack of progress. Whereas the first trains on the eastern section ran in 1838, by August 1839 there was little sign of any trains running on the western part. Hopes of opening between Bristol and Bath by spring 1840 were hit by a wet winter, which not only caused floods but also made excavation of land almost impossible. The navvies must have felt as if their work was cursed.

At Reading, Brunel wanted to make life as convenient for the townsfolk as possible as the town was virtually all to the south of the railway. Rather than having a conventional station with platforms arranged between the tracks Brunel opted for a single-sided arrangement with separate arrival and departure platforms. While the theory of this was reasonable – that passengers wouldn't have to cross the tracks and thus risk their lives – in practice it was soon proved a very difficult system to operate as trains calling from the west would have to cross over the eastbound lines to get to the platforms and then again on their way to London. It limited capacity and vastly increased the risk of mishap but with so few trains running when the station opened on 30 March the layout's limitations would not be immediately obvious.

For his part, Daniel Gooch had been busy too. After the success of *North Star* he was given the green light to design his own locomotives. The first, *Firefly*, arrived on 12 March 1840, two days before the first preview trip for directors to Reading ran and on 17 March recorded an average speed of 50mph on the return journey from the water stop at Twyford. By comparison with most other railway operations this really was lightning quick and it showed vividly the potential of railways to go far faster than anything else mankind had been able to travel in or on thus far.

For the Great Western in general and Gooch in particular the delivery of *Firefly* and its sisters over the next couple of years transformed things. At one point Gooch had been under pressure for the failures of Brunel's odd initial locomotives but the arrival of modern equipment proved his ability beyond all doubt. Just as importantly it meant the railway could offer a service that by the standards of the day was reliable, punctual and above all, extremely fast.

The completion of Sonning Cutting and the opening of the line to Reading really spurred things on, and by 1 June 1840 a further 20 miles was opened as far as Steventon, the nearest point on the Great Western Main Line to Oxford at the time. A further 7¼ miles to Faringdon Road (later renamed Challow) were completed by 20 July.

The impending opening of the line west from Reading must have acted as a spur to press on with efforts on the Bristol to Bath section because despite all the difficulties the directors insisted the railway would open on 31 August 1840, five years to the day since the Act of Parliament was won.

With just ten days to go before the directors' self-imposed deadline, they took a preview trip from the engine shed at Bristol (the station was not yet finished) and reached Bath in 33 minutes. Even so, with the Bath viaduct and river bridge unfinished (not to mention Bristol Temple Meads) it looked like a tall order to run the first trains by 31 August. It certainly was. The first train *did* depart from Bristol that morning but the last rail had only been laid half an hour before the train left shortly after 08:00. Crowds came to see it depart and lined the trackside. The locomotive, *Fireball,* was dressed in flags and bunting.

Amazingly things were even less complete at Bath, with little more than hastily knocked-up platforms providing the station. The debut train arrived in 33 minutes (compared with around 11 minutes today) and arrived back in Bristol at 10:08 following a half-hour delay. Ten trains ran per day, providing a link that eclipsed the best the stage-coaches could offer.

This just left the section from Bath to Faringdon Road to complete, and section by section it opened, from Faringdon Road to Hay Lane (between Swindon and Wootton Bassett) by 17 December 1840; then Hay Lane to Chippenham on 31 May 1841. This day also saw the start of services on the Cheltenham & Great Western Union Railway from Cirencester to Swindon Junction. With more and more of the works being completed, the railway started to reach critical mass – though the final stretch, Chippenham to Bath, contained Box Tunnel.

Box Tunnel had seen a Herculean effort thrown in to get it completed in time for the hoped for opening in May 1841. Around 1,200 men (and some sources say up to 1,600) were involved, working in shifts 24 hours a day on the tunnel most of the time but MacDermot claimed that in the last six months a staggering 4,000 men and 300 horses were thrown at the project. The statistics are staggering – 247,000 cubic yards of spoil were excavated; 30 *million* lining bricks were used. Almost 100 navvies were killed and countless more injured during the tunnel's construction. Incredibly, when the two halves of the bore met up, the alignments were just two inches out, barely a shovel's scrape. And this was in just one structure: add together all of the railways being built at the time and it's little wonder that many have claimed since that building the railways was the greatest human endeavour since the pyramids.

It wasn't just the Great Western Railway that was nearing completion either: the Bristol & Exeter's first section from Bristol to Bridgwater would be ready on 14 June 1841, and finally the GWR directors promised the line would be open throughout from London to Bristol on 30 June. Even so, the railway was in reality far from finished, with the government inspector finding deficiencies in ballasting, bridges and fencing. They only let it open at all because Brunel had promised that the most crucial measures would be completed before the trains ran.

On 30 June 1841, a special train carrying the directors and other guests left Paddington with little if any ceremony at 08:00, reaching Bristol in four hours and Bridgwater in another 90 minutes. They were the first passengers to travel from London to Bristol by rail throughout, even if they were beaten on the Bath to Chippenham section by the 07:00 Bath to London.

There was a big price to pay for the opening of the railway however. It cost £6,500,000 – more than double the original estimates – and with funding running short, a decision was taken which would have long-lasting and detrimental ramifications.

It was originally intended to rely on outside builders for the provision of locomotives, carriages and wagons, with only servicing being undertaken at a series of depots along the line. However, the rapid growth of the Great Western and the impending opening in part of its two associates meant that by 1840 it was becoming clear that this arrangement could present difficulties in the longer term. With a great degree of foresight, Brunel and Gooch decided to build a major new works where heavy repairs could be undertaken by the railway itself, limiting its reliance on outside contractors.

The site they chose was near the small town of Swindon, which for centuries had been a backwater although the advent of the Wilts & Berks Canal in 1810 had changed this somewhat. The story goes that Brunel and Gooch were travelling along the railway to decide the site for the works and that Brunel threw a sandwich out of the window where he wanted the works to be built. As tempting as it might be to believe this, the reality is that there were sound reasons for choosing a site near Swindon. Most importantly of all it was where the CGWUR joined the main line, meaning that it was a logical place to base and maintain locomotives for that route. It was also near enough to both Bristol and London so as to not incur a lot of unnecessary movements of locomotives to and from repair. Finally, as Gooch himself reasoned, because it was next to the canal (and thus connected with the national canal network) it would be possible to obtain coal and coke cheaply.

As for the Bristol & Exeter locomotives, Gooch again argued correctly that routine servicing could be undertaken at Bristol and that only when heavy repairs were needed would the locomotives be sent to Swindon. Basing a major facility at Swindon meant that locomotives could be changed mid-route if necessary and it would also provide a handy refreshment stop for passengers as there were no lavatories or dining cars on trains at the time. The works was largely built using stone excavated from Box Tunnel and other cuttings nearby: it was free to acquire and the only cost was of transportation. Although the material was cheap the buildings would be elegant and stylish, including a pair of stone reliefs showing a locomotive and tender.

The plan for Swindon Works was to build a comprehensive maintenance and overhaul facility for Great Western locomotives and rolling stock but it would also be necessary – as was often the case when the great railway works were built – to construct houses for the workers. The problem was that by 1841 there was simply no money to build any of this. In a desperate deal to get the works, accommodation and station built without having to raise capital, the contractor J & C Rigby agreed to build the railway works, 300 staff cottages, the station and refreshment rooms in return for a 99-year lease on the refreshment room and an agreement that all bar a few trains would stop there for 10 minutes: there would be no 'rival stopping place for refreshments' between London and Bristol. It was like the proverbial magic porridge bowl which never ran out, and successive owners of the lease milked it for all it was worth.

This deal, which ran from Christmas 1841, was born out of desperation to finish the railway. It would play havoc with attempts to speed up services in the future and played a major part in giving railway catering the poor (and often undeserved) reputation which endures today. However, despite this funding crisis the focus was already shifting towards expansion and in 1842 the Great Western received the highest endorsement of all.

On Monday, 13 June 1842 Queen Victoria wasn't sure if she would be amused by her first train journey. It was the custom for her to spend weekends at Windsor Castle and the working week in Buckingham Palace. The journey to and from Windsor was by road. It was dusty, slow, and uncomfortable. In winter it must have been even worse – and often her carriage had to slow for crowds wanting to see her close up. Surely, she must have thought, there must be a better way.

Her husband, Prince Albert, was an enthusiastic advocate of the railways and made the first high-profile romantic journey on the railways in November 1839 when he travelled on the Great Western Railway from London to Slough – the nearest station to Windsor Castle – in order to propose to the young Queen, who had taken the throne in 1837. Understandably there were concerns about the safety of royalty travelling on the railways. Viewed on a national basis, accidents and injuries were frequent; staff were often overworked, and the technology, though maturing rapidly was still very much a newcomer. It's not surprising it took two-and-a-half years from Albert's first journey for him to persuade the Queen to try out this new form of transport.

The Great Western had long been conscious of its proximity to Windsor Castle and had built a special coach dedicated for Royal use. It was a big vehicle, 21ft long and was originally built for Victoria's aunt, Queen Adelaide, who became the first British Royal to travel by rail in 1840 from Wallingford Road to Slough, and very quickly its four wheels were replaced by eight in order to improve the ride. It had three compartments, with the largest central section devoted to Royal passengers. The carriage contained silk hangings, Louis XIV sofas, chequered matting on the floor and a rosewood table, a big improvement on even the best first-class coaches of the time. Two other coaches were included in the train for the rest of Victoria's entourage, along with three luggage trucks and the crucial brake carriage. Gooch chose one of his newest locomotives, the '7ft single' *Phlegethon*, to haul the train and would supervise the driver, Jim Hurst.

Joining Gooch on the footplate was Brunel, and it is difficult to imagine that Brunel wouldn't have driven the train himself – it would have been too much of an opportunity to miss for a man like him! The train was waiting safely in Slough station an hour before departure at midday and it was surely one of the most exciting moments in the lives of many in the crowds that must have thronged there. Today, in 2010, the sense of anticipation and occasion from observers is almost palpable when the present-day Royal Train is expected – one can only imagine what it must have felt like for those watching history in the making.

The train left Slough safely, and 22 mins 30 seconds later arrived in London Bishops Road station, which had been spruced up for the occasion with a red carpet laid along the platform. Wisely, given the interest in the event, a detachment of the 8th Royal Irish Hussars was there, alongside various dignitaries awaiting the arrival. The train's average speed was 48.7mph and Victoria wrote to her Uncle, King Leopold of the Belgians, that day, saying: 'I am quite charmed by it. By railroad from Windsor in half an hour, free from dust and heat.'

The journey was a success and Victoria was soon using the railway regularly to travel for many of her duties; most often on the Great Western but also elsewhere as the other railway companies had also built lavish royal trains. One thing that would cause difficulties later, however, was Victoria's aversion to speed. The first run had been so fast that Prince Albert – who despite his public image, was something of a nervous and earnest man – asked for the train to be slowed and from then on Victoria refused to be carried faster than 40mph in daylight and 30mph at night.

Despite the precautions and the success of this first run there were the inevitable opposing voices. According to O.S. Nock, one newspaper thundered: 'A long Regency in this country would be so fearful and tremendous an evil that we cannot but desire in common with many others, that these Royal railway excursions should be, if possible, either wholly abandoned, or only occasionally resorted to.'

Although safety was something of a problem for all early railways, the speed and comfort of rail travel compared with road meant that the Royal Family would quickly come to depend on it. For the Great Western, it was enough to be able to say that in June 1842 it was the first railway company in Britain to carry the reigning monarch. As seals of approval go, they simply didn't come any better than that.

Chapter 4
The Railway Expands

By the time full services started in 1841, the Great Western found itself in an enviable position in being able to operate services far beyond its original plans. In August 1840 the Bristol & Exeter (B&E) had agreed to lease its line to the GWR for five years at a cost of £30,000 per year, charging a farthing per mile for each passenger or ton of goods carried. It meant the B&E wouldn't have to pay for the cost of building stock and running trains – and had a guaranteed income. This lease would prove to be a good deal for both parties.

By 1844, the agreement would allow through-trains from Paddington to Exeter, a distance of 193 miles. The B&E's terminus at Bristol was at right angles to the Great Western's Temple Meads station, which has given rise to a legend that trains could only pass from one line to another by means of small turntables on which each carriage would be laboriously rotated through 90 degrees. While that may have been the case initially, provision was made for through-access from the start and indeed, the bridge over the Floating Harbour was being widened at the end of the year to provide extra through tracks from the B&E to the Great Western.

The other broad gauge line which received Parliamentary assent in 1836, the Cheltenham & Great Western Union Railway (CGWUR) was opened from Swindon to Cirencester on 31 May 1841 and again the Great Western leased this part of the line, with the Birmingham & Gloucester Company undertaking to open the section from Cheltenham to Gloucester which was needed in order to reach Gloucester. A series of financial, and ultimately Parliamentary, measures ensured that the GWR would eventually acquire it outright.

Both of these companies were separate from the GWR – indeed, the

B&E didn't even share a director with it – but they were allied with it. The common gauge they shared forced them into co-operation but with Brunel's involvement in them as well, it was logical that they would share many of the same principles.

Elsewhere there were other key extensions of the broad gauge network in the planning stages. The Oxford Railway Company was a nominally separate entity that proposed to build a 9 mile, 57 chain branch from Didcot to the university city. It was not the first attempt to link Oxford with the Great Western: the first was in 1837, another in 1838, and one more in 1840. Unsurprisingly, all schemes encountered vociferous opposition from landowners and the university itself but by 1843, at the fourth time of asking, Parliament finally consented to allow the construction of a railway to the city and it opened in June 1844. This short but important line illustrates vividly how the Great Western expanded. In some cases, such as this, a separate company would be set up but with capital provided by the GWR in the names of its own directors; in other cases, the Great Western would invest in a railway and become a major (if not a majority) shareholder with its own directors on the board. The second mode proved most popular as it gave the GWR influence and very often, operational control of a railway without having to stump up the full construction cost. Later, when funds allowed, the GWR would invariably acquire all of the shares and amalgamate the company fully with its own operations. The GWR acquired the CGWUR entirely on 1 July 1843, the first of many acquisitions and largely a preventative measure to deny competition access to its metals. The Act of Parliament confirming this as well as the formal acquisition of the Oxford Railway Company was passed in 1844.

The year 1844 was particularly significant as on 1 May, the Bristol & Exeter finally completed its route to Exeter, which by dint of the GWR's lease on the line gave the company a main line of almost 194 miles, the longest by some margin of any railway company in Britain. The B&E cost just £2 million to build.

Gooch took charge of the regulator of *Actaeon* that spring morning, leaving Paddington at 07:30 and arriving in Exeter at 12:30 before a celebratory dinner was held in the goods shed. At 17:20 Gooch took to the footplate again, this time arriving in London at 22:00. One of the party, Sir Thomas Acland MP, went directly to the House of Commons in order to reveal that just five hours before he had been in Exeter. Never before had the possibilities of rail travel been proven in such emphatic fashion.

After spending ten hours on the footplate, Gooch recorded in his diary: 'It was a very hard day's work for me, as, apart from driving the engine a distance of 387 miles, I had to be out early in the morning to see that all was right for our trip, and while at Exeter was busy with matters connected with the opening, so that my only chance of sitting down was for the hour we had at dinner. Next day my back ached so that I could hardly walk.'

It was hardly surprising that even Gooch should be so tired but he had proved his point: for the first time it was possible to travel from London to the South-West and back in a day.

The success of these early railways – and growing inevitable concern about their safety and practices – led the government, under the leadership of Sir Robert Peel, to introduce the Regulation of Railways Act 1844, also known as the 'Gladstone Act'. It contained provision for state acquisition of railway companies but of far more importance was its demand for every railway to run at least a train a day along the full length of its lines, calling at every station, with fares limited to a penny a mile. The trains had to average at least 12mph and passengers were to be provided with seats and shelter from the elements. The Great Western, like many other companies, opposed the Act but was forced to abandon its open-sided second-class coaches. Instead, the GWR provided something rather like a cattle truck with a roof and no windows but seats for sixty people. Furthermore, by meeting the requirements of the Act there was, as Stuart Hylton points out in *The Grand Experiment*, nothing to stop railways running lesser services to whatever standard they liked.

While this was happening, the stage was set for an extension of the broad gauge farther west still to Plymouth, via Newton Abbot and Totnes. To this end, the Great Western would invest £150,000 in the South Devon Railway with Charles Russell and two other GWR directors on its board. In addition to this move, the South Wales Railway from Standish to Fishguard with two branches would add 211 miles; the Cornwall Railway from Plymouth to Falmouth a further 66 miles; the Wilts, Somerset & Weymouth Railway from Chippenham to Weymouth via Frome, Yeovil and Dorchester and related branches another 148 miles; and the Oxford, Worcester & Wolverhampton 97½ miles. The Great Western itself established subsidiaries to build railways from Reading to Basingstoke and from Newbury to Hungerford (the Berks & Hants); the Oxford & Rugby Railway and the Monmouth & Hereford Railway, which would run from Standish to Hereford with a branch to Monmouth. All bar the Cornwall Railway would receive Parliamentary Assent in the following year, 1845.

This was the beginning of the 'Railway Mania', a frantic period of expansion which saw investors eager for a better return than from government bonds plough their savings into railways promising far better rates of return. It had started in autumn 1844 when around 800 miles of new railways were authorised by Parliament. To put this in context, Christian Wolmar asserts in *Fire and Steam* that just 50 miles were authorised between 1838 and 1843. Yet in 1845, 240 bills were presented to Parliament seeking approval to build a combined total of 2,820 miles of new railways – double the national network at the time. Wolmar calculated that if all of these had been built (in the event only half were) the investment needed would have been double Britain's gross national product of the time. Seldom has there been such a concerted national drive – only the war efforts in 1914–18 and 1939–45 materially surpassed the Railway Mania. The mania further accelerated in 1846 when 3,350 miles were sanctioned, and between 1844 and 1847 a total of 9,500 miles were authorised, and of these schemes around two-thirds were actually built.

It was this meteoric expansion of the railways that prompted Parliament to look closely at the question of gauge because at places such as Gloucester, the transfer of passengers and goods between broad and standard gauge (a process known as transhipment) was causing chaos.

*

Very soon after the initial decision to adopt the broad gauge was taken, there were warnings of the problems that would occur when it met the standard gauge: passengers would have to change trains and goods would have to be laboriously transhipped from wagons, but for a while these problems didn't matter. The Great Western had no direct interfaces with standard gauge railways and neither did the Bristol & Exeter. It was a different story at Gloucester, however.

Gloucester was the ultimate terminus of the Cheltenham & Great Western Union Railway (which was broad gauge and controlled by the Great Western) but it was also the junction between the Birmingham & Gloucester and Bristol & Gloucester railways. The former was from the outset built to standard gauge, and the intention was for the two lines to form a standard gauge link from Birmingham to Bristol. Initially it was planned that the Bristol & Gloucester be standard gauge too – and even at the end of 1842 this was still the intention. Yet by the start of 1843, the directors of the Bristol railway had a massive change of heart and decided to adopt broad gauge instead. Perhaps they were conscious that with the likely takeover of the CGWUR by the GWR there would be an extremely powerful company using the broad gauge nearby – perhaps, as MacDermot suggests, they were frightened by this prospect. Certainly the B&G tried to reach agreement with the GWR to operate trains on the line and they were confident enough in broad gauge's viability to invest £50,000 in the South Devon Railway. Whatever the reasoning their decision to abandon the standard gauge for which they had Parliamentary authority would cause a major operating headache.

The whole concept of through-running from Birmingham to Bristol was in tatters: passengers and goods had to transfer from one train to another, and Brunel's assertion that there was a 'very simple arrangement' for transferring goods was nonsense, because he never, ultimately, came up with such a device.

Parliament established a Royal Commission in July 1845 to examine the problems and when the Railway Commissioners visited Gloucester, the Goods Manager of the Birmingham & Gloucester, Mr J.D. Payne, made sure they saw what they expected to. Finding two trains that had already been dealt with before the Commissioners arrived, he ordered that they be unloaded onto the platforms and be reloaded when the guests appeared. The result was predictable chaos with a clamour of voices shouting out destinations for packages and utter confusion.

The problems weren't restricted to Gloucester: there were more than thirty locations on the network where transhipment took place with similar results. Even so, the Commissioners were determined to evaluate the merits of the rival gauges even-handedly and the Locomotive Superintendent, Daniel Gooch, gave them a tour de force demonstration of the technical superiority of the Great Western's operation. Figures produced by Gooch showed that the Great Western was running more trains and carrying heavier weights at far higher speeds than any of its standard gauge competitors could manage. And when it came to locomotive performance, even though the standard gauge companies used various ploys such as making flying starts with hot water in the tender (which meant the locomotives would generate more steam), none of their locomotives could get close to the best of the Great Western.

In essence though, although the Commissioners acknowledged the technical superiority of the broad gauge, the bottom line was that out of 2,175 miles of railways laid at the time, 1,901 miles – 87 per cent – were of standard gauge. On a practical level, there was no argument: it would be cheaper and easier to convert the broad gauge lines to standard gauge rather than vice versa.

The Commission made recommendations that the national standard should be a gauge of 4ft 8½ins and immediately the Great Western responded unsuccessfully in its defence of the broad gauge. It wouldn't wash. When the Oxford & Rugby Railway was going through Parliament in 1846, it was specified that it should have a standard gauge rail added. This was the thin end of the wedge.

When Parliament finally got round to making its mind up about what to do on the question of gauges the result was a characteristic fudge. The Gauge Act 1846 expressly forbade the use of any gauge other than standard for the carriage of passengers but then, incredible though it seems today, excepted:

> any Railway constructed or to be constructed under the provisions of any present or future Act containing any special enactment defining the gauge or gauges of such railway or any part thereof, or any Railway which is in its whole length southward of the Great Western Railway, or any Railway in the Counties of Cornwall, Devon, Dorset, or Somerset, for which any Act has been or shall be passed in this Session of Parliament, or any Railway in any of the last-mentioned Counties now in the course of construction.

So a company couldn't build a broad gauge railway unless special dispensation was obtained – or if it was in a large swathe of south-west England! Exemptions were granted too for the Oxford & Rugby and Oxford, Worcester & Wolverhampton Railways. It was a mockery of the whole purpose of the Gauge Commission and furthermore, when the Birmingham & Oxford Railway's Bill passed through Parliament, no mention of the gauge was made. Because the Bristol & Oxford would connect with the Oxford Worcester & Wolverhampton, it was always likely that broad gauge rails would eventually reach as far north as the Black Country.

In the face of all logic (the outstanding performances of Gooch's locomotives against their standard gauge competitors notwithstanding), Parliament had sealed the ultimate fate of the broad gauge while at the same time giving it a lengthy stay of execution. Needless to say, Brunel, Saunders and Gooch were delighted.

*

To modern eyes, some of the operation of the Great Western in the early days appears horribly dangerous and chaotic – and it was. By the time the first stretches of the line opened, railways had been operating for thirteen years, so you might imagine that even what now appear to be very basic safety rules would have been imposed. This wasn't so.

Take, for example, the practice when a train was delayed. Rather than sending someone to walk up the track to look for it, a locomotive was sent along the track to look for the train, travelling on the same track in the opposite direction! Worse still, experiments took place in and about the regular service. As early as 26 September 1838, an experimental train run by Dionysius Lardner collided with a service train, injuring, as Gibbs put it, 'three of the carriages very much'. A month later a similar accident happened, killing one of Lardner's pupils. The early railways were disasters waiting to happen.

Brunel seemed to have something of a blasé attitude to safety too. Back then any official of the company with enough bravery could board a locomotive and drive it wherever he liked at whatever speed he chose. Brunel had a near miss after doing just that at speeds of 50mph. When asked what he would have done had he seen a train coming towards him, he replied: 'In such a case I would have put on all the steam I could command with a view to driving off the opposite engine with the superior velocity of my own.' All Brunel's actions would have achieved was to make a bad (and entirely avoidable) accident much worse!

It took until 1840 for Daniel Gooch to put his foot down and specify that locomotives must always run forward on the left-hand track except when specifically authorised and only then at low speed. Prospective passengers could have been forgiven for thinking they were taking their lives in their hands when travelling on the Great Western, and in a very real sense, they were.

For many of the staff, conditions were dreadful too. The lack of proper brakes and signalling meant that if a train split en route, the driver and railway policemen might not be aware of this; another train could then be sent into the path of the stranded carriages with inevitable results. Brunel suggested in 1847 that a man should sit on the back of each locomotive's tender to keep an eye on the train and alert the crew. He installed iron seats on the backs of four tenders and paid the men 25 shillings a week to sit on as look-outs. In summer, the vibrations of the trains were jarring enough to risk the porters, as these brave fellows were known, falling off. In winter, the rushing air quite literally froze some of them to their seats. No wonder they dubbed the seats the 'iron coffins'.

Things were little better for the railway policemen, who stood in 3ft-square sentry boxes by the side of the tracks. These could be pivoted away from the wind so were one better than the iron coffins but would still have been freezing in winter. Each box was allocated to two men who worked twelve. They alternated eighteen-hour shifts on Sundays to give one at least a day off per fortnight. This was a difficult, demanding job and the Great Western paid bonuses of a week's wages to those who could go a year without making a mistake.

With no cover for meal breaks or calls of nature, it was inevitable that accidents would happen, though it wasn't until 1848 that one of the most serious occurred. At Shrivenham, a Porter called Weybury had held a farmer at a level crossing for a late-running train; when it arrived around fifteen minutes late, he opened the level crossing then went to a pub to answer nature's call. While he was doing this, some shunting of goods wagons onto the main line was taking place to allow a coal wagon to be unloaded. As they were doing this, an express for Exeter was haring west, blissfully unaware that there was an obstruction ahead. The driver of the train saw the situation just 150 yards ahead and ordered the guard to apply his brakes (oddly he didn't apply his own) but it made little difference. There was a huge collision. One of the wagons on the main line tore open the leading second-class carriage, the locomotive then struck a horse box, annihilating it and sending lethal splinters in all directions. When the dust had settled, four passengers were dead and fourteen seriously injured – and all because one of the men charged with the safety of the railway had to go to the toilet! This disaster exposed the lethal operating practices of the time, but little was done by GWR to prevent it from happening again, except to urge greater vigilance on the part of the staff.

The oddities of early rail travel did not end with the poor operating practices. Buying a ticket was a bizarre and complicated process. Passengers were given a ticket showing their destination, date and time of train and on boarding gave this ticket to the conductor who showed them to a coach allocated to a certain destination. Once all the passengers had boarded, the doors were locked from the outside and the booking clerk handed a waybill to the conductor, who was only then able to start the train. At intermediate stations, the conductor then unlocked the doors of the appropriate carriage to let the passengers out.

Of course, this system was open to abuse. Passengers were not obliged to prove their destination, and couldn't in any case so, as a letter written by a Mr Hammond in September 1838 pointed out, a dishonest passenger could buy a cheap ticket to their nearest station and then continue all the way to the end of the line if they wanted: the only check was the conductor's memory and naturally, many got away with it.

We have already seen that conditions for passengers in second and third classes were poor even by the standards of the day but one thing the broad gauge did offer was wider coaches than later standard gauge equivalents. The difference wasn't vast – perhaps a foot or so – but it was noticeable, and today, at the Great Western Society's carriage workshop in Didcot, the comparison is clear when you look at the difference between a GWR standard gauge coach from the Victorian era and one of its replica open coaches for broad gauge. Swapping from broad gauge to standard gauge trains must have been rather like transferring from a TGV to Eurostar in Paris today.

Despite the risks (and these applied to most other railways in Britain at the time) to staff and passengers, the railways were popular because of their speed and convenience and in the mid 1840s a new railway was opened in Devon which has continued to delight and infuriate passengers and railwaymen to the present day.

Chapter 5
The Atmospheric Farce

Connecting the great Devon port of Plymouth with Exeter and the wider railway network was a matter of significant strategic importance. The town was one of the country's most important naval bases and helped guard the entrance to the English Channel, as well as projecting Britain's naval power into the Atlantic Ocean. The problem for railway builders was that Dartmoor lies astride the most direct route between there and Exeter. Building a railway through Dartmoor would have involved long, steep gradients and served few people along the way, so the only sensible options were to run around its northern or southern edges. The southern route was far more attractive as it offered the chance to serve towns and ports along the south coast and this option is what Brunel chose for the South Devon Railway (SDR) when he was appointed its engineer in 1844.

For the twenty or so miles from Exeter St David's station to Newton Abbot, Brunel surveyed a flat sinuous railway that skirted the River Exe as far as Dawlish Warren, then followed the coast to Teignmouth, along a section known today as the sea wall, heading inland for five miles until it reached Newton Abbot. From there, however, Brunel proposed a route based on the supposed capabilities of a system which would supersede the steam locomotive, offering far greater power – the 'atmospheric system'.

The principle of the atmospheric system was that rather than being hauled by a steam locomotive, trains would be connected to a pipe that ran between the rails and be sucked along by a vacuum created by steam-powered pumping stations at regular intervals along the line. The pipe had a narrow gap at the top running along its length to allow a crosshead to pass from a piston running inside the tube to a four-wheeled truck which was then connected to the carriages of the train. To ensure an airtight seal, the gap was covered by a continuous leather flap which was sealed by sticky grease after the train had passed. The atmospheric system offered the possibility of fast, silent and above all cheap-to-run trains, and Brunel believed he had hit on a revolution as great as the steam locomotive itself. A 1¼ mile stretch of railway in Dublin using this principle convinced Brunel that the concept could be scaled up to suit the South Devon. He wasn't alone in his advocacy of this new idea – names as great as Charles Vignoles, William Cubitt and Sir Robert Peel also found it appealing – but the fact that his trusted lieutenant Daniel Gooch, along with the eminent engineers George and Robert Stephenson, immediately recognised its weaknesses should have given him pause for thought.

The directors of the South Devon, having received advice that the atmospheric system would be suitable, wrote to Brunel asking his opinion. Brunel enthusiastically supported it and even attacked the likes of Robert Stephenson, who had warned of its impracticality. 'I have no hesitation in taking upon myself the full and entire responsibility for recommending the adoption of the atmospheric system on the South Devon Railway and of recommending as a consequence that the line and works should be constructed for a single line only,' he wrote.

In this statement, Brunel was being disingenuous at best: he must have known full well that under the atmospheric system, it would be impossible for trains to switch from one track to another as the vacuum pipe would have to be broken to allow that. For a railway as important to the nation as the South Devon, it was a critical weakness.

It didn't stop Brunel from surveying a route that was as much a contrast with his London to Bristol Railway as it is possible to imagine. From just over a mile west of Newton Abbot the railway immediately starts up a steep incline at Dainton, rising as steep as 1-in-36 in places before careering downhill into the little town of Totnes. Straight out of Totnes station, Brunel's route climbs again for more than nine miles to a summit at Wrangaton. From there it's around a 15-mile descent to Plymouth with a series of vicious sections steepening to as much as 1-in-42 down Hemerdon Bank. No sane engineer of the day would have considered such a route for steam traction, but Brunel, blinded by the way the atmospheric principle had worked on a short stretch of railway in Ireland, ignored convention. The only benefit in doing this was that the line ought to be cheaper to build.

In fact, the opposite proved to be the case. Brunel estimated a cost of £190,000 for the 52½-mile line from Exeter to Plymouth but he spent £380,000 getting to Totnes alone, and as Vaughan sardonically added, that didn't include wasted money in ordering 4,400 tons of 13-inch tube from his neighbour, Mr Hennett, even before the London & Croydon atmospheric railway (which he had promised to evaluate before installing a similar system in Devon) had ordered any tube of its own. When the L&C opted for 15-inch tube, Brunel then ordered that instead and the South Devon Railway was forced to pay for its scrapping.

This was Brunel at his arrogant worst. Never mind that trains couldn't switch tracks or even reverse; never mind that Gooch had worked out as early as September 1844 that it would be much cheaper to work the railway with locomotives; or that Brunel's friend Charles Saunders wrote to the South Devon's chairman, Thomas Gill to affirm that the GWR was against it. For Brunel the degree of informed opposition can only have spurred him into proving them wrong.

The problems mounted. Brunel designed beautiful ornate pumping houses between Exeter and Newton Abbot for the stationary engines but these had been designed to work with 13-inch tubes, so an auxiliary engine had to be installed too. The London & Croydon began atmospheric services in January 1846 but by May the airtight seal was failing. Brunel assured the directors of the SDR that all was well but they were beginning to suspect they had been sold a pup and ordered Brunel to a board meeting on 11 June that year. Brunel, who had stayed away from the South Devon due to other projects, seemed to want to distance himself from it. In August 1847 when the directors not unreasonably wanted to know why their railway still hadn't been opened, Brunel blamed the contractor for not getting the stationary engines ready in time. The contractor, Rennie Brothers, demolished Brunel's excuses by reminding the directors that the steam engines had been ready for two years and that it was Brunel who was at fault because he was still frittering his time away getting the details of his engine houses just right.

Services between Exeter and Teignmouth finally began on 16 August 1847 but within a month the airtight seal was already failing – hardly a surprise given the salty sea air. Passengers must have loved the smooth and quiet ride but the operating problems mounted. Although trains still ran to Newton Abbot, from 17 December a hard frost froze the leather seal, preventing trains from running at all. In summer the following year, the seal dried out due to the hot weather, and waves crashing onto the track on the Sea Wall section corroded the metal seal that held the leather hinge in place. The one thing that didn't happen, contrary to popular myth, is that rats acquired a taste for the sealing grease and ate that and the leather, thus rendering the system inoperable. Even if the rats had eaten the ingredients, there were plenty of problems of a more fundamental nature to derail the atmospheric railway.

Brunel was called on to solve the problem. He couldn't and even recommended that the atmospheric system should not be extended further west than Newton Abbot. It was the final straw and on 9 September 1848 the atmospheric railway was suspended; the steam locomotives Brunel believed to be so inferior took its place.

With steam operation now in force, the branch to Torre, near Torquay, opened on 18 December 1848, with services to Plymouth starting on 2 April 1849. It took eleven months longer to complete the route from Laira Green, two miles outside Plymouth.

Between Newton Abbot and Plymouth Brunel's legacy was a noxious mixture of steep gradients and sharp curves which limit speeds and make the journey time between Plymouth and Exeter far longer than it needs to be – but between Newton Abbot and Exeter he bequeathed us one of the finest stretches of railway in the world. The sea wall section between Dawlish Warren and Teignmouth is justly renowned for its beauty and accessibility. The way the railway skirts the coast and the way that when you poke your head out of a drop-window heading west it feels like you're skimming the sea – the experience of travelling along the sea wall is an elemental pleasure that even those who travel on it every day look forward to if they're not in a hurry. It is redolent of holidays on the beach, of sunny weather, of endless days spent doing nothing

Despite the atmospheric system's weaknesses, in seeking an alternative to the steam locomotive, Brunel was years ahead of his time: in essence, modern electric trains do the same thing, with power generated remotely but transferred through overhead wires or a third rail. Even so, for an engineer as great as Brunel to seriously consider the atmospheric railway was a gigantic mistake that continues to impose a real and severe cost on the railway to this day; trains inevitably run much slower over the steep gradients west of Newton Abbot than they would otherwise have done if the route had been designed from the outset for locomotive traction.

Chapter 6
Swindon

Gooch anticipated early on that Brunel's use of the atmospheric principle in Devon would end in failure and that nothing would be replacing the conventional steam locomotive in the foreseeable future. Fortunately for the Great Western, Gooch was a brilliant practical engineer and, as the railway's main engineering base at Swindon came on stream in the early 1840s, he began to consider whether the company should expand this to build its own locomotives.

The Great Western was fortunate that the CGWUR had acquired a parcel of land next to its branch from the London to Bristol railway and it was here that the works was built despite the financial troubles it had in the early 1840s. At the time, most railways bought their locomotives – and invariably their carriages and wagons – from outside contractors. Building rail vehicles was a specialist business that was for obvious reasons beyond the ability of most railways, which tended to focus on running a service.

While in time many other railways would build their own locomotives, perhaps the biggest imperative for the Great Western was that the broad gauge itself effectively prevented shipment of any new locomotives by rail from contractors served by standard gauge lines. Furthermore, the success of the *Firefly* passenger locomotives designed by Gooch hinted that the Great Western could build locomotives perfectly suited to its needs as well as any contractor and probably at a substantially lower cost (providing it hired the right expertise to assemble them).

It wasn't until late 1845 that a conscious decision was made to bring locomotive building in-house but once the die was cast it didn't take long for the first machines to emerge. The first was a 0-6-0 freight locomotive called *Premier* in February 1846, though the boiler for this and the other eleven locomotives of the first batch were built by outside contractors as there wasn't quite the expertise in Swindon Works at the time. However, having proved that Swindon was well capable of building all of a locomotive bar the boiler, it wasn't long before the first entirely Great Western locomotives were built.

This bold business move was prompted by the board's desire for the broad gauge to be seen to be superior to its standard gauge rivals and in January 1846, Gooch had been ordered to build 'a colossal locomotive working with all speed'. With ambiguity as to whether that meant the board wanted a fast locomotive or one delivered quickly, Gooch hedged his bets by delivering a fast locomotive in haste. Helped by his friend Archibald Sturrock (who had first met Gooch in Dundee and since moved to take up a position in the works), the pair designed, built and raised steam in the first of a new generation of locomotives that made the most of the broad gauge's spaciousness by the end of April 1846 – thirteen weeks from the order.

Appropriately christened *Great Western*, this 2-2-2 was a giant for the time, and after running-in and trials, it took a train from London to Exeter in 208 minutes – a good hour and a half faster than Gooch had managed in *Firefly* a few years before. *Great Western* proved Gooch's ability, although it had to have an extra pair of wheels added at the front after it fractured its front end in service at Shrivenham. Thus modified as a 4-2-2 (or more accurately, a 2-2-2-2 because the two pairs of carrying wheels at the front weren't installed in a bogie), *Great Western* set the template for broad gauge express passenger locomotives and future modifications of its design proved astoundingly robust in traffic.

The works staff worked what might today be considered extremely long hours – around a 57½ hour week. The working day started at 06:00 with a break from 08:15 to 09:00, grafting again, then an hour for dinner at 13:00, with the day's labour finally finishing at 18:00. On Saturdays they worked until 13:00. The workforce numbers rose accordingly as more locomotives were built: in 1847 around 1,800 were employed at Swindon. However, by the end of that year, the abrupt end of Railway Mania and the cost of acquiring or fighting off potential competitors meant funds were so tight that the workforce was cut to just 600. Gooch and Sturrock must have been dismayed by this action, having worked hard to build up a skilled and capable workforce but in time Swindon Works would recover strongly.

Although the engineering developments in Swindon would prove enduringly fascinating over the years, the role the Great Western Railway played in the development of that town in the Victorian era is, if anything, even more so. The 99-year lease of Swindon's refreshment rooms would prove an operating albatross for the railway but in return, the contractors built one of the finest factory villages in the country at the time. The houses are thought to have been designed by Matthew Digby Wyatt and were built, like much of the works itself, from stone excavated from Box Tunnel. For the time, the houses were extremely good: each had a privy and sewerage was provided too – and all this for unskilled men. Skilled workers such as engine drivers and craftsmen were given even better accommodation and foremen better still. Recreation and allotment areas were also provided, as well as two grand houses for the Works Manager and Stationmaster.

As the works expanded, this fine railway village proved too small for requirements and the railway built a barracks for single men employed at the works. These however proved unpopular, many choosing to live in the houses built by speculative developers banking on the railway's growth instead.

The railway, like some other companies of the time, also took an interest in the employees' spiritual welfare. When G.H. Gibbs died in 1842, he bequeathed £500 to build a church which, after further funds were raised via a public appeal, was consecrated in 1845. One Colonel Vilett also donated a piece of land for use as a cricket ground and recreation area, while the railway itself bought land for a school.

The school was particularly interesting given the lack of formal education available to most people back then. It opened in 1845 and railway employees could send their children there for 2d or 4d a week depending on age, though families with four children already at school could send any further arrivals for free. The children received five hours of education a day with two weeks' holiday at Christmas and three in the summer. A move by Reverend Mansfield of the new church to demand compulsory church attendance for pupils was rejected by Charles Saunders (still the company secretary) – on the grounds that religion was a matter for the parents, not the company.

Unlike other industrial villages of the time, Swindon was not a dry town, though endemic drinking and fighting seems to have been the exception rather than the rule. If anything, many of the employees had an almost Quaker-like desire for self-improvement and in 1843 some decided to set up a library, which by March 1844 had fifteen members. Small beginnings, maybe, but it wasn't until 1852 that the first state-supported library opened in Salford, Manchester. Gooch took an interest in the welfare of the staff too and in 1844 the GWR Mechanics Institute was founded to develop the library further. Its purpose was 'disseminating useful knowledge and encouraging rational amusement of all classes of people employed by the GWR at Swindon'. The company provided space in the works for its activities and very quickly the Mechanics Institute played a central part in the social life of the town.

The Mechanics Institute became a place of learning for those that wished to use it for that purpose but it also hosted dances, plays and lectures. Handbills from the late 1840s promote a series of lectures on subjects as varied as the work of Charles Dickens, the rise of language, mineral acids, chemistry, paper-making and printing, amongst others. Clearly there was a thirst for knowledge and this isn't surprising when you bear in mind that although the skilled labourers weren't educated in today's sense, they were generally intelligent and interested men working in an industry that was at the very forefront of technology.

There was one other aspect of the GWR at Swindon that backs up the idea that the railway was rather like a state within a state, and that was the provision of basic healthcare to its staff. The cuts of the late 1840s, combined with relatively poor drainage and sanitation, provoked a real fear of an outbreak of cholera and other diseases (although the railway cottages had sewers, it seems they were rarely maintained). In a bid to maintain the health of Swindon's workers, Gooch proposed that the practice of some of them to band together to fund healthcare should be extended to all employees and made a mandatory condition of employment. Gooch's argument was that some injured employees could not afford treatment from the private practitioners in the area and that a surgeon should instead be directly employed by the railway. With around one accident a week requiring the services of the doctor, Mr Rea, Gooch felt this would be money well spent.

In 1847 the Medical Fund Society was founded and it was made a term of employment at Swindon that a fixed portion of people's wages would be subscribed to the fund. In return the fund would provide medical assistance to the men employed at the works, as well as their wives and families. Contributions varied from 1 ½d for youths earning less than 10s. a week to 4d per week for married men with families earning more than £1 per week. The committee which ran the medical fund pushed hard for improvements to living conditions and gradually won improvements that made Swindon's workforce and its families some of the best provided for in Britain at the time.

The significance of Gooch's suggestion of a form of health insurance cannot be understated: more than a century before the state provided free healthcare for all, the Great Western had instituted a universal health service of its own at Swindon. It was free at point of use, available to the workers' families as well as themselves – and for the next hundred years offered a degree of security and reassurance lacking almost everywhere else in Britain. The Great Western's healthcare system at Swindon Works was nothing less than the template for the National Health Service itself.

There was, naturally, a degree of self interest in providing education, healthcare and recreation facilities to its workers – the works would need literate, numerate staff in the future, it would need healthy staff willing to undertake dangerous work, and by playing a central role in the social fabric of Swindon the GWR could extend its influence beyond the factory gate. All of this may be true but underlying it is the idea of the Great Western being a kind of hybrid between a co-operative and a public limited company. The glimmerings of a bond of mutual trust and respect between the company and its staff are evident and while the next two decades would be tough, that bond helped the railway through until better times arrived.

The Great Western drew inspiration from industrial housing in Cromford, Derbyshire, New Lanark on the River Clyde, and most importantly of all, the London & Birmingham Railway's settlement at Wolverton, which was built in 1838. The railway town of Crewe was a contemporary of Swindon and thus had little influence although it followed a similar pattern. Swindon cannot claim to be the first industrial village but in its scale and beauty it is without question amongst the most important – and overlooked – of all.

*

The vicious cuts at Swindon Works in 1847 were down to a very simple problem: the Railway Mania had sucked so much money from the economy that raising capital to fund investment in new equipment was hard to the point of near impossibility: improvements would have to be paid for from profits rather than issuing new capital.

However, schemes approved in the early days of the mania stood a much greater chance of success and would lead to the broad gauge (and by extension, the Great Western) reaching as far as Penzance, south-west Wales – and most intriguingly of all, Birmingham and Wolverhampton. In 1848, the furthest north the broad gauge reached was Cheltenham but plans were in hand for the Oxford, Worcester & Wolverhampton, Oxford & Rugby, Birmingham & Oxford and Birmingham, Wolverhampton & Dudley railways, the first two of which received Parliamentary assent in 1845 with the other pair following in 1846.

The Oxford & Rugby Railway was planned to link the Great Western with Rugby, which was widely considered to be the gateway to the north. This was by virtue of the many routes which joined at Rugby, connecting Derbyshire, Birmingham, Yorkshire and beyond with London and the south. The strategic need for a connection seemed critical at the time.

The Oxford, Worcester & Wolverhampton (OWW) meanwhile, was promoted by mining and manufacturing interests in South Staffordshire who asked the GWR's board for assistance in promoting a broad gauge line. The GWR proposed that the railway should instead join the Oxford & Rugby at Banbury – a move which was agreed to at the time, alongside provision for the GWR to lease the line when it was completed.

This expansion of the broad gauge empire northwards did not escape the notice of the London & Birmingham Railway (LBR), which hurriedly promoted a rival scheme. A lengthy parliamentary battle ensued in which the GWR lost support for its two schemes but submitted them anyway and, against the odds, won approval. However, Parliament insisted that much of the OWW should be dual gauge, and that the Rugby line should be so if the Board of Trade insisted.

The London & Birmingham's anxieties were further stoked when the Bristol & Oxford Railway began rallying support for a route that didn't depend on the LBR. The plan was to build a railway from Birmingham that would join the GWR at Oxford (the junction later changed to Fenny Compton after the Oxford & Rugby was approved). Provision was made for the GWR to lease this dagger into the heart of the LBR's territory. Oddly there was no mention of gauge for this railway, meaning that under the terms of the Gauge Act it would have to be built to standard gauge. One more railway, the Birmingham, Wolverhampton & Dudley, was proposed at the same time and this was to share a station with the Birmingham & Oxford at Snow Hill, joining the OWW at Priestfield, just outside Wolverhampton, to where it would share tracks. The directors soon realised that as they would be sharing Birmingham Snow Hill station and also that the routes were really continuous, the companies should merge. This they did and immediately proposed to sell the combined company to the Great Western.

The reaction of the London & North Western Railway (LNWR) –

the giant successor to the London & Birmingham following a series of mergers – was initially to try politely to head off the arrival of the Great Western by use of a joint lease. After the LNWR was rebuffed, its redoubtable General Manager, Captain Mark Huish, started to play dirty. His company acquired four-fifths of the 50,000 shares in the Birmingham & Oxford Railway, which were split amongst railway employees into batches of ten to maximise voting rights. Meetings and appeals followed in a bitter struggle. So desperate was the LNWR to prevent the GWR's incursion that it even forged a copy of the Oxford & Birmingham's seal in a bid to get its way. Despite these dirty tricks, the GWR won through and was cleared to acquire the Oxford & Birmingham and Birmingham, Wolverhampton & Dudley, and won powers to extend the broad gauge as far north as Wolverhampton.

While the railways north of Oxford were being planned, surveyed and financed, the situation in the West Country was somewhat different. Although a bitter and expensive decade-long fight for territory ensued between the Great Western and the LSWR for a more direct route from London to Exeter than the one via Bristol, in general terms things ran more smoothly than in the north.

The Berks & Hants was one of the railways the Great Western was to build and operate, and it ran from Reading to Basingstoke, and also to Hungerford. Unusually the whole line was let as a single contract and the 25½ mile section from Reading to Hungerford opened on 21 December 1847. The second section, 13½ miles from Southcote Junction, two miles west of Reading, opened to Basingstoke on 1 November 1848. In September that year another broad gauge route opened from Thingley, two miles west of Chippenham, to Westbury, which would soon become a key junction station in its own right.

Another major route, the South Wales Railway, was also under construction in the 1840s; this would link Milford Haven with Gloucester. Although the company was nominally independent, it was laid to broad gauge and designed by Brunel – and had been promoted, canvassed and supported by the Great Western, which appointed six of the eighteen directors. Brunel originally wanted the railway to run to

Fishguard, where a vast new harbour would be built to rival Holyhead for Irish traffic, but the cost of doing this was far too high and the financial situation in 1849 compelled work to go no further west than Swansea. In 1852 it was extended to Carmarthen and in 1854 the rails reached Haverfordwest. Brunel originally wanted to build a bridge across the River Severn at Hock Cliff, near Frampton-on-Severn, but the Admiralty refused permission, despite the fact that Gloucester was seldom if ever used by large ships and so the original Act of Parliament only allowed the railway to run from Milford Haven to Chepstow. In anticipation of this the Great Western, which had appointed six of its directors to the South Wales Railway's board, had arranged for the Gloucester & Dean Forest Railway to extend its line seven miles from Grange Court to meet a short extension of the South Wales from Chepstow. It avoided an expensive and difficult-to-engineer river crossing but it added many miles to the route that was later avoided by tunnelling under the Severn.

One of the distinguishing features of this railway that would soon spread to Cornwall was the use of timber for the construction of two spectacular viaducts at Landore (Swansea) and Newport. At 580 yards long, the Landore Viaduct had 37 spans supported by trusses on cast iron pillars. Where it crossed the River Tawe, the railway was supported on 100ft wooden polygonal double arches 75ft above the river. At Newport, over the River Usk, the design was similar but shorter, and caught fire just before it was completed in 1849, by which time iron of good enough quality made it feasible to use in major bridge construction. An iron bridge was planned over the Wye at Chepstow which would suspend the railway under a tubular arch structure. The first trains ran from Chepstow to Swansea on 18 June 1850, using rolling stock displaced from the Bristol & Exeter Railway, where the Great Western's lease had expired.

The other major expansion of the broad gauge underway at that time was the Cornwall Railway, which would run from Plymouth to Truro and Falmouth, then a key port for the famous Packet-ship service. Brunel was appointed engineer for the railway and immediately faced an obstacle in the River Tamar. Because of Plymouth's importance as a naval base and the need for large sailing ships to navigate the Tamar, many thought a bridge would be impossible to construct – but Brunel was working on a design which would carry the broad gauge over the Tamar. Construction on the project started quickly but soon foundered due to a lack of funds in 1848. However, it wasn't just railways under construction which suffered in this period: the abrupt end of the railway mania and consequent shortage of capital came close to bringing three of the most important railways in Britain to their knees.

*

It was possible in 1847–8 to see that with a fair wind, the Great Western Railway and the broad gauge would carve out a sizeable slice of Britain on which they could hold a virtual monopoly thanks to the incompatibility of the broad gauge with standard. At the same time though, once the railway mania had burst it would put most railways in a depression that would take some years to recover from.

Christian Wolmar suggests in *Fire and Steam* that the end of the railway bubble started in 1845 when the Bank of England raised interest rates, share prices then slowed, levelled and eventually started to decline. The state of the economy wasn't helped by the abolition of the Corn Laws in 1847, which pushed corn prices up rapidly. When share prices fell, banks went bust and interest rates soared from 3.5 per cent at the start of the year to 10 per cent in November. The economy was plunged into recession and the Great Western wasn't immune.

In August 1847, the board of directors decided to delay new construction and spread it out until the recession eased. With interest rates soaring, it was simply too expensive to borrow money for major projects. The dividend for the second half of the year was cut from 8 per cent (a rate that had remained constant for the past three years) to 7 per cent. Worse still from the point of view of issuing new capital, the share price had fallen. From an index value high of 146 in July 1847, the £100 shares fell to 95 a year later. Other railways were in even worse straits and in September 1848 the boards of the Great Western, London & North Western and London & South Western railways met to discuss a possible merger in order to provide at least some capital for developing infrastructure. In November 1848, they formally announced their plans but an alteration to the proposed terms by the LNWR was refused by the other two companies. It's a sign of how desperate the railways were that these three companies were prepared to put their differences aside and merge.

In 1849 dividends fell further, to 6 per cent in February and 4 per cent in August. Economies were made too, and not just at Swindon Works, which had its workforce slashed by two-thirds: auditors recommended across-the-board pay cuts. The directors naturally opposed this but when Charles Saunders agreed to have his own pay cut, they eventually fell in line – it was yet another example of how this remarkable man put what he considered the railway's interests above his own. New railways were halted with the exception of the Birmingham, Wolverhampton and Dudley extension. Things were helped a little in April 1849 when the Great Western's lease of the Bristol & Exeter expired, releasing rolling stock for use elsewhere. The companies would remain on good terms but the mileage of railways operated by the GWR was cut from 312 to 227.

As the 1840s drew to a close, two other matters began to come to the fore. The most pressing was the need to improve facilities at London, where Bishop's Road had reached capacity, while in the Midlands two plucky little companies based around Shrewsbury began to sound out Charles Saunders for help in defeating the bullying tactics of Captain Huish of the LNWR.

The 1840s had seen the GWR complete its initial main line and expand its reach as far as Plymouth with a raft of extensions underway. The 1850s would see the core of the Great Western completed, along with some of Brunel's greatest achievements of all.

Of all railway stations great and small, none justifies the railway enthusiast cliché of a 'cathedral of steam' more than Paddington – the Great Western Railway's presence in London. It had always been the plan to replace the cramped and inconvenient temporary terminus at Bishop's Road with something grander and much more fit for purpose. Such was the need that, even given the financial situation in the late 1840s, the go-ahead was given. Brunel was responsible for the design of the new station and he took inspiration from the architect Joseph Paxton, whose pioneering use of prefabricated components made from iron metal and glass formed the basis of the spectacular Crystal Palace of the Great Exhibition of 1851. Brunel thought a similar approach would allow a spectacular station to be created that would give plenty of space for growth. He seems somewhat bewildered by the freedom that Paxton's pre-fabricated method of construction gave him, coming up with sketches full of eclectic, fussy, slightly confused designs that were most unlike him.

He wrote to the architect Matthew (later Sir) Digby Wyatt in January 1851 for assistance. 'I am going to design in a great hurry and I believe to build a station after my own fancy – that is with engineering roofs etc without any architectural or attempt. It is at Paddington in a cutting and admitting of no exterior, all interior'– all roofed in,' he wrote.

In a rare admission, Brunel acknowledged he didn't have the knowledge he needed of metal construction and sought Digby Wyatt's help on the detail, though Brunel would be in charge of the overall appearance. The grand hotel that would front the station was to be designed by Philip Charles Hardwick.

It took some development and it looked for a while as if the distinctive triple-arch train shed would use semi-circular arches tied together at their bottoms with tie rods. The contractor responsible for the station, Fox, Henderson – which also built the structure for the Great Exhibition – suggested elliptical arches would obviate the need for tie rods and Brunel agreed.

The design was extravagant and elegant in its conception. Three arches – 68ft, 102½ft and 69½ft wide – sat next to each other, covering an area 700ft long by 240ft wide. It might have looked like three long tubes from the end except for a dash of inspired brilliance.

The trainshed is divided at two points by 50ft wide transepts crossing at right-angles to break up the length. These had oriel windows forming gable ends and balconies on Platform 1 that generations of station-masters gazed out from. The transepts are what give Paddington its cathedral-like splendour. Although some have suggested they existed to provide space for traversers to swap locomotives and coaches from one track to another, it was more than anything a grand visual touch which added to the splendour of the station. At the outer ends, Digby Wyatt designed swirling arabesques to detail the windscreens, and the glass roof over the centre of the arches (the sides were originally covered with corrugated iron) made it light and airy. The detailing is beautiful in its simplicity and elegance, and was matched by the buildings along Platform 1 that included a royal waiting room (now partially restored and forming part of the first-class lounge) and station offices. Platform 1, the left-most platform looking out from the buffer stops, opened in January 1854 and the arrival side on 29 May 1855. In Paddington, the Great Western had a presence in London that was unmatched until the rebuilding of St Pancras in the twenty-first century, and possibly not even then. Strapped for cash the Great Western may have been, but nobody could dispute that its investment in Paddington paid for itself many times over.

For those that believe that what goes around comes around, it is perhaps just that Brunel, whose withholding of payments from contractors was legendary, was a victim of this tactic himself with Paddington. He spent £3,000 of his own money on planning the station believing the Great Western would pay him back on the basis of its long-standing agreement with him. The GWR directors interpreted it differently, offering him just £1,000. Brunel threatened to resign but the directors held firm and called his bluff. The great engineer gave in.

Chapter 7
The Shropshire Lions

With work underway on Paddington station, the Great Western now turned its attention northwards once again. The Shrewsbury & Chester and Shrewsbury & Birmingham railways were small independents and both were being put under pressure by the LNWR to merge with it to ensure a monopoly in Shropshire and Cheshire. Unlike most of the LNWR's other smaller rivals, who folded readily, the two Shrewsbury companies put up a fight to retain their independence.

The Shrewsbury & Chester (S&C) opened throughout on 14 October 1848, with the Shrewsbury & Birmingham (S&B) following on 12 November 1849. The latter ran as far as Wolverhampton from where it had agreed to share the LNWR's line to Birmingham. In itself this would not have posed a major problem for the LNWR, which had acquired the Shropshire Union Railway from Stafford to Shrewsbury via Wellington from where it shared metals with the S&B for the 10 miles into Shrewsbury.

But when the S&B and S&C pooled resources to compete against the LNWR for traffic from Chester and Birkenhead to the Midlands, this could not be tolerated by the LNWR, which had access to Shrewsbury and Chester from its citadel at Crewe. It immediately tried to acquire or eliminate the new upstarts.

Mark Huish of the LNWR wrote to the S&C expressing his hope that competition would be avoided: 'I need not say that if you should be unwise enough to encourage such a proceeding [competition] it must result in a general fight by our Railway from Shrewsbury to Liverpool and by our Shropshire canal, the only gainers being of course the public and the Shrewsbury & Birmingham Company,' he warned.

The S&C's secretary, Mr Roy, rebuffed Huish in almost casual terms, making it clear that the smaller railway *would* compete for traffic. To Huish it was war and very quickly the LNWR refused to allow passengers to be booked via Shrewsbury from Chester and when this didn't deter the S&C, dragged its booking clerk out of his office, throwing his tickets after him. The Birkenhead Company, who the S&C relied on to gain access to Birkenhead, was thoroughly cowed by the LNWR and barred third-class passengers of the S&C from all except two inconvenient trains. The S&C ran omnibuses to provide a service instead and in turn the LNWR barricaded the approaches to Chester station – which the S&C part-owned! – to prevent the buses getting access. The S&C sought an injunction against the LNWR and was successful and there, for a little while, things rested.

In 1850, Huish succeeded in bullying the Birkenhead Company into refusing through-booking, interchanging carriages and forwarding cattle trucks. On 4 May, when the S&C sent empty cattle trucks to Birkenhead for loading they were returned empty, the cattle having been loaded onto LNWR trucks instead. Incredibly the S&C still refused to give in, chartering a boat to move cattle. The LNWR responded in kind at huge loss to itself, doing everything it could to undermine its lesser rival. Somebody had to blink and it was the chairman of the Birkenhead Company, whose shareholders were furious that it was refusing legitimate traffic because of the LNWR. Sanity was restored and the S&C was able to resume something approaching normal operation.

In the West Midlands, the LNWR started a ferocious price war with the S&B, hoping to out-muscle it financially, even though its journey from Shrewsbury to Birmingham was 16½ miles longer than the S&B's 29½-mile route. When the S&B tried to lay a siding for goods traffic on the Birmingham Canal, it was prevented from doing so and after legal appeal the S&B started work, only to find a veritable army of LNWR navvies had turned up to forcibly prevent it doing so. Only police and military intervention prevented a riot.

Inevitably, the financial warfare took a toll but when the S&B approached the LNWR to pool fares for through traffic, the S&C,

whose assent was needed, refused to ratify the deal. In retaliation, the LNWR slowed construction of the Stour Valley line from Wolverhampton to Birmingham: it would happily cut off its own nose to spite its opponent's face, particularly as it had a route which passed near Wolverhampton. What mattered was beating the competition, not serving the public.

It was clear the two Shrewsbury companies were too small to fight off the LNWR but rather than seeking a merger they turned to the Great Western, whose routes to Birmingham and Wolverhampton were underway. Furthermore, the S&B had hedged its bets in Wolverhampton by signing a deal for access to the proposed low-level station there – which the GWR would use. The companies went to see Charles Saunders, who quickly signed a deal for co-operation and interchange of traffic between the three companies.

Predictably, Huish was enraged. Having already been beaten once by Saunders on the Birmingham & Oxford Railway, he tried similar tactics, buying shares in the Shrewsbury & Birmingham Railway and giving them to residents around London Euston station. He sought to create a climate of opinion against the S&B's directors and proposed a resolution effectively giving control to the LNWR. In April 1851, a four-day meeting to consider the deal was demanded and obtained by Huish's lackeys, and despite a solicitor confirming that the deal would be totally illegal without an Act of Parliament, the motion was carried.

The Great Western wasn't to be defeated so easily, however and made the shareholders a counter offer that bettered the LNWR's proposed terms. Saunders proposed a future amalgamation of the S&B and S&C in 1856 or 1857 – the smaller companies to decide – on terms based on their revenues in the previous year. A fixed percentage of revenue from London traffic to places beyond Birmingham was also guaranteed – and most importantly of all, the Great Western promised to seek an Act of Parliament to ratify the deal, which Huish had not.

Although Huish made use of a forged seal again to apparently endorse the proposed effective merger with the LNWR, when the S&B's directors held a special meeting on 8 May 1851 his forged document was not produced, his party merely protesting against the agreement with the Great Western, whose proposal was passed. He tried similar tactics with the Shrewsbury & Chester in June 1851 but he failed here too, the S&C shareholders voting overwhelmingly in favour of the Great Western's offer.

The LNWR continued its opposition almost in spite, it seemed, and there were still legal wrangles to resolve. However, in November 1851 the S&B was finally able to run trains into its joint Wolverhampton High Level station on LNWR metals, and finally on 1 July 1852 into Birmingham via the LNWR's route after yet more obstructive tactics from that company. When the Great Western's own rails reached Wolverhampton two years later, the LNWR's opposition would become completely irrelevant.

The Great Western had acquired two extremely useful railways and extended its reach from Wolverhampton all the way to Merseyside (although the railways from Oxford to Wolverhampton were not open at the time of the merger); in addition GWR gained a well-equipped repair shop in Wolverhampton headed by an extremely competent engineer called Joseph Armstrong. The crucial aspect of the Shrewsbury railways though, is that they were standard gauge and Parliament would not sanction their conversion to broad. With the Great Western obliged to lay dual gauge track from Birmingham to Oxford and from Reading to Banbury, it had ceased to be an entirely broad gauge railway.

These acquisitions – as important and useful as they were – came at a cost to hard-pressed shareholders given the economic situation in the early 1850s, but in time would prove their worth. It wasn't all plain sailing when it came to the planned railways either. In 1851, the Oxford, Worcester & Wolverhampton (OWW) – which was engineered by Brunel and received financial support from the GWR – rebelled and descended into open warfare with its parent company over a disagreement about how much the Great Western would pay it. The OWW directors believed the GWR had guaranteed to pay interest of 4 per cent on the whole construction cost, but the Great Western disagreed and said the agreement placed a cap of £2.5 million on the amount of construction costs it was prepared to guarantee. After wrangles about funding and completion of the route, which ran into 1851, it was decided to complete the OWW to standard gauge and deny the GWR its lease. So bitter was the dispute that the OWW proposed to abandon its route into Wolverhampton and use the LNWR's instead – all to spite the GWR. The Great Western appealed to Parliament, which eventually forced the OWW to lay dual gauge track from Priestfield to just beyond Wolverhampton, allowing access to the Great Western. For the time being at least, the OWW would reside firmly in the LNWR's camp.

The year 1852 also saw completion of Brunel's distinctive bridge over the River Wye at Chepstow, which allowed services to run to South Wales from Gloucester for the first time – and in the Midlands, the Great Western was preparing to run to Birmingham.

By Autumn 1852, the Oxford to Birmingham Railway was ready to open and on 30 September, an inaugural special for directors, officers and friends was chartered, leaving Paddington at 09:00, then calling at Oxford at 10:20 before running to Birmingham to pick up more guests and return to Leamington for the traditional feast. On the way up, it caught up with a mixed passenger-and-goods train from Didcot to Oxford which regularly ran late and when it left Oxford the special was running half-an-hour late but it still caught up with the service train at Aynho. Two wagons were being detached from the mixed train when the special, hauled by Gooch's *Lord of the Isles* and with Gooch himself on the footplate, crashed into the wagons. Miraculously, none of the passengers on the service train or the special were hurt but the loco-motive was damaged. The trip to Birmingham was abandoned and the locomotive of the service train took the special party to Leamington, where they met the Birmingham guests, who had been brought down by another special train. The cause was simple: none of the men on the footplate knew the new route as intimately as they ought and misread a disused signal which they thought gave them the 'All Clear' as they approached Aynho. When they saw the station signal at 'Danger' the train's brakes were woefully inadequate and unable to stop them in time. It was a lucky escape but despite the accident, passenger services started on the following day, 1 October 1852, with the 129 miles from Paddington to Birmingham covered in 2¾ hours. This incident again emphasised the lack of effective safety standards at the time.

At Swindon, which had seen such vicious cuts in the 1840s, locomotive building had resumed on a small scale and in 1853 the works was extended in order to meet the requirements of the Birmingham line, as well as to a lesser degree the Shrewsbury railways (being standard gauge there was no easy way to send any locomotives, carriages or wagons there before the route to Wolverhampton was opened throughout).

The following year, 1854, saw the completion of the Birmingham, Wolverhampton & Dudley Railway; there was considerable pressure to finish this as the amalgamation with the Shrewsbury railways had been brought forward to 1 September 1854, when the agreement with the LNWR to run on its tracks expired. In the event, a weak bridge which had collapsed before the route opened had to be replaced and five other bridges also had to be replaced or strengthened, which delayed the opening of Wolverhampton Low Level to 14 November 1854. From the very beginning, broad and standard gauge trains operated on the Wolverhampton to Birmingham stretch of line with no difficulties, proving such operation was feasible.

For a while, matters rested. Charles Russell, the company's long-serving Chairman, retired on 2 August 1855. A portrait had been commissioned of him three years before and 1,900 staff had contributed to the £420 cost. The portrait was hung in the boardroom and, for many years, being summoned before the directors was known as 'going to see the picture'. Russell had warned the Board that his increasingly poor health and age meant that his retirement would be imminent but since 1853 he had twice been persuaded to stay on. In his sixteen years' service, Russell had transformed the Great Western from a single main line into an empire which, either directly or through allied companies reached from London to Plymouth, Swansea, Chester and the Mersey,

Weymouth (the Wilts, Somerset & Weymouth would open the following year) and could soon see its influence spreading as far as Cornwall. The growth had been massive and continuous but Russell had, as much as Brunel, Gooch and Saunders, laid the foundations for the great things that would follow. Sadly, he did not get to enjoy a long retirement and died on 15 May 1856.

Chapter 8
The Final Pieces

Construction of the Cornwall Railway, of which the Great Western, South Devon and Bristol & Exeter railways all had stakes, resumed in 1852 with Brunel, as ever, at the helm. Cornwall's terrain was difficult and expensive to build a railway through, and with only a small population it was impossible to justify the expense of providing the flat and straight route that might otherwise be ideal.

The Cornwall Railway was to run from Plymouth, crossing the Tamar, before running via St German's, Liskeard, Lostwithiel and St Austell to Truro and then down to Falmouth. In its 53 miles it would need thirty-five viaducts crossing valleys, estuaries and creeks – and with the exception of the Tamar crossing, there was no money to pay for the expensive stone or iron structures found on other routes.

Brunel had used timber structures on the West Cornwall Railway from Truro to Penzance, which was originally built to standard gauge. This was another independent railway that aimed to serve the key towns of West Cornwall and although it opened in 1852, it would be some years before it came into the Great Western's orbit.

Timber may seem an unlikely material to build railway viaducts out of (especially given the propensity of early steam locomotives to throw out sparks) but used properly it is immensely strong. Brunel's experience with timber structures on the West Cornwall – and of course, the South Wales – railways meant that he knew how to build structures which were able to cope with the strain of passing trains and also to be easily maintained, with timbers able to be replaced without compromising the viaduct's integrity.

Of these structures, the 378yd-long Notter Viaduct over the River Lynher at St Germans was incomparably the finest – and although it looked extremely fragile when viewed from a distance, it still prevented two goods trains which had collided head-on from falling into the water. Most of these viaducts supported the lattice-like timber structure on substantial stone piers. Some were re-used when they were later reconstructed in stone but others were simply abandoned and stand sentinel next to their more robust counterparts today.

The advent of railways to Devon and Cornwall meant that Great Western even affected time itself in the 1850s. There was no standard time throughout Britain, with towns and villages all working to the exact local time. When the fastest means of travel was a stagecoach this didn't matter so much but the speed of the railways presented problems; the local time in London is twenty minutes ahead of that in Truro, and neither the railway nor passengers could be expected to compensate for the difference. The decision was taken to adopt London time as a standard as early as 1840 and from 1 November 1852, when telegraph communication was completed from London to Plymouth, a standard time signal was sent to all stations at 10:00 so they could adjust their clocks accordingly. Telegraph operators were ordered to keep their lines clear from 09:58 in order to synchronise clocks. It was this innovation, lead largely by the Great Western, that led in 1880 to Greenwich Mean Time being recognised as the standard time throughout Britain. It was an idea whose time had come.

*

The estuary of the River Tamar at Saltash is deep and wide. It was also of considerable strategic importance to the Royal Navy, which demanded that any bridge should offer enough clearance for its ships of the line to pass under. Very few bridges had been constructed over such challenging and demanding waterways: Robert Stephenson had designed the Britannia Bridge which crosses the Menai Straits to link Wales with Anglesey and this opened in 1850, but there was nothing else of comparable scale — and even Stephenson's bridge didn't require a pier built in deep water.

The big problem Brunel faced was that a wide span was needed to allow ships to pass safely. A conventional masonry structure would have been virtually impossible to design, while Stephenson's approach of using tubular girders couldn't be considered: *that* would look like copying. Brunel took an approach that was elegant in its conception, rational in its construction and above all beautiful in its execution. Taking a lead from his bridge over the Wye at Chepstow, Brunel opted to create a two-span steel-arch bridge from which the railway would be suspended. The weight of the deck would counteract the tendency of the arches to try to flatten, meaning each span could be considered a self-contained structure in its own right. The bridge would be connected to the shore by approach viaducts built of wrought iron, which were substantial structures in their own right.

The biggest challenge was to build a pier in the centre of the estuary and for this feat Brunel exercised every last ounce of his genius. The central pier was key to the entire structure but deep foundations had to be excavated underwater into the hard rock below. Brunel designed a 'great cylinder', a 90ft-tall wrought-iron tube which was 35ft in diameter for the first 50ft, increasing to 37ft for the remaining 40ft. The bottom of this tube was angled to fit the profile of the rocks, and a pressurised domed roof effectively creating a diving bell was fitted 20ft above the base. A 4ft-wide pressurised annulus – a ring – ran around the edge of the cylinder's inside to allow men to excavate rock and build a ring on which the granite piers could be built. There was a 10ft-wide tube that connected a deck at the 'Great Cylinder's' top and a 6ft tube inside that allowed pressurised air to flow to the annulus, preventing water ingress and giving the workers air to breathe.

This ingenious structure was built at a temporary works on the Devon side of the river and floated out in May 1854: four precisely positioned pontoons would keep it stable. Having been floated out on its side, more Brunellian genius came into play: the cylinder could be partially flooded to tilt it to the vertical. Once all was ready the cylinder was lowered in exactly the right position and its 300-ton weight cut through 16ft of mud to rest on the river bed, but not the rock the bridge needed to be built on.

Then it was the turn of the workers using hand tools to first excavate the mud and then to level the stone within the annulus. Once a granite wall had been built around the annulus the mud in the centre of the great cylinder was excavated and more granite blocks laid. The men were working under pressure in every sense of the word and once they returned to the surface, many suffered the bends like today's under-water divers. Initial shifts were seven hours but this was very soon reduced to three in recognition of the appalling conditions. Slowly and painfully the central pier reached upwards and by November 1856 it had cleared the surface of the Tamar.

There are ten approach spans to the bridge on the Cornish side and seven on the Devon; because the spans of these were no greater than 93ft it was possible to build them conventionally using wrought-iron girders on masonry piers. Brunel made the spans shorter as they approached the land, not for any engineering reason but simply to make the main spans look more impressive: it was a visual trick which still delights.

For the giant main spans, Brunel built two 455ft-long trusses formed of an elliptical arch made of a riveted wrought-iron tube 16ft 3in wide and 12ft 3in high – large enough to drive a car through and almost, but not quite, a train. The tube itself is elliptical in order to reduce wind resistance. As later experience with suspension bridges would prove, if the underside was flat, strong winds could turn them into aerofoils with disastrous results. For the Tamar Bridge, Brunel deliberately incorporated aerodynamics into a static structure before most engineers had even considered these possibilities. From the tube arches are suspended two tiers of chains (although they are more like bicycle chains than anchor chains) on either side of the arches and the trackbed was suspended from these. The structure is made more rigid by eleven vertical supports hanging from the tubes to the deck and these are cross-braced in turn. The railway was to be carried in a trough with walls 16ft 9in apart, enough for a broad gauge track and tall, wide Great Western locomotives.

The main spans – elliptical tube arch, chains and most of the decks – were assembled on land as it was much safer and simpler than trying to construct all of the bridge over water. They were then floated into position and jacked up 3ft at a time, the piers being built underneath as the spans were raised. The landward piers of masonry and the central pier of four wrought-iron columns extensively braced together.

The Cornish span was floated out on 1 September 1857 after extensive tests to prove its strength that showed very little deflection of the arches even when heavier-than-anticipated loads were placed on it. Bit by bit the span was jacked up and by 31 May 1858 was at full height. The Devon span followed on 10 July 1858 and was completed by 16 February 1859. By April 1859 the bridge was ready for the first trains.

The directors of the Cornwall Railway inspected the bridge by train on 11 April 1859, and the Board of Trade inspected it for itself on 20 April, finding nothing to fault. Prince Albert, who had given his blessing for the structure to be named after him, officially opened the Royal Albert Bridge on 2 May 1859 with a crowd of thousands lining the shores on both sides of the bridge, but Brunel wasn't there. His health was failing rapidly due to the pressures of completing his giant steam ship SS *Great Eastern* allied with high blood pressure and inflammation of the kidneys. He was conveyed on a carriage truck fitted with a couch for him to rest on and driven over the bridge by a Gooch steam locomotive in May 1859.

Brunel had made amends for his atmospheric railway debacle with the first of Britain's three great railway bridges (the others are the Forth and Tay bridges in Scotland). He had paid absolute attention to the design of the structure to the smallest detail – even to where the rivets would be placed – and how the components should be made and assembled. The Royal Albert Bridge across the Tamar is perhaps his crowning achievement – more so than the Clifton Suspension Bridge in Bristol, or Paddington or even the Great Western Main Line from

London to Bristol itself. The structure is visible not just from the adjacent road bridge completed in 1961 but also from miles away on a clear day and it continually inspires with its grace and elegance. It stands as eloquent testimony to Brunel's sometimes misguided but so often brilliant genius.

The bridge may have been completed but time was running out for Brunel himself. After *Great Eastern* made her maiden voyage on 7 September, he gamely went to Millwall in London to see her and stood on deck, but as a picture was taken of him on his ship he suffered a stroke. Isambard Kingdom Brunel passed away on 15 September 1859 at the early age of fifty-three, and with his departure something of the Great Western's élan went with him. It would be another two generations before there was anyone comparable at GWR again.

Daniel Gooch was devastated. In his diary he wrote:

On the 15th September 1859 I lost my oldest and best friend in the death of Mr Brunel. He had been far from well for two or three years past, and during that time had been much worried by the *Great Eastern* steamship. This was his last great work; not satisfied with the size of the *Great Britain*, he conceived and designed this noble ship.

By his death the greatest of England's engineers was lost, the man of the greatest originality of thought and power of execution, bold in his plans but right.

The commercial world thought him extravagant, but although he was so, great things are not done by those who sit down and count the cost of every thought and act.

He was a true and sincere friend, a man of the highest honour, and his loss was deeply deplored by all who had the pleasure to know him . . . I shall ever feel a deep sense of gratitude to Mr Brunel for all his kindness and support, from the day I first saw him in 1837.

Chapter 9
Losing the Way

With the broad gauge network largely complete by the start of the 1860s, it's instructive to now look at some of the operation. In 1841, when the main line was open throughout from London to Bristol, the fastest train was the Night Mail, which took 4hrs 10 mins for the 118¼-mile journey. Considering that so much was made of the speed potential of the broad gauge, one might imagine that speeds rose fairly quickly after that.

In fact, by 1845, four years later, ten minutes had been *added* to this time, and the journey time to Exeter was 7hrs 10mins – far slower than the first train that Gooch so expertly drove all the way from Paddington in 1841. Far from being the fastest railway in England, the Great Western's average speed exclusive of stoppages was 33mph, slower than the 36mph of the Northern & Eastern from London to Bishop's Stortford. If the broad gauge was to prevail, something needed to be done – and it was.

In March 1845, the Great Western suddenly accelerated its fastest London to Exeter train to five hours, and this was cut by a further thirty minutes in May by cutting the mandatory stop at Swindon to just a minute – to the wrath of Swindon's refreshment room tenant, Griffiths of Cheltenham. After a legal appeal, a ten-minute stop was reinstated in January 1846 and Gooch then suggested that his locomotives of 1840 could make up the time, which they did until 1847.

As the first of Gooch's new more powerful and faster Swindon-built locomotives – headed by *Great Western* (the famous '7ft singles') – came on-stream, the journey time to Bristol was cut by 13 minutes to 2hrs 30mins, though an additional stop at Bridgwater meant the journey time to Exeter was only cut by 5 minutes. Between Paddington and

Didcot, the fastest train was allowed just 55 minutes for the 52½ miles; an average speed of 55mph which gave the Great Western by far the fastest trains in Britain, if not the world.

Gradually however, the insertion of extra stops frittered away these fast journey times and the recession of the early 1850s slowed things further, with 45 minutes being added to the fastest London to Bristol and Exeter times in 1853. There things would rest for another nine years. Between London and Birmingham, in 1852 the fastest trains ran the 129 miles in 2hrs 45mins but poor weather caused damage to the infrastructure and in December that year the journey time had increased to 3hrs. Additionally, improvements to locomotives and use of more daring timetabling was allowing the standard gauge railways to catch up with the Great Western's performance.

Services began to be accelerated again from London to Birmingham in 1859, but it was the London & South Western Railway's decision to speed their services from London Waterloo to Exeter to 4hrs 45mins in February 1862 – 25 minutes faster than the best Great Western service – which prompted the reinstatement of the 4hrs 30mins journey time from the 1840s. Again though, complacency seemed to creep in rapidly, with the Great Western slowing the London to Bristol journey time from 2hrs 25mins to 2hrs 58mins. The Bristol & Exeter tried to make up the deficiency by speeding its part of the service but it failed and soon it slowed to 5hrs 5mins. Of course, with the LSWR offering comparable journey times the broad gauge's alleged superiority in speed was proved to be a myth. It was the start of a gradual decline in standards which would give the Great Western the reputation of being rather slow and staid.

But, in spite of it all, what a spectacle the broad gauge railway must have been, particularly in those days when the standard gauge hadn't yet penetrated Paddington. Gooch's beautiful green 8ft-diameter driving wheel 4-2-2s with their gothic-arched fireboxes gliding with their trains through the west of England, no hint of outside valve gear or motion spoiling their lines; the quaint four-wheeled chocolate-and-cream coaches in short trains behind; the glistening copper, the burnished brass and the sense of unchallenged superiority engendered by Brunel's brilliant engineering.

And what of the men who drove and fired those locomotives? They must have been made of iron and steel and with fire in their bellies. They suffered vibration and jolting thanks to Brunel's insistence on the unforgiving baulk road but there was little protection for them from the elements. Working on those locomotives might have been rather pleasant in the summer but when the weather broke it must have been hell. Lashed by the wind and rain – and sometimes snow – and with little even to prevent them falling off the footplate, it would have been as much as they could do to stay on board. They might have been instructed to pay complete attention to their locomotive, the signals, the timetable (without even a rudimentary speedometer) and to conserve coal but I agree with the railway author W.A. Tuplin, who reckoned that when the weather got really bad the driver and fireman spent as much time as possible huddled around the firebox behind the weatherboard (where there was one), relying on the rear view of signals to indicate that it might be worth paying a little bit more attention.

Working on a steam locomotive was tough even on more 'modern' designs (including *Tornado*, which made its debut in 2008), and more so on a typical Great Western locomotive of the 1930s but by comparison, the broad gauge locomotives were the definition of torture. The railway policemen might have suffered in their sentry boxes and the porters in the iron coffins certainly did, but when it came to the demands of their daily duties it is hard to deny that the drivers and firemen of the broad gauge railway were the real heroes of the early days.

But never mind that the trains didn't have very good brakes, or that journey times were long and facilities poor! Just to stand at somewhere like Didcot or Maidenhead for an hour or two and watch these gilded if already outdated creations strut their stuff in the 1850s must have been magnificent. Sadly the most telling word in that flight of fancy is 'outdated'. Gooch's express locomotives would continue to deliver good service until the end of the broad gauge but by 1860 they were starting to look a little obsolete. Their sheer size and relative lightness gave them a good amount of power so they were able to keep time on the light trains of the period but if schedules had accelerated or trainloads increased they would soon have been found wanting. Thankfully for the Great Western there was no need and no money to replace them, which was a good job because from the early 1860s, it was becoming clear that the broad gauge's days were numbered.

*

The opening of the Cornwall Railway marked the end of widespread expansion of the broad gauge and the beginning of a lengthy process of consolidation for the Great Western. This process began in 1860 when the Birkenhead Company sought to relinquish control of its railway to the Great Western and the London & North Western. This practice of two companies jointly owning and operating a railway was quite common: the short stretch of line from Shrewsbury to Wellington in Shropshire ran on the same principle, and although there were niggling differences between the GWR and LNWR, in practice it was a fairly straightforward process for the two to agree which was finally completed in July 1860.

The operation of standard gauge railways north of Wolverhampton and the refusal of Parliament to countenance further extensions of the broad gauge in that part of the world meant that it was impossible to run through trains from London beyond the Black Country, and although the Great Western had run its first passenger train to Birkenhead in 1857 it was clear that it was missing out on a great deal of through traffic from south of Birmingham because passengers could reach Merseyside via the LNWR without the inconvenience of enforced train changes due to the break of gauge. Perhaps more important to the Great Western than passenger traffic was the inevitable loss of goods traffic heading to London from Shropshire and Cheshire, for which the break of gauge meant it simply couldn't compete.

Gradually the Great Western's hand was being forced into extending standard gauge rails from Reading (where it already allowed goods trains to run from the north through to Basingstoke and the south coast) to Paddington. A further consideration was that the Oxford Worcester & Wolverhampton (OWW) was planning to merge with the Worcester & Hereford and Newport & Abergavenny railways to form a new company called the West Midland Railway. As the Great Western already had a substantial stake in the OWW and saw the potential to acquire a great deal of business from the region, it decided to look closely at extending standard gauge to London.

This was a matter which must have caused a great deal of soul searching by Saunders in particular, who was still Company Secretary and whose advocacy of the broad gauge had seldom wavered. He believed that if the amalgamation to form the West Midland Railway was approved, 'great good would result to both companies' and in a report to the directors in August 1860, he wrote that 'it would be difficult to overestimate the flow of traffic which would flow off the Oxford and Worcester lines from South Wales for London,' after the Worcester & Hereford Railway was completed.

In another report in October that year, the cost of extending standard gauge rails to Paddington was estimated at £225,000 and the cost of acquiring new locomotives, carriages and wagons to run the services another £230,000. The directors finally acknowledged the inconveniences caused by the breaks of gauge and the shareholders approved the recommendation to go ahead with the plans readily.

Work didn't start on laying the standard gauge until May 1861, by which time the Great Western directors had been thoroughly spooked by the West Midland Railway's plans to build a new railway to London in competition with the GWR and agreed to acquire the West Midland Railway at a cost of paying 17.5 per cent of the net revenue of both companies. Saunders seems to have been unconvinced of the high cost of the deal but acceded because he believed that bringing the West Midland Railway into the Great Western system would ultimately be worth the price. Although Parliamentary approval was needed to formally ratify the deal, by 1 July 1861 the West Midland Railway and

Great Western were essentially operating as a single entity under a joint operating committee.

The dual-gauging of the Reading to Paddington section which started in May was completed in mid-August 1861 with minimal disruption to traffic and on 14 August, an engineer's inspection train was hauled throughout from Reading to Paddington using a standard gauge locomotive. The standard gauge and broad gauge locomotives and rolling stock were never mixed into a single train – to do so would have been dangerous even if it had been possible – but a standard gauge train could follow a broad gauge train on the same route, and of course, vice versa.

Little time was wasted in making full use of the standard gauge connection and on 1 October 1861 the first through train from Paddington to Birkenhead departed, leaving London at 09:35. The standard gauge wasn't entirely complete: new platforms had to be built at Reading, and at Didcot trains had to use the avoiding line around the station so they couldn't call there, but the Great Western was finally starting to make good use of potential suggested by a quick glance at its route map. The Windsor branch was also in line for dual-gauging and when this was completed in early 1862, Queen Victoria was finally freed from the perils of the break of gauge, travelling all the way to Scotland on standard gauge tracks in April that year.

Although the West Midland Railway's Oxford Worcester & Wolverhampton route offered a roundabout way to the Midlands, it potentially offered the chance to compete with the South Wales Railway for goods traffic to London. Mindful of the fact that the Great Western operated the South Wales Railway and that to compete with it would be akin to a tiger eating its own tail, the Great Western proposed a merger with the Welsh concern in 1861 which would see the existing operating agreement replaced with a fixed rent of £170,000 from 1 January 1862 and, once the merger with the West Midland Railway was approved, South Wales Railway shareholders would receive between 10.7 per cent and 10.9 per cent of the joint revenue of all three companies. In a sense, the Great Western acquired the West Midland and the South Wales on the never-never, banking on increased revenue more than offsetting the high dividend payments — which were far higher than those paid to the Great Western's own shareholders.

The Shrewsbury & Hereford Railway, meanwhile, found itself in the position of being surrounded by the Great Western, which would be able to steal traffic from both ends of its route. Not surprisingly, its directors were not happy about this prospect and approached the LNWR to seek a big partner who might wish to acquire the company. The LNWR initially offered to lease the line in partnership with the Great Western but Saunders refused, fearing the LNWR would have too much control. The LNWR and Shrewsbury & Hereford took matters into their own hands and proposed that the LNWR should take sole control of the route and promoted a bill to rubber-stamp that. The Great Western appealed and failed and finally on 1 July 1862 a bill was passed giving half of the Shrewsbury & Hereford to the LNWR and the remainder to the Great Western and West Midland railways. It wasn't actually a bad deal in that it gave neither company a monopoly on traffic from South Wales to the North West and although the Great Western could have sent traffic the long way round via Hereford, Worcester, Wolverhampton and Shrewsbury to the north, in practice the 'North and West', as the route became known, was and is a vital artery which continues to perform useful service to the present day.

In the early 1860s there were some additions to the broad gauge network but these were by and large short branches, though some would later be extended to form through routes. The most unlikely of all was the dual gauge Metropolitan Railway from the Great Western Railway at Paddington to Farringdon Road, with an extension to the Central Meat Market at Smithfield where the Great Western and Metropolitan railways would lease a station in the basement.

The extensive tunnels on the Metropolitan line — it wasn't entirely underground but much was — required the provision of locomotives with low emissions. Gooch, still Locomotive Superintendent after all these years (although he had pursued many other ventures over the

years alongside his GWR activities) designed some 2-4-0 tank
locomotives for the line which were the first fitted with condensing
apparatus. This equipment diverts the exhaust steam normally vented
out through the chimney and instead returns it via pipes to the side tanks
that contain the water. This process not only eliminates much of the
smoke and steam coming from the chimney, it also saves water. The
cost is that without the draught provided by the exhaust blasting
upwards through the chimney, the fire struggles to burn hot enough –
so steam generation is limited. The problem was that the water tanks
were too small and as the returning steam condensed, it heated the
water inside them, preventing the water injectors from working
properly. Six of these locomotives were built by the Vulcan Foundry in
1862, followed by another ten at Swindon in 1863–4.

Services began on 10 January 1863, the Great Western using its new
condensing tank locomotives and a fleet of eight-wheeled coaches,
which for the first time were lit by gas rather than the oil used on the
railway's other rolling stock. Disagreements between the GWR and the
Metropolitan sprang up quickly. First the disagreements were about
finance but then about the service frequency, which the GWR limited
to four trains per hour. The Metropolitan not unreasonably felt this was
rather low but Saunders retained an old-fashioned view of safety and
refused to increase this, believing there was no demand for a greater
service. As the dispute escalated the Great Western told the
Metropolitan on 18 July 1863 that it would operate no services after
the end of September.

The Metropolitan refused to be cowed and promised to take over the
service the day after. Saunders then said the Great Western would
withdraw its stock on 10 August in a high-stakes bid to retain control of
the situation. It was rather like the situation with the Shrewsbury
railways but this time with the GWR as the aggressor. The
Metropolitan took matters into its own hands and borrowed standard
gauge stock from the Great Northern Railway – whose Locomotive
Superintendent was Archibald Sturrock, who had left Swindon Works
to take up the position. Sturrock modified some locomotives with

condensing gear and from 11 August 1863 the Metropolitan worked its trains using standard gauge equipment. The point proved, the Great Western began to be more reasonable and started running through-services from Windsor to Farringdon Road that autumn.

It was, all things considered, rather unlike the normally pacific Charles Saunders to be so obtrusive but in 1862, then aged sixty-six, he was suffering from heart trouble and offered to resign. He was persuaded to stay on until the amalgamations with the West Midland and South Wales railways were completed in 1863. He was given a hostile reception at the first meeting of the now much-expanded Great Western in September 1863, with many of the Bristol shareholders who blamed Saunders for the costly northern extensions opposing a plan to give him a pension – an unusual provision for the time. He finally left at the end of that September. Despite this setback, Saunders *was* highly regarded and shortly after his retirement Queen Victoria sent him a silver centrepiece in recognition of his services to the Royal family's journeys from Windsor. Charles Saunders died a year later, on 14 September 1864 having done more than anyone – Brunel, Russell and Gooch included – to ensure the success of the Great Western.

On Saunders' death, Gooch wrote:

On September 22nd 1864 [Gooch's mistake] my old and good friend Mr Saunders died. He was one of the most able of our railway men, and in his time had probably had a greater amount of influence than any other. He was a perfect gentleman and much liked by all the officers. We presented him with a very handsome testimonial in January. We had worked together for nearly my whole life and never had a disagreement. He was always a good friend to his brother officers and a man of high honour.

Gooch was the last of the 'big four' Great Western men left and it wouldn't be long before he too departed the scene, albeit temporarily.

Chapter 10
Into the Frying Pan

The Great Western Railway of 1864 was a very different company to that of even a decade before. Its acquisitions in the Midlands and South Wales had changed it from a company that ran services to Bristol, Birmingham and Chester with allies running into Wales and Devon, into a giant with 1,100 miles of track of which more than half were available for standard gauge trains. The addition of successive companies had changed the composition of the board of directors, bringing in new ideas of railway operation and commercial priorities and chief amongst these was the abolition of the broad gauge.

The railway's long-serving and brilliant Locomotive Superintendent Daniel Gooch had long had activities other than the railway, and from 1860 was heavily involved in Brunel's last great steam ship, SS *Great Eastern*. That year he had been elected onto the board of the company which owned her and played an integral part in its first transatlantic journey and accompanying tour of the North American coast to show her off. Money quickly ran short and for the winter of 1860 the ship was laid up in Milford. In 1861 she grounded on the Irish coast, with expensive repairs needed.

Gooch's involvement in *Great Eastern* prompted him to turn his mind to a career beyond the railway and in 1861, after persuading the Great Western's board of directors to invest in a rail mill at Swindon so the company could manufacture its own rail, wrote:

> I now began to think of retiring from the Great Western. I had ample income independent of them, and, in my own mind, settled to give up at the end of twenty-five years' service, which would end in August 1862. I was further inclined to this by the prospect of an amalgamation between

the three companies; viz., the great Western, the South Wales, and the West Midland.

Gooch was unhappy with his relationship with the board of directors. Most of the old guard with whom he had worked so closely had gone and when the Chairman of the West Midlands Railway, Richard Potter, was appointed to the top job on the GWR, Gooch was appalled. He had had long experience through the Oxford, Worcester & Wolverhampton of Potter's methods and thoroughly disliked him. The feeling was mutual, and Gooch made his preparations to leave.

He helped set up a gun company in Manchester which would later become famous as Armstrong Whitworth, partially at least so he could secure a good role for one of his sons, because that looked ever less likely at Swindon under the new regime. In March 1864, he discussed the matter of his succession with Potter. Although Gooch wasn't surprised that his brother, William, was passed over for the job, he was astonished that Joseph Armstrong, who headed the standard gauge engineering operation at Wolverhampton, was to be ignored in favour of a locomotive engineer from the Manchester, Sheffield & Liverpool Railway. Gooch was now furious and wrote personal letters to his old friends on the board urging them to overrule Potter's plans. For the last time as Locomotive Superintendent he got his way, and Armstrong moved from Wolverhampton to Swindon in order to prepare for the handover.

Gooch retired in September 1864 to concentrate on a new attempt to lay a transatlantic cable using *Great Eastern*. Despite the ship's great size in the intervening years it had been impossible to make a profit from her and Gooch was instrumental in setting up a new company that would use her to better effect.

He departed at an opportune time. Another mini railway mania broke out in the mid 1860s, which saw a plague of new and often unnecessary railways being promoted across the country. Because the issue of the break of gauge was still present in parts of the Great Western's network, many proposals were made for railways that would avoid this inconvenience, and a huge and costly effort was made to defeat these plans. In the 1865 session of Parliament, 160 bills were put forward which affected the Great Western alone. The other major railways were in a similar predicament and had similar costs.

To make matters worse, there was a real lack of clear leadership in the period after Charles Russell retired in 1855, with five men taking the chair between then and 1863 – the Rt Hon. Spencer Walpole in 1855–6; Viscount Barrington (1856–7); the Hon. Frederick Ponsonby in 1857–9, Lord Shelbourne from 1859–63 and the aforementioned Richard Potter in 1863–5. The Parliamentary workload, allied to the inevitable challenges of integrating the new acquisitions into the Great Western also took the focus away from railway operations and in 1865 there were three accidents that bore testimony to this.

The first was on 7 June that year when thirteen passengers were killed and thirty injured at Rednal, north of Shrewsbury, after an excursion train from Birmingham and Manchester to London ploughed into a section of track which was being ballasted and re-laid; the only protection was a green flag on a pole 1,100 yards before it. That same evening, the night passenger train from London was hit by a postal train at Keynsham with no deaths, but fourteen injuries. And on 28 June, a ballast train ran at full speed into a siding at Bruton, through the goods shed, the buffer stops and onto the road below, killing the driver and fireman. All bar the latter could have been avoided with proper signalling and use of the electric telegraph to communicate when a train had safely passed a given section of track. Sadly for those injured, safety was felt to be a poor investment by the Great Western, just as it was on other railways.

The leadership vacuum continued when in 1865 Richard Potter resigned at the end of September due to the sheer volume of Parliamentary business. Nobody wanted or was able to remain in the top job on the Great Western for long. The directors searched high and low for a successor to Potter but there were no suitable candidates other than Daniel Gooch, whose engineering and commercial expertise was beyond repute. Gooch had been away on his first unsuccessful voyage with *Great Eastern* to lay a telegraph cable across the Atlantic and when he returned to London in August 1865 wrote that he was surprised to find a proposal to elect him Chairman. The vote was carried and he was elected on 2 November 1865.

Gooch quickly discovered that the company's finances were, to put it mildly, in a mess because Potter, perhaps imagining that the Great Western was wealthier than it was, had loaded the company with huge debts as part of a major expansion drive. Amongst these plans was to build a carriage works at Oxford (hitherto the GWR had bought its carriages and wagons from contractors), firmly on former West Midland Railway territory. Gooch quickly halted every proposal that hadn't firmly started and reviewed what the company needed and could afford. It's perhaps untrue to suggest that the Great Western was nearing bankruptcy at this stage, but under Potter's aegis it had certainly been sailing close to the wind.

With – for the moment – the Great Western's finances stable if still somewhat precarious, Gooch resumed his bid to lay a transatlantic telegraph cable again, this time successfully, and it was he who sent the first ever telegram from America to Ireland. For his work on this, he was made a Baronet by Queen Victoria.

When he returned to GWR, the brief railway boom of the mid 1860s had turned firmly to bust. It was prompted not by falling share prices but by a banking crisis rather similar to that in the late 2000s. Banking was unregulated and many banks lent money to contractors who were now funding the very railways they built. It was a risky business, given the unprofitable nature of some of the projects (many were for overseas railways with uncertain prospects) and contractors borrowed against their future success. They increasingly found it impossible to pay their debts, and when the finance house Overend Gurney went bust in 1866, it took several other banks with it as well as major contractors. Panic ensued – creditors laid siege to other banks and the Bank of England suspended the Bank Act of 1844 so that paper money could be issued instead of gold to investors. The financial crisis this prompted led to the London Chatham & Dover, the Great Eastern and London, Brighton &

South Coast railways going bust, only being kept operational by their receivers – and the Great Western wasn't doing much better.

The response of investors was predictable: the value of railway shares fell and when rumours started to circulate that the Great Western was unable to meet some of its obligations, things became even more serious. The Great Western had borrowed heavily to fund its acquisitions. It had somewhere between 13 and 14 million debentures, some of which were due to be paid every month. In addition, it had £1,286,837 of short-term funding which had to be renewed every two months at an interest rate of 8.75 per cent.

In desperation, and in order to pay these temporary loans and fund much-needed new rolling stock, in October 1866 the GWR tried to issue £2.66 million of preference shares offering a 6 per cent dividend – but by the end of the year, barely £250,000 of this issue had been taken up. The loans had to be paid from revenue and although by the end of 1866 half had been, it still left £859,000 on the books, still at a cripplingly high interest rate. It was starting to look suspiciously as if the Great Western's growth forecasts had been woefully over-optimistic for its recent acquisitions and that the company could even go bust.

Gooch applied for a loan from the Bank of England but was refused and all the while the interest payments continued to cripple the Great Western's ability to run all but the most basic train service. Together with Edward Watkin of the South Eastern Railway and Samuel Laing of the London, Brighton & South Coast Railway, Gooch went to see the Chancellor of the Exchequer, Benjamin Disraeli, seeking a £1 million loan. For a self-reliant, honoured man such as Gooch to go with the begging bowl must have been a sign of how bad things were.

The deputation Gooch took to Downing Street on 7 March 1867 may not have asked for it in name, but in practice they were seeking nothing less than the complete nationalisation of the railways. If Disraeli had granted the GWR its loan, every other indebted railway in Britain would have sought and inevitably gained government funding. As writers ever since have noted, this would have been nationalisation by stealth and that was never going to happen in those free-enterprising times. Disraeli replied to Gooch on 13 March saying that it was not the duty of the Government 'to interfere in the affairs of the company [the GWR].' The message was clear: you got yourselves into the situation – and it's up to you to get yourself out of it.

Thus rebuffed, Gooch took immediate measures to save money. Express trains were abolished and refurbishment of broad gauge coaches was stopped; safety improvements, gauge conversion, and station improvements were all postponed. In 1867 the twenty-eight-man board of directors was cut to sixteen.

It was a mess, and of the really big railways, the Great Western was alone in suffering so much. Share prices for the likes of the LNWR certainly dipped but there was never a question of that company having to go cap in hand to the government seeking emergency funding. Fortunately for the Great Western, the creditors never sought immediate payment – it wouldn't have done them much good if they had because the company couldn't have paid them – but because the farebox revenue remained broadly stable, the short-term loans that caused so much pain were gradually paid off.

However, the price for this rescue strategy was the collapse of the GWR's reputation. Its trains were slow and outdated, stations dilapidated (to quote MacDermot) and fares high. Passengers and freight customers often had little choice other than to use the Great Western's services, but where they had a choice of one of the railways that hadn't been so badly affected by the financial crisis, very often they took it, even if the journey took longer. For freight customers in particular this was hardly surprising, as the GWR took forever to deal with claims for losses, damaged goods or delays. For businesses that depended on the railways, if there were a choice it would have been crazy to use the Great Western at the time.

The Great Western survived the financial crisis of 1866 but at huge cost in treasure and an even greater one to its image. It takes many years to build a good reputation but only a second to ruin it – and many years more to rebuild it. Nonetheless, with Gooch at the helm it wouldn't be long before things started to improve for good. The recovery was evident more than anywhere else in the impending expansion of Swindon Works.

*

The Swindon that Joseph Armstrong moved to in 1864 was rather larger than when we last looked at the town in 1847. The population of Swindon and nearby Stratton St Margaret had more than doubled from 4,024 in 1841 to 8,498 in 1861 and would continue to rise steadily through the following decade to 14,247 in 1871.

Succeeding Gooch was a daunting task for anybody and Armstrong's workload was if anything higher, following the decision to include carriages and wagons within his remit. He was born in Bewcastle, Cumberland in 1816, the same year as Gooch and, following his education in Newcastle, had become familiar with George Stephenson's locomotives at Wylam colliery. He was given a chance to drive locomotives on the Stockton & Darlington and by 1836 was a driver on the Liverpool & Manchester Railway, later moving to the Hull & Selby. From there, where he was made Foreman at Hull shed, he followed his Chief Engineer, George Gray to the London Brighton South Coast Railway (LBSCR) and then moved to Chester where he was made Assistant Locomotive Superintendent. In 1853 he took over the fleet of the combined Shrewsbury & Birmingham and Shrewsbury & Chester railways and when they merged with the Great Western he became Gooch's principal assistant at Wolverhampton, where he was given the title Northern Division Superintendent. He was thus a very experienced and competent engineer when he took over from Gooch.

Armstrong faced two distinct challenges. His first and most important was to ensure the provision of enough locomotives, carriages and wagons to operate the railway's trains. The second was to plan a complete re-equipment of the Great Western's fleet in light of the aspiration to abandon the broad gauge and also in view of the chaotic state of the standard gauge fleet, which had a wide range of locomotives made by different manufacturers and with different characteristics. The

standard gauge fleet in particular made operation and maintenance an
absolute nightmare, and a costly one too. Swindon had built its first
standard gauge locomotive in May 1855, one of twelve goods
locomotives which had to be ferried north to Wolverhampton on
special flat wagons. Another twenty 0-6-0 locomotives emerged from
Swindon in this time as well as two tank locomotives.

After Gooch dropped plans to build a carriage works in Oxford in
favour of Swindon, Armstrong also had to plan and build a carriage
works; he was conscious as well of the need to prepare a new
generation of standard gauge locomotives. To help with the former, he
sent for the abrasive but dynamic Thomas Clayton, and for the latter the
much more palatable and extremely able engineer William Dean. Both
men were from Wolverhampton. Dean also bought with him his
confidential clerk, W.H. Stanier – who himself would rise on the Great
Western and whose son would become a legend in Swindon and
far beyond.

The planning and construction of the new carriage works, as well as
expansion of the locomotive works to accommodate the major new
building programme, occupied much of the period from 1865 to 1869.
By then, Swindon Works was capable enough for the first major
combined order the railway had ever placed. Sixteen locomotives, 76
carriages, 460 wagons, 130 pairs of spare wheelsets and extra tarpaulins
for wagons, were ordered at a cost of £95,340, a huge sum given the
financial constraints earlier in the decade.

Swindon itself was developing too, and Armstrong and other Great
Western men played a major part in the town's life. The town's first
building society was formed in 1868, with Gooch as President,
Armstrong as one of three trustees and four members of the works
management on its board of directors. This new venture quickly proved
popular and allowed the construction and purchase of houses by many
works staff – which was a good job, as overcrowding was something of
a problem. Armstrong was also instrumental in setting up the Swindon
Water Works Company to provide a guaranteed and safe water supply
to the new town. As the GWR had a vested interest in securing a

sustainable water supply for the works and locomotive shed, it funded construction of a new reservoir four miles south of the railway. The Mechanic's Institute now boasted baths as well as a band and in 1868, the first 'juvenile fete' was held, specifically to provide entertainment for the children, while one year later, a much larger swimming pool was opened by the Medical Fund Society.

Swindon's working population — at least, those who worked for the Great Western — were relatively well paid compared with the agricultural workers in the area and became increasingly literate as the first generation of railway worker's children passed through school — and in turn entering service in the works. The process of the Great Western becoming rather like a family-run business was underway.

Neither the works nor the town were yet at anything approaching peak production but despite the recession, in the 1860s Armstrong and Gooch laid firm foundations that would be needed imminently because the end of that decade saw the process of abandoning the broad gauge resumed, as well as some extremely significant acquisitions.

*

One of the consequences of the financial crisis of 1866 was the delay in converting routes for standard gauge operation. The same arguments that prompted the extension of standard gauge rails to Paddington in 1861 clearly applied across the whole of the broad gauge network, and it fell to Gooch to formulate an expanded gauge conversion policy. At a general meeting of the company on 1 March 1866, he spelled out why:

> There is no doubt it has become necessary for us to look the matter of the narrow gauge fairly in the face. We have had within the past few days a memorial signed by nearly every firm of any standing in South Wales wishing that the narrow gauge might be carried out in their district. It is also pressing upon us in many other districts, and it will be necessary for us now to consider how this matter should be dealt with. That it will be

a costly question there can be no doubt. We cannot look at it without
seeing that it involves a large expenditure of money.

One of the problems, ironically, was that the Gauge Act of 1846 had
made it imperative that Parliamentary approval was required to alter
the gauge. In earlier years, this had provided the Great Western with
protection against allied companies changing their minds on the
question of gauge but now it was something of a pain, not least because
there were some 600 miles of broad gauge line that the Great Western
owned, leased or worked over. It wasn't simply the main routes either
– sidings and engine sheds had to be converted, and new rolling stock
delivered to operate standard gauge services. When Gooch said it
would be expensive he wasn't joking.

It took some time for gauge conversion to really begin again though
– and in 1866 the West Cornwall Railway, Truro to Penzance, had
actually added broad gauge rails to its route, enabling trains to run
through from Paddington for the first time. It was 1868 before the first
meaningful progress on conversion was made, on a short stretch of line
in Wales, followed by the Aylesbury branch of the Wycombe Railway
– a separate concern but allied with the Great Western in this.

In addition to the complications of gauge conversion, the Regulation
of Railways Act 1868 forced the Great Western to allow smoking on
stations and trains; the GWR had previously abhorred the practice and
prosecuted anyone found smoking on its property. More significantly
for passengers, however, the act also made it mandatory to provide a
communication cord between the carriages and locomotive in order to
alert the locomotive crew that something was amiss. A cord ran from a
wheel and bell in the guard's van (to alert him), along the eaves of the
carriages and to a whistle or gong on the locomotive. It was eventually
adopted on 1 August 1869, the first meaningful safety improvement for
passengers in years.

By this time, although broad gauge rails ran from Paddington to
Wolverhampton, all passenger services between Wolverhampton and
Birmingham were operated by standard gauge trains (bar one express

each way between Birmingham and Oxford). Four goods trains also ran to Victoria Basin, Wolverhampton, but these too became standard gauge when the broad gauge rails north of Oxford were removed in March 1869.

Attention now moved southwards and the broad gauge rails were removed between Basingstoke and Southcote Junction near Reading in April 1869. Next was between Gloucester and Grange Court, where the Great Western had joined the South Wales Railway. Around 21 miles of single-line railway had to be replaced and for those sections using longitudinal sleepers akin to Brunel's baulk road, this was fairly straightforward: cut the horizontal transoms between the rails to standard gauge lengths, shift the sleepers, rail and all from broad gauge to standard, and fix them together. For other stretches it was a more challenging affair but even so it was completed in five days on 15 August with some important lessons learned.

In the early 1870s, attention continued with an ambitious plan to convert the entire route between Swindon and Milford Haven, and furthermore, to remove the broad gauge rail from the route, making it standard gauge only. The cost was estimated at £226,000. The rationale was simple: coal mining and other industries had really taken off in South Wales and the broad gauge prevented the Great Western from winning all bar a tiny fraction of the traffic. Conversion to South Wales would give the Great Western good access to London from those markets. It was a huge, complex job that would tax the company's track gangs to the full. One hundred and eighty-eight miles of double track and 48 of single track would have to be converted, and when sidings were included, if all of the tracks had been laid end to end they would have been 500 miles long. Standard gauge rails were added between Didcot and Swindon (dual gauge tracks would run to Paddington until the very end of the broad gauge), which went without hitch, finishing in February 1872. Then it was the turn of the huge section between New Milford and Grange Court. Obviously the route would have to be done in stages and the policy was to convert the eastbound line to standard gauge first, with a limited train service running on the other broad gauge line, and then converting the westbound route. It started on 30 April 1872, and by 12 May the first standard gauge trains could run.

In the two days before work started on converting the westbound broad gauge line a massive logistics operation took place to ensure that all broad gauge locomotives, carriages and wagons were out of the way, including those on allied railways that connected to the Great Western. The released rolling stock was to be sent to Swindon but there was no space there, so the eastbound line between Newbury and Hungerford was used to store the wagons.

The last broad gauge trains ran in South Wales on 11 May 1872. In less than six weeks, the South Wales Railway from New Milford to Grange Court and all the associated branches had been converted from broad to standard gauge. The stretch from Gloucester to Swindon was converted in May 1872, with the first standard gauge trains running on 26 May. In that month alone, a whopping 295 miles of broad gauge railway had been converted to standard gauge. Throughout 1873 and 1874, the process continued, and to all intents and purposes the broad gauge only remained to provide a through service between London, Bristol and the West Country, for the Bristol & Exeter, South Devon and Cornwall railways were still broad gauge and the Great Western had no powers to force them to convert, though it was increasingly in their best interests to do so. By August 1875, all of the Great Western Railway's lines apart from the Henley branch had standard gauge rails.

The pioneering spirit of the Great Western was resurgent and it wasn't just gauge conversion which proved this. The company was part of a £1.8m scheme to cross the River Severn on a bridge to cut the long route from London to South Wales via Gloucester. However, when Charles Richardson – who had been heavily involved with the Box and Thames tunnels – suggested that a tunnel under the Severn Estuary would be cheaper than a bridge, the Great Western was receptive. It would also be safer as there was no danger of shipping striking it. When the famous engineer John Hawkshaw – who had been involved in the early battles over the broad gauge – endorsed the proposals the die was cast. An Act of Parliament was passed in August 1872 and the first preparatory works began on 22 March 1873.

The Severn Tunnel would prove, as we shall see, an almost insuperable engineering challenge but in nearby Bristol, a dramatic reconstruction of Temple Meads station was also underway. The need was compelling because the joint Great Western/Bristol & Exeter station was approaching the limits of its capacity. The basis of the new station was the connecting curve that joined the two companies' main lines and Brunel's original terminus. More tracks and platforms were added to this curve, which was covered with a fine pointed-arch roof that complemented Paddington's elliptical arch perfectly. Far more striking however, was the new frontage which was designed by Sir Matthew Digby Wyatt — most appropriate, given the success of Paddington. This spectacular structure was built in the gothic style so in vogue at the time (and best exemplified by London St Pancras). The new Temple Meads facade was built in variegated grey stone, with an imposing central tower. It had six crocketted pinnacles complete with battlements and twisted chimney stacks. None of this was strictly necessary and indeed its fussiness drew criticism at the time, but Digby Wyatt's aim was to give an air of permanence to the undertaking, the implication being that the railway had been here a long time and would remain even longer. The rebuild of Temple Meads started in 1865 and wasn't completed until 1878 but it gave Bristol a station that could rival Paddington for splendour, albeit in rather different fashion.

Safety still remained a major problem at this time. The Great Western was gradually extending two systems which would make services much safer, but they were far from complete. These were the provision of absolute block signalling with safety interlocks, as well as the accompanying electric telegraph. The old-fashioned time-interval signalling was proven to be unsafe because it couldn't stop trains from entering a section of track already occupied by another; somewhat tardily (not least because even the railways recognised that to run more trains would have greatly amplified the risks), the Great Western was addressing this. The principle of these new systems was simple. When a train entered a section of track, no other trains were allowed into that section until it was proved the train had cleared it. This required the signalman at the next section along the line to pass word back down the line via the electric telegraph to confirm that the train had now entered his section of track. Only once this message had been received, via bell codes, could the first signalman allow another into his section. Furthermore, mechanical interlocking of points and signals was designed to physically prevent the signalman from switching points or other signals which could send a train running on another track into the first train's path. It wasn't and isn't a totally foolproof system – it relied on drivers stopping at signals at danger which told them the line ahead was occupied – but by only allowing trains to proceed when the route was proven to be clear, it was vastly safer than any other method.

At the end of 1872, the Great Western had what for the time was a pretty good safety record. 'Just' one passenger had been killed and 247 injured in the preceding seven years. The Board of Trade had been given powers to order railways to prove their progress in installing modern safety systems. When in 1873 the Board sent a circular to the chairmen of all railways pointing out that the vast majority of accidents were preventable, Gooch responded robustly:

Whilst admitting without reserve the expediency of adopting and applying every improved means of securing safety, as and when proved reliable, I think it is my duty, as one who has been actively engaged in the railway work of this country from its very commencement, and who has had daily experience in its working and in the conduct of the men engaged therein, to express my opinion that grave and serious dangers may arise from too great a reliance on mechanical appliances as substitutes for manual labour . . . I am satisfied that if this substitution is not adopted with caution and under due limitations, we shall only be changing the nature of the risk, and may increase rather than diminish danger.

Gooch's words came back to haunt him with a vengeance the

following year. First, on 6 February 1874, the broad gauge Up (railway parlance generally but not always meaning 'towards London') 'Flying Dutchman' hit a stationary goods train at West Drayton at full speed – around 60mph. The goods train was supposed to sound a mechanical gong to alert the signalman when it was clear of the main line, but poor communication resulted in the points remaining locked against the siding: the goods train never stood a chance. Then, to prove the gods weren't smiling on the Great Western that day, a standard gauge express from Paddington to Worcester hit the wreckage across the tracks. Amazingly, only the guard at the front of the 'Flying Dutchman' was killed but twenty-four passengers were injured.

Next, on 16 May, a coupling snapped on a coal train as it was entering Merthyr Tunnel in Wales. The loose wagons ran out of control down the hill, hitting a passenger train slowing to stop in Merthyr terminus. Fifty-two were injured and one later died.

Finally and most terribly of all, was an accident at Shipton-on-Cherwell on 24 December. The 10:00 Paddington to Birkenhead was heavily loaded and running late, not helped by the addition of an extra four-wheeled third-class coach which had been marshalled immediately behind the two locomotives assigned to the train. As the train passed Kidlington at around 35mph, the metal tyre of the front right-hand wheel of the third-class coach shattered and fell off, followed soon after by part of the wheel. A derailment was inevitable but was not immediately obvious to the drivers. When they discovered the problem (probably only a matter of seconds later), they slammed on the brakes and put their locomotives into reverse. The immediate effect was disastrous and fatal. The derailed third-class coach was squeezed between the locomotives trying to go backwards and the forward momentum of the heavy carriages behind. The timber construction wasn't designed to cope with anything like these forces and the whole coach shattered apart. With events now completely out of control, nine of the remaining fourteen carriages were thrown off the line and down an embankment, splintering, twisting and breaking as they did so. Once the third-class coach had shattered, the locomotives sprang ahead, unable to exert any further influence on events. Thirty passengers died in the crash itself, and four later died. Another sixty-five were injured, as were four railway staff. It was, wrote MacDermot, the blackest day in Great Western annals thus far.

All three of that dreadful year's accidents were avoidable: proper signalling and thorough observance of the procedures would have prevented the first; effective brakes would have stopped the second, and the third was caused by the dangerous practice of securing the coach's tyres to the wheels with rivets – something the Great Western had promised to change from 1855, but still hadn't implemented by 1868 (when that particular tyre was replaced). The drivers were pilloried for making completely the wrong decision – they should have let the locomotives coast to a stand rather than imposing additional strain on the coaches. Added to this was the lack of continuous braking from the locomotive to the train, which would at least have slammed on the brakes in the other carriages after the third-class coach had disintegrated. The communication cord would have been little use to the passengers – that was on the outside of the coach and at times when it was needed most, when survival depended on it, even those tall enough to reach it might not have had the presence of mind to remember where it was. Gallingly, although the Board of Trade had withdrawn its approval to this method of communication – demanding something rather more useable – it continued in operation until 1900.

At least conditions for passengers began to improve a little. In response to the Midland Railway's decision to admit third-class passengers to all trains, the Great Western had followed suit on all bar a handful of London to Bristol expresses, but when the former said it would drop first-class fares to the second-class rate of 1.5p per mile and abolish second class completely the Great Western joined a number of other railways in opposing such a move as responding in kind would slash its margins. A legal appeal failed and the Great Western was forced to match these rates, though it retained second class. Conditions were still poor though, whatever class one travelled in. The carriages had no heating, no toilets and only the gloomy illumination provided by oil lamps. Regular travellers took food, water and blankets but for those that did not, the only source of heat came from metal hot water bottles known as foot warmers which could be hired. When winter set in, even comparatively short journeys would have been a real endurance test.

The Great Western, like other railways, was certainly investing in its infrastructure but seemed curiously reluctant to sanction expenditure on anything that would improve the lot of passengers. It's no wonder the railways' collective reputation was so poor. Even so, in 1875 the Great Western made the sensational decision to acquire another 287 miles of broad gauge and 127 of mixed gauge by taking over the Bristol & Exeter, South Devon, Cornwall and West Cornwall railways, and as ever, it was the threat of another company impinging on its monopoly which provoked it.

*

The Somerset & Dorset Railway Company (S&D) had managed by July 1874 to connect Bournemouth and Bath by building a lengthy single-track standard gauge railway and linking it with the London & South Western and Midland railways. The big problem was that by the time the S&D had built its main route from Evercreech to Bath, it was broke, unable even to afford enough locomotives and rolling stock to run the line, so needed to look for a suitor to acquire it.

When the S&D approached the Great Western for help in May 1875, the General Manager, James Grierson, readily started negotiations for a joint purchase with the Bristol & Exeter Railway, and that really should have been it. But then Grierson, in a rare misjudgement, ordered his staff to open negotiations with the LSWR's manager, Archibald Scott, to divide the S&D's route in three. This made some logical sense but Scott demurred on the Great Western's proposal, and while keeping it at arm's length went to see the Midland Railway's General Manager, James Allport, about a joint bid of their own. Why it didn't occur to the Great Western that the Midland Railway would have an interest is a mystery, especially as the S&D shared the Midland's impressive Green Park station in Bath. Very quickly Scott and Allport prepared a bid that was far more generous than the Great Western and Bristol & Exeter's and unsurprisingly the S&D accepted, with a long-term lease starting on 1 November 1875.

Gooch was livid, complaining to the LSWR's chairman that the railway had abused the trust placed in it when the GWR offered its involvement. The acquisition went to Parliament for approval but it was so obviously in the public interest for a north–south railway in that part of the world to be successful, that the Great Western didn't seriously challenge the deal on that basis. It did, however challenge the Midland Railway for its apparent breach of a deal signed in 1863 that the company would not extend south of Bath. The Great Western's objection was overruled, largely on the basis that the agreement was anti-competitive.

With the acquisition of the S&D ratified (it was known thereafter as the Somerset & Dorset Joint Railway and became iconic in its final years thanks to John Betjeman's and Ivo Peters' loving coverage of it) the Bristol & Exeter looked to the future and didn't like what it saw. It now had potentially serious competition in its heartland and it feared the strength of the S&D's new owners.

The B&E Board meeting of 22 September 1875 had included some lengthy discussion about the longer-term prospects for the railway. The board concluded that the brokering of a sell-out deal with either the Great Western or the Midland would ensure the best possible terms for its shareholders and, in the longer term, a successful continuation of its operations, albeit in a different guise. However, the Board was split between the choice of company most likely to offer the most lucrative terms for a proposed merger.

The B&E's General Manager, J.C. Wall, wrote to Grierson offering enticing terms for the two Boards of Directors to meet the following month at Paddington and agree to the leasing of the B&E to the GWR at advantageous terms, followed by amalgamation when it could be approved by Parliament. The GWR was keenly aware that its new acquisition had always been more evenly prosperous than its own operation, the B&E's annual dividend having only twice fallen below 4 per cent. The mileage worked by the company stood at 213½ miles – of which 138½ was owned outright. The total capital was £4,253,552 split between £2,022,460 Ordinary and the remaining balance of Preference Stock. Debentures and Loans stood at £1,106,224.

The GWR found little to change in the running of the line, for much of its substance was GWR in origin thanks to the GWR's operation of it until 1849. However the B&E was infinitely safer than the Great Western (as was the South Devon), the company having introduced Absolute Block Telegraph and starting signals from 1865, replacing the GWR 'standard issue' time interval system. In its twenty-five years of independent operation, there were no fatal train accidents – probably the best safety record in Britain at the time. The lease of the Bristol & Exeter Railway was to start on 1 January 1876, followed by an amalgamation Act as soon as possible.

At the same time – GWR presumably being thoroughly determined to secure its position in the South-West – negotiations were taking place with the South Devon Railway, which was vulnerable to losing traffic from Exeter to Plymouth and beyond from the LSWR's new line over the top of Dartmoor. The shareholders ratified a lease deal with the GWR and this started on 1 February 1876. As the South Devon owned the West Cornwall Railway outright, and gave the Great Western control of the Cornwall Railway (it was leased to a consortium of the GWR, Bristol & Exeter and South Devon railways), the Great Western had added another 438 miles of mostly broad gauge railway into its empire. The Cornwall Railway would remain nominally independent until 1889 but in practice it was Great Western from the mid 1870s. All of West and South Cornwall was now Great Western, though the north of the Royal Duchy as far west as Padstow would largely remain dominated by the LSWR. With all but a few small additions the Great Western Railway's principal network was now complete.

Chapter 11
Winds of Change

Joseph Armstrong died in harness in June 1877 aged sixty-one. His tenure had seen dramatic changes in the company's composition and operations. From a position of having 702 steam locomotives in 1864 – 360 broad gauge and 342 standard – Armstrong had overseen the construction of 850 new standard gauge locomotives, of which 600 were built in Swindon and the remainder at Wolverhampton by his brother George.

Armstrong's designs were a break with the broad gauge tradition. Whereas the principal express locomotives on the broad gauge were 'single wheelers' – so called because the only wheels which provided any traction were a pair of giant driving wheels – Armstrong had introduced a series of 2-4-0 locomotives which offered double the grip and could get heavier trains on the move when conditions were less than perfect. He also designed a range of 0-6-0 goods locomotives as well as tank engines for local work, including the popular and spritely 2-4-0 'Metropolitan' tanks for use on short-distance lightly loaded passenger services. Although the boilers couldn't be as large as on the broad gauge locomotives, technical advances meant that they could provide every bit as much power, and generally speaking, much more than equivalent standard gauge designs on other railways. Some of Armstrong's locomotives remained in service until the 1930s, a sure measure of their success.

Armstrong had also devoted a lot of time to improving the welfare of the 13,000 engine drivers, firemen, depot staff and others whom he was responsible for (with the exception of providing his locomotive crews with proper cabs), and played what can only be described as a patriarchal role in Swindon. He chaired and represented many of the key societies that played such a part in the social fabric of Swindon, and also made sure he was active in supporting them. In this he was, he believed, only fulfilling his responsibility, and his successors would all – with one exception – strive to match this. Joseph Armstrong's funeral in June 1877 was attended by thousands of people, including deputations from other railways, so high was his standing. The Great Western's directors were led, of course, by Sir Daniel Gooch.

Armstrong's successor was his principal assistant, William Dean, a man very much in the same mould. With his long beard, bald head and Patrician stare, Dean looked every inch the stern Victorian manager, yet in this case first impressions were far from accurate. Though a typical product of the Victorian age he was a shy but friendly man who didn't believe in the latter-day management policy of shouting first and asking questions later. He was a team builder, preferring to develop and encourage his staff rather than browbeat them and this policy was absolutely critical in ensuring the smooth running of the locomotive department. He was also a talent spotter par excellence and two of his main assistants were Joseph Armstrong's namesake son, and a young man from Devon who revelled in the name of George Jackson Churchward. Both would play an integral part in Dean's engineering developments in the 1880s.

From the start Dean had a slight problem in that Joseph Armstrong's brother George was in charge at Wolverhampton, which had a significant locomotive building capacity of its own. Thus there were detail differences in the appearance of the locomotives and rolling stock in terms of fitments and finish, and Dean could have enforced a change, but he seemed reluctant to have a confrontation and let George Armstrong continue with a light rein: things were generally working well and he must have felt there was no need to upset the apple cart.

One of the oddest things that he did, to today's eyes, was to produce locomotives that could be converted from broad to standard gauge. His approach was simple: take a standard gauge design with double frames with a set of frames either side of the wheels, extend the axles to the broad gauge and fit new wheels, and set the locomotive to run. The use of double-framed locomotives, incidentally, was because it was felt on the Great Western and a few other railways that relying on a single set of frames inside the wheels was risky – but more on that later.

Changes were generally few from around 1875: the Great Western finally adopted a continuous brake which relied on a vacuum holding the brakes off: should the vacuum be disrupted either by the driver admitting air into the system, a passenger pulling the communication cord (which was connected to the continuous brakes on new coaches), or by the hoses which connected the coaches parting, the brakes would apply.

At least Dean could draw upon the resources and expertise that had been re-focused by the opening in 1869 of the new Carriage Works at Swindon. A programme of new broad gauge vehicles kicked off in 1876 to complement the existing standard gauge carriage production. The gloom induced by the financial crisis of the 1860s had meant that no new broad gauge carriages had been built since 1863 and the existing stock had got into a thoroughly dilapidated condition due to the enforcement of a minimal repair plan. Although an earlier weeding-out process and a new four-stage condition grading system (Best Express, Second Best, Ordinary and Excursion) had improved the situation, Dean clearly had much catching up to do to improve the company's standing in this department.

The new broad gauge carriages were of both six- and eight-wheeled types, the latter being 46½ft long, 10ft wide and 8½ft high, boasting continuous footboards, clerestory roofs and two lamps for each compartment. December 1877 saw the introduction of the first two six-wheeled GWR sleeping cars to run as part of the Night Mail services between Paddington and Plymouth. Each car was divided into two 'dormitories', one for gentlemen containing seven beds and one for ladies with four beds. Provision was also allowed for two small lavatories but passengers subsequently complained of having to 'sleep in close-packed rows like recumbent cod on a fishmonger's slab'. These carriages were subsequently replaced in 1881 by a pair of eight-wheeled cars with six double-berth compartments, three lavatories and a side corridor, very much superior to anything else offered by the other railways running sleeping car services at the time. They were the first coaches to be built with standard gauge bodies with extended foot-boards on broad gauge frames and the introduction of the sleeping cars began a much-loved service which continues to this day even though it is now possible to travel between London and Plymouth in three hours by rail.

This practice of using standard gauge bodies on broad gauge frames continued for the next few years and included the introduction of three eight-wheeled Travelling Post Offices. Improvements to internal comfort saw the bare wooden seating of third class covered with upholstery from 1878, carpets on the floors of second class and gas lighting replacing the rape-oil roof lamps from 1882.

When it came to technical and operational developments Dean proved remarkably open to new ideas and the introduction in 1882 of the Great Western's first on-board toilets in day coaches must have been a relief to cross-legged passengers who had previously had to wait until the next stop before getting relief. Still, however, there were no corridor connections between the coaches, which made it impossible for passengers to escape from the occasional drunk who could quite literally make a journey hell. Vaughan records one case of a drunk shouting abuse at the passengers in a compartment, downing most of a bottle of whisky and then urinating in front of them. He (the drunk, not Vaughan!) was hauled off the train at the next station and arrested but even so it wasn't a pleasant experience for the rest of the passengers and, if not the norm, was far too common an occurrence.

Dean is most famous for creating two very different designs of locomotives. His most important design soon became a recognised masterpiece: it became known very quickly as the 'Dean Goods'. In essence, the 'Dean Goods' was a simple o-6-o tender engine designed primarily for freight; the first emerged from Swindon Works in 1883. The design broke with Great Western tradition by having no outside frames at all, but was wonderfully elegant, almost dainty in its appearance. Two hundred and sixty would eventually be built, operating all over the Great Western's network. The last would survive in front-line service until the 1950s.

Dean's other great design came in the early 1890s and was a derivative of some of his 2-2-2 convertible locomotives. With only a pair of wheels providing any traction, this type had fallen out of use for some time on most railways but the advent of better sanding gear which sprayed sand onto the rails with more force, allowed them to get a slightly better grip when the rails became wet and prompted a brief final flowering. In their broad gauge form they looked ungainly and quaint, yet when they were converted to standard gauge something remarkable happened: the ugly ducklings turned into swans. Dean retained the outside frames when they were converted, and with no outside motion at all they glided along the rails with little sign of mechanical effort. They were, however, somewhat nose heavy thanks to a larger boiler fitted on the later version and when one derailed in Box Tunnel, Dean fitted them with bogies at the front to guide them round curves – from a 2-2-2 to a 4-2-2. The transformation was complete, balancing the design and giving it real poise. The '3031' class as they were known, were some of the most beautiful locomotives ever to take to the rails and they had a turn of speed – given the right conditions – to match.

Dean was the first locomotive and carriage engineer on the Great Western since Gooch's early days who wasn't afraid to experiment in a bid to improve the breed. He tried compounding, where exhaust steam is sent from the cylinders to another set in order to use all of its energy before being exhausted to the atmosphere. He also spent a lot of time focusing on the suspension of locomotives and carriages in a bid to improve the ride and reduce the forces acting on the track. In addition to the 'Dean Goods' and the '3031s' he would also design some locomotives of the 4-4-0 configuration which offered double the grip of the 'singles' and which, with input from Churchward in the 1890s, would point the way forward powerfully.

In other respects though, the Great Western was distinctly sluggish. The absolute block system and electric telegraph were gradually being extended over the network, yet the service remained poor: the Great

Western seemed unable to shrug off the malaise of the 1860s. It may be that there were no funds to address this, or that management's attention had been occupied elsewhere but the most likely explanation is that the man responsible for organising the company's traffic, the Superintendent of the Line, wasn't up to the job. His name was G.N. Tyrell and it was said with some justification that he detested any speeds of more than 40mph. MacDermot, usually the most measured and flattering of railway writers, described him as 'probably the most unprogressive traffic chief of that or any other time' and was right to do so.

In the 1860s, when the need was for economy, Tyrell's approach was probably fair enough but by the late 1870s profitability was rising. Dividends rose from 3.75 per cent in 1878 to 6.37 per cent in 1883: the Great Western was not a cash-strapped company any more. If there had been a serious competitor in the Great Western's patch, it wouldn't have been hard to offer a much faster and more comfortable service: it was only the company's largely monopolistic situation which allowed it to proceed in the way it did. Admittedly there was a lot of infrastructure expenditure, much of it on the Severn Tunnel, which was proving incredibly difficult to engineer, but for the Great Western to sit on its hands and stick to speeds of little more than 40mph was ridiculous.

An equally ridiculous decision, given that the broad gauge's days were numbered, was the opening of the St Erth to St Ives branch as broad gauge in 1877 – within fifteen years it would be converted to the standard gauge it really should have opened with.

The acquisition of the B&E and Devon and Cornwall railways meant the Great Western would need a lot of additional motive power, and as the mid-1880s loomed, so too would the opening of the Severn Tunnel, which after many hardships was nearing completion.

Chapter 12
Epic Development

The 8-mile-long Severn Tunnel is one of the crowning engineering achievements of the Victorian era. Over the thirteen years of its construction, it proved to be perhaps the most challenging project in all that time – far more so even than any of the great bridges of the era. Building it cost the Great Western dear but it was without question a worthwhile endeavour.

It was appropriate that as the Great Western celebrated its golden anniversary in 1885, the men charged with building this vast structure could see, as it were, light at the end of the tunnel because from the start it had been plagued by all sorts of unforeseen problems. The plan was for lengthy cuttings on both sides of the Severn estuary to be built before the tunnel bored underground. It was to run two miles from near Pilning on the Gloucestershire side of the estuary to the eastern edge at a gradient of 1-in-100, levelling out for a few yards and then rising again at 1-in-100 to emerge near Sudbrook Farm, Caldicot. The first works took place by sinking a shaft near Sudbrook Farm for preliminary work to take place and work started on 18 March 1873. By August however, it had only been driven 60ft of the planned 200ft depth because two large springs of fresh water were discovered which completely overwhelmed the pumping capacity, preventing further excavation. More steam-driven pumps were hastily added but it took until December for this preliminary shaft to reach the target depth.

From there, work began on building a small seven-foot-square heading eastwards. The workers initially used explosives and hand drills to cut through the rock, but the strata were tough and just 12ft of progress per week was made at the start. The introduction of air-driven drills from January 1875 finally allowed progress to accelerate to 50ft a day but it was still long, hard progress and as the length of the heading increased so did the ventilation problems, prompting the man in charge of construction, Charles Richardson, to install a steam-driven extractor fan.

In June 1875, construction began on a lengthy bridge over the River Severn at Sharpness, which would connect the Midland Railway routes in Gloucestershire with the Great Western's in South Wales, saving 30 miles on the lengthy deviation via Gloucester. The Great Western was a partner in this but never gave it its full support as understandably it was focussed on building the tunnel.

By July 1875, around 300yds of heading under the river had been driven but water ingress from freshwater springs continued to trouble construction and, in order to avoid flooding the whole of the heading, a wall with a thick iron door was installed 340 yards from the main shaft. Work continued laboriously and slowly through 1875 and 1876; in 1877, conscious of the need to provide permanent pumps to drain the tunnel, another shaft (known as the iron shaft because it was clad internally with iron sheets) was dug next to the first. It would later prove a vital escape route.

Initial attempts to let a contract for the whole tunnel horrified the directors, as the highest bid was £1.3 million to complete the works. It was pointed out, however, that this was an engineering work of extraordinary magnitude and that the River Severn might well have more surprises in store. The contract was won by Thomas Walker, who bid £948,959, and it was decided to continue to fund the heading directly all the way under the river, by which time conditions would be known and the tunnel could be completed.

A shaft on the Gloucestershire side and two on the Monmouthshire side were sunk at this time to accelerate work on the landward sides and to allow for the construction of the gradients that would take the railway uphill and out of the tunnel. From this point on, work progressed quickly and by mid October 1879 just 500ft remained between the westbound Gloucestershire shaft (known as the Sea Wall shaft) and the original shaft on the Monmouthshire side. A big push was all that was needed for men to be able to walk underground from one side of the Severn Estuary to the other.

And then disaster struck. On 16 October, men employed by the contractor Oliver Norris were working westward from the original shaft when one of the men drilled into a new source of fresh water that became known as the Great Spring. It crashed in at a rate of 360,000 gallons per hour, flooding the entire heading to river level in 24 hours. Incredibly, nobody was killed: only a few men were working at the time and after they had tried and failed to stem the flow of water, made their escape. The rest of the workforce, by a rare miracle, was in the process of changing shifts. All underground work was suspended.

New pumping engines had already been ordered from Harvey & Company of Hayle, Cornwall, but these and their engine houses were not yet ready. The Great Western appointed Sir John Hawkshaw to take over from Richardson (who would act as an advisor) – the situation needed comprehensive engineering know-how right away. Hawkshaw accelerated construction of the new pumping engines and on 6 January 1880, after almost three months of inactivity, they were started up to give divers a chance to seal the area affected by the Great Spring. New seals made of heavy oak sealed with tar were installed by 24 January, but pump failures meant that it wasn't until 5 February 1880 that pumping resumed.

In light of the Great Spring, Hawkshaw ordered the headings to be lowered by 15ft to increase the depth of rock above the tunnel. It meant the gradient on the western side would steepen from 1-in-100 to 1-in-90, and that the construction shafts would have to be deepened but it was a price worth paying.

More pumping problems plagued progress on the Western side throughout 1880, but by early November the water level in the tunnel had dropped to 160ft below the surface. No matter how hard the pumps were worked though, fresh water continued to enter at a hefty rate because in their panic to escape, the workers hadn't closed the headwall to seal the tunnel properly. A diver called Alexander Lambert was sent down to close it, but the heavy air hose he needed was too cumbersome for him to reach the headwall. The debris from construction constantly threatened to puncture it too.

The situation was at deadlock until the introduction of a primitive form of aqualung that had been developed by Henry Fleuss was introduced. Although Fleuss attempted to reach the heading, he failed and it fell to Lambert to head down there, remove the rails for the construction tramway that passed through the doorway, close the door and seal the valve. His first attempt failed, as he was unable to remove one of the rails but after Fleuss returned to collect more oxygen, Lambert managed to remove the rails and close the door. He also sealed the valve – or so he thought. The pumps were started but the water level only fell by 3 inches per hour, and at high tide not at all. It took from 10 November to 7 December 1880 to bring the level down to 2ft in the headings, shallow enough for a man to walk through with care.

The pump foreman James Richards walked down the heading to the door and checked it to find water pouring out of the valve. Lambert had turned it the correct number of turns, but in the wrong direction: nobody had told him the valve had a left-hand thread! When Richards closed the valve, almost immediately the pumps could be slowed. When it was possible to inspect the area affected by the Great Spring, it was decided to build an 8ft-thick brick headwall to stop it and allow other work to continue. By 4 January 1881 the Great Spring was sealed.

In May, with work on the rest of the headings progressing well, the door to the Great Spring was opened. The long task of clearing the heading now took place, and workers were ordered to take their breaks underground. The Great Western men resented this and went on strike demanding a return to their previous conditions. Hawkshaw's main contractor, Thomas Walker, called their bluff and sent them on their way. Afterwards he said he was glad of the strike as it got rid of a number of 'bad characters'.

With just over 130 yards separating the two headings, Walker now opted to concentrate on completing the tunnel. Opening it out from the 7ft headway to the 26ft width and 20ft height at the peak of the arch would be difficult enough anyway but Hawkshaw's decision to lower the headway meant that for much of the length the workers would have to dig down as well as up and outwards, making the job more difficult. Hawkshaw was worried too that they would strike another freshwater spring, so keeping separation between the two tunnelling efforts would provide another headwall and extra safety.

It was a good job he did. An area 600ft west of the Sea Wall shaft suddenly had a break-in from above in January 1881, with water pouring down. It came from a small tidal pool known as the Salmon Pool and after trying to seal it from below, a group of men were ordered to rope themselves together and walk out at low tide to find it. When one of them disappeared from view in the waist-deep water, the location was known and the hole was promptly sealed with vast amounts of loose and bagged clay after Walker allowed the water level in the eastern tunnel to rise to the level of the tide. The water was pumped out and work resumed.

During the excavations it was found that much of the material dug out was suitable for making bricks, and with an eye for convenience and reducing costs, a brickworks was opened at Sudbrook to supply the gargantuan construction effort. With progress going well, Hawkshaw ordered Walker to accelerate works. Walker increased his workforce and built extra accommodation at Sudbrook as well as wooden houses on the Gloucestershire side directly over the line of the tunnel.

At the start of 1882, just before bricklaying took place under the river, there was a major collapse at the eastern end when a slab of coal shale collapsed, incredibly without killing anyone. It took two months to clear the debris. At the same time, because construction of the tunnel had drained several wells near Caldicot, Walker built a water main to serve the villages. It was a welcome gesture of goodwill from a project that for the locals must have long outstayed its welcome.

The workers were put up in temporary accommodation and one of the reasons the buildings on the Gloucestershire side were built of wood was because they were thought to rest on a 6ft layer of marl above the tunnel. In fact, it was just 6 inches deep and on 13 November the inevitable happened – it collapsed. Because the structures were wooden, the floors remained largely intact but a chimney breast fell straight down into the heading below – a lucky escape for all involved.

As 1883 dawned, work was progressing well until an accident in February when a skip of loaded clay being taken up one of the shafts fell onto another lift bringing workers to the surface from the end of their shift. It killed three men in the cage itself, another at the bottom of the shaft and injured three more. The dangers of tunnelling are always present and this was one of the worst accidents. Construction of the extensive cuttings leading out of the tunnel began on the Monmouthshire side in March and in May 1883 attempts were made to tackle the Great Spring, which was still sealed up. Fallen debris blocked the door in the headwall and after two months of hard labour it was decided to drive another heading under the Great Spring to get behind the headwall where it was found the roof had fallen in – leaving a cavern large enough to fit a house but with little water ingress. It seemed work could continue once the area was made safe, but on 10 October the Great Spring burst in from the bottom at a rate of 27,000 gallons *per minute*. The men tried but failed to close the headwall and ran for it, surviving by the skin of their teeth. Three construction horses died but in comparison with how bad it could have been, it was yet another lucky escape.

By 12 October the water level was up to 132ft below sea level and rising – the pumps couldn't hope to handle the amount of water rushing in from what was thought to be an underground reservoir. This event was followed by an extremely high tide on 17 October which saw the water rise 6ft above the land. It extinguished fires in the pumping engines and sent a torrent of water careering down the Marsh Shaft on the low-lying western bank. The men in the tunnel couldn't escape using the shaft so they ran up the gradient of the tunnel to a wooden platform built for installing the roof's brick lining and waited. There was nothing else they could do. A boat was lowered down the shaft and eventually rescued all eighty-three men.

This flood was a double-whammy of colossal proportions and only closure of the headwall door to the Great Spring by Lambert allowed pumping to start again. By this time it was clear to Walker that even more pumping power would be needed to deal with the Great Spring, which obviously wasn't going to run dry any time soon. He ordered two more giant pumping engines from Harvey's of Hayle along with sixteen Lancashire boilers but it would take time for them to be delivered and Walker was already out of pocket to the tune of £100,000 due to cost overruns. Until then, the Great Spring could not be dealt with.

The other sections of the tunnel could, however, and by now, late 1883, the brickworks at Sudbrook was unable to keep up with progress despite making a gigantic 600,000 bricks per month. Despite additional supplies from Cattybrook Brickworks near Bristol of 100,000 bricks a month, and another two works in Staffordshire of 500,000 bricks a month, this was still nowhere near enough. Another one million bricks a month were eventually secured from five brickworks in Staffordshire: completing the Severn Tunnel was consuming 2,200,000 bricks every month at this stage in construction.

At the end of 1883, two miles of tunnel were completed and the cuttings at both sides well underway. As building a cutting was cheaper than the tunnel, it was decided to shorten the tunnel slightly from 7,942 yards to 7,666, but otherwise progress continued in 1884 on digging and lining all bar the Great Spring section. To solve the Great Spring problem, Hawkshaw decided to drive a new heading 40ft north of the main tunnel to act as a drain. It was driven at a constant gradient to end up at a level 3ft below the bottom of the tunnel. A 12in cast-iron pipe would be run along it from where it intercepted the Great Spring and the water pumped out. It worked and the water level fell enough so that when Daniel Gooch paid a surprise visit to the construction site on 17 October 1884, it was finally possible to squeeze through a gap in the headings and cross the River Severn underwater. He wrote in his diary:

I went this morning to the Severn Tunnel. Lord Bessborough met me there before lunch, and we inspected the surface works and after lunch went below. It fortunately happened that the headings were just meeting and by the time we had finished lunch the men had got a small hole through, making the tunnel open throughout. I was the first to creep through, and Lord Bessborough followed me. It was a very difficult piece of navigation, but by a little pulling in front and pushing behind we managed it and the men gave us some hearty cheers.

I am glad I was the first to go through, as I have taken great interest in this great work, which is now getting fast towards completion. The spring is now about 7,000 gallons per minute but is fully under the control of the pump; and a fresh pump is just ready to start, which will give us more than ample power, more than double our present wants.

A heading is being driven parallel with the tunnel, so as to turn this water from the line of tunnel and so enable us to complete this short length of about two hundred yards. The side heading will then be built out. I hope by June or July next the tunnel will be finished.

There were still problems – water ingress continued to trouble workers but by and large, the way was clear for work to be completed. The last of the brickwork was completed on 18 April 1885, and on 5 September Daniel Gooch was hauled through the tunnel by train.

However, there were still some ongoing issues. A build up of water pressure caused by overoptimistic forecasts that no pumping would be needed inside the tunnel delayed the opening and threatened to flood the whole enterprise. A permanent pumping station had to be built but a trial coal train from Aberdare to Southampton tentatively ran through the tunnel on 9 January 1886. As the directors' report of February 1886 put it, coal that had been raised at the colliery in the morning was delivered to the port in the evening of the same day. Approval was given for freight traffic to start on 1 September 1886, with passenger traffic following three months later on 1 December 1886.

The statistics for the Severn Tunnel are staggering: 74.6 million bricks were used, of which 28 million were made on site. At its peak, 3,628 men worked on its construction, using almost 37,000 tonnes of Portland cement and 250 tonnes of explosive. Taken together with its approaches, the tunnel cost £1.8 million to build but would shorten

Bristol to Cardiff journey times by up to 90 minutes. The Severn Tunnel was an absolute bargain – even though it couldn't bring its full potential to bear until the twentieth century because of capacity constraints around Bristol! This daring feat of civil engineering was Gooch's final and perhaps his greatest achievement.

*

Sometimes, despite advancing years and poor health, people hang on to life until something of great importance to them is completed. It probably happened with Brunel, who died shortly after the Royal Albert Bridge was completed and, just after the Severn Tunnel opened, a number of key senior managers were lost to the Great Western.

The first was the General Manager, James Grierson, who passed away on 7 October 1887, just three days before his sixtieth birthday. He was Goods Manager from 1857 to 1863, when he took on his last role as General Manager and did his best to drive progress through the increasingly conservative Great Western management. He was a worthy successor to Charles Saunders and would be sorely missed. He was succeeded by the Chief Goods Manager, Henry Lambert.

Not so sorely missed was the stubborn Traffic Manager G.N. Tyrell, who finally retired in June 1888 as Superintendent of the Line. His constant, grating opposition to change and service improvements meant that he would have been cursed by passengers and freight customers had they known his name. It is no exaggeration to say that in his twenty-four years in position, he had dragged the Great Western's reputation into the mud by his refusal to countenance improvements and, to modern eyes – irrespective of his length of service or relationships with the directors – should have been removed from his post many years before.

The greatest loss was on 15 October 1889 when Sir Daniel Gooch died aged seventy-three. He had been ill for years and had stood down from Parliament in 1885, where he represented Cricklade for more than twenty years. Before he stood down he wrote: 'I have taken no part in any of the debates, and have been a silent member. It would be a great advantage to business if there were a greater number who followed my example.'

Even though Gooch had become more cautious and conservative as he aged, particularly about matters of safety, his contribution to the Great Western and to railways in general was vital. As a mechanical engineer, he had designed locomotives which served until the last days of the broad gauge and set an enviable reputation for speed, but it was as Chairman that the Great Western owed him most. Without his steadying hand in the 1860s, it is possible the railway might have gone bust with unthinkable consequences ranging across a huge wedge of England. Gooch not only saved the Great Western from oblivion: he also set in motion plans to abandon his beloved broad gauge and was instrumental in completing the Severn Tunnel when lesser Chairmen might have cut their losses in the late 1870s. He is without question one of the greatest railway engineers of all time, as deserving of a place in popular folklore as George Stephenson and Brunel yet, even for Great Western admirers, his importance is often overlooked. Without Sir Daniel Gooch, the Great Western would never have approached the greatness it had in its early days and would recapture in the early twentieth century. He was succeeded as Chairman by another steadfast servant of the railway, Frederick George Saunders.

There was one other death of huge significance in the 1880s that has barely merited a mention in most histories, that of Joseph Armstrong junior on 1 January 1888. Eight years before, William Dean had spotted the twenty-four-year-old's talent (which he doubtless inherited from his father) and set him to work developing the continuous brake for use on the company's passenger trains. Armstrong didn't have the best of health but he was regarded as a visionary and imaginative genius in Swindon and was assisted by George Jackson Churchward. His colleague had moved from the South Devon when it was acquired by the Great Western in 1876 in order to work at Swindon as a draughtsman. The consensus amongst the few accounts of this partnership is that Armstrong was the innovator, while Churchward translated his ideas into practical engineering. Armstrong was sent to Wolverhampton where he was assistant to his Uncle George in order to gain experience. This was at the time considered to be the springboard to the top engineering position – it was where Dean had been promoted from – so the message was clear: Joseph Armstrong would in all likelihood succeed Dean when he retired in the early twentieth century. Sadly on New Year's Eve 1887, Armstrong went to inspect the running shed at Wolverhampton to ensure everything was running properly. On his return, he was hit by a freight train and killed. It was a great loss and even Churchward later told Armstrong's nephew that if Joseph had survived, Churchward would never have got the top job as Joe was 'far more clever' than he was. But out of death comes rebirth and Churchward was elevated to a position of increasing influence as Dean's right-hand man.

All that was now standing in the way of the proverbial great leap forward was the last remaining stretch of broad gauge, the 177 route miles from London to Bristol, Exeter, Plymouth and Penzance. Perhaps it was as well that Gooch didn't live to see the end.

*

Although the railway from London to Exeter was dual gauge throughout, between Exeter and Truro it was still broad gauge all the way in 1892. Between Truro and Penzance, which was dual gauge, a few local mineral trains ran on standard gauge but otherwise the broad gauge continued to dominate.

With the Great Western having to maintain complicated trackwork in addition to broad gauge locomotives and rolling stock for only a relative handful of services, the need to complete the elimination of the broad gauge was growing more pressing by the day and finally it was decided to change over for good on the weekend of 21–22 May 1892. One of the key driving forces for this was the quadrupling of the line between Taplow and Didcot; if the broad gauge was to be retained, it would have to be installed on all four tracks and the complexities and

The Great Western Railway's inspirational engineer, Isambard Kingdom Brunel, at the launch of his ship SS *Great Eastern*, 1857. © *Science & Society Picture Library*

Charles Saunders, 1796 – 1864. The Secretary of the GWR, 1840 – 1863, he was perhaps the most important person in the company in those early years. *STEAM Picture Library*

Sir Daniel Gooch, Locomotive Superintendent and later Chairman of the GWR pictured in the 1860s. © *Science & Society Picture Library*

Fire Fly, one of Gooch's pioneering broad gauge locomotives, built in 1840.
STEAM Picture Library

The striking portal of Brunel's Box Tunnel near Bath.
Getty Images

The Royal Albert Bridge at Saltash under construction in spring 1858.
© *Science & Society Picture Library*

Men at work in the GWR's Swindon Works in 1875. *Getty Images*

Men working on the construction of the Severn Tunnel at the cutting at Patskewett *c.*1880. It was one of the greatest engineering achievements of the Victorian era. *Getty Images*

Brunel built elegant timber viaducts in Cornwall to save construction costs, and many were huge structures. This is Liskeard Viaduct in 1894. *Getty Images*

The broad gauge in its pomp was a unique spectacle. In this undated view, 4-2-2 *Bulkeley* stands at an unidentified location, probably towards the end of the broad gauge era. *Rail Archive Stephenson*

Passengers and luggage being moved from a broad gauge to a narrow gauge train at Gloucester. Scenes such as this prevented wider use of the broad gauge. Originally published in the *Illustrated London News*, June 1848. *Getty Images*

GWR broad gauge locomotives dumped at Swindon Works in 1892 shortly after total conversion of the railway from broad to standard gauge. © *Science & Society Picture Library*

William Dean, 1840 – 1905. GWR Locomotive and Carriage Superintendent, 1877 – 1902. *STEAM Picture Library*

William Dean's '3031' single-wheelers were some of the most elegant locomotives ever built. 3026 *Tornado* leaves Teignmouth with an Up (Eastbound) train in 1903.
Robert Brookman/Rail Archive Stephenson

Sir James Inglis, 1851 – 1911. GWR General Manager 1903 – 1911. *STEAM Picture Library*

George Jackson Churchward. GWR Chief Mechanical Engineer 1902 – 1921. Born 1857, died 1933. *STEAM Picture Library*

Perhaps the single most important British steam locomotive of the twentieth century, Churchward's brilliant 4-6-0 'Saint' class No. 98 waits to leave Paddington in *c.*1903. *Rail Archive Stephenson*

Mechanics Institute Luncheon, July 1908. George Jackson Churchward is at the back of the room to the centre of the image. The Mechanics Institute was built in 1854 and was at the heart of the Railway Village. *STEAM Picture Library*

Medical Fund Dispensary Waiting Room, *c.*1910. The Medical Fund Society in Milton Road housed swimming baths, Turkish and Russian Baths, a dispensary and a dentist. It was built in 1892. *STEAM Picture Library*

Large Swimming Bath. The large coloured window at the end was made by Mr T. Rice, an employee of Swindon Works. *STEAM Picture Library*

Passengers boarding the 'Cornish Riviera Express' at Paddington Station, 1914. *Getty Images*

Charles Collett, 1871 – 1952. GWR Chief Mechanical Engineer, 1922 – 1941. *STEAM Picture Library*

Mr Bird from the National Union of Railway workers addresses the members at a rally in Victoria Park, London, 1919. Industrial action such as this paved the way for road hauliers to begin winning goods traffic from rail. *Getty Images*

Viscount Churchill 1864 – 1934. Chairman of the GWR, 1908 – 1934. *STEAM Picture Library*

King George V tries his hand at driving No. 4082 *Windsor Castle* on a visit to Swindon Works on 28 April 1924. Beside him are Queen Mary, Viscount Churchill, the General Manager and the Chief Mechanical Engineer. *Getty Images*

The 'Castles' shocked observers during the famous GWR/LNER locomotive exchange of 1925 by outperforming larger rivals. No. 4079 *Pendennis Castle* departs King's Cross with the 1.30p.m. express to Leeds and Bradford.
F.R. Hebron/Rail Archive Stephenson

The 'Kings' were the ultimate GWR passenger locomotives. In 1929, No. 6000 *King George V* (complete with bell marking its visit to North America in 1927) passes Taunton with the 11a.m. Paddington to Penzance.
F.R. Hebron/ Rail Archive Stephenson

The GWR wasn't just about railways: GWR Thorny-croft bus No. 930 Reg No. YK 3824 pauses in South Wales *c.*1930.
C.R. Gordon Stuart/Rail Archive Stephenson

Locomotive shells at the GWR works in Swindon, July 1934. Swindon Works was the hub of the GWR's engineering capability.
Getty Images

The GWR was the first widespread user of diesel railcars in Britain, and in 1935, Railcar No. 4 calls at Straford upon Avon. *F.R. Hebron/ Rail Archive Stephenson*

Bristol Temple Meads Station from the GWR's old Control Office, 1934. The station, designed by Sir Matthew Digby Wyatt, opened on 1 January 1878. The spire on the clock tower was destroyed by a German incendiary bomb in an air raid on 3 January 1941. © *Science & Society Picture Library*

No book on the GWR could be complete without a glimpse of one of the ubiquitous 'Pannier' tanks. '57xx' No. 3759 looks characteristically busy at Bristol Temple Meads in *c.*1939. *Rail Archive Stephenson*

Women oiling tracks on the GWR in Reading, March 1943. During the World Wars women were called to work on the railways in order to release men for service in the forces, numbering 114,000 nationwide by 1944. *Getty Images*

Welsh coal was the lifeblood of the GWR and later of British Railways. On 13 April 1957, No. 7232 hauls a coal train through Aberbeeg. *J.F. Davies/Rail Archive Stephenson*

Modernisation started early on the former GWR routes. D600 *Active* looks in pristine condition hauling the London-bound 'Cornish Riviera' just after passing Teignmouth on 2 September 1958.
K.L. Cook/Rail Archive Stephenson

Quintessential branch line scenes just about lasted into the 1960s. One of the little '48XX' 0-4-2Ts, No. 1451, waits at Hemyock with the 1.42p.m. train from Tiverton Junction on 8 August 1962.
M.J. Fox/Rail Archive Stephenson

The pioneering 'Castle', No. 4073 *Caerphilly Castle* was saved for the nation and moved to the Science Museum, London in 1963. © *Science & Society Picture Library*

One of the founder members of the Great Western Society, Graham Perry (and Chairman from 1967-2001) stands on Southall footbridge in about 1960. *Courtesy of Frank Dumbleton*

The moment the Great Western Society steamed its own locomotive, No. 4866, at Totnes in April 1964. *Courtesy of Frank Dumbleton*

The new diesel-hydraulics were notable for their short careers, but the Westerns outlasted all others. D1008 *Western Harrier* calls at Exeter St. Davids with the 8a.m. Cardiff to Plymouth on 12 July 1974. ***R.O. Tuck/Rail Archive Stephenson***

1986 was the Great Western Society's 25th anniversary year. Left to right are Angus Davis, Graham Perry, Mike Peart and Jon Barlow.

A delegation of MPs, sleeper staff and users presented an 8,000 signature petition to 10 Downing Street on 14 September 2005 during the Save Our Sleeper Campaign. The author is centre, holding the petition with then Falmouth and Camborne MP Julia Goldsworthy. *Paul Bigland*

First Great Western's 'Night Riviera' sleeper train is still the umbilical cord linking Cornwall with the capital, and business is booming. 57602 *Restormel Castle* waits at Paddington's Platform 1 on 1 July 2010 shortly before hauling the train west. *Andrew Roden*

The Great Western Society's headquarters at Didcot plays host to the most complete collection of GWR locomotives and rolling stock in the world. This glimpse of the main shed shows only a small fraction of the huge site devoted to preserving the GWR's memory. *Andrew Roden*

expense of the pointwork would have been horrendous. Of course, where the tracks were already dual gauge, the broad gauge rails could be left until it suited the railway to remove them; so, while in practice it was really the section from Exeter to Truro and associated branch lines through Devon and Cornwall that needed to be converted, it was still a massive task.

The planning was – and needed to be – meticulous. The General Manager, Henry Lambert, issued a fifty-page manual detailing when and how conversion was to take place, and a further thirty pages were provided for the men in charge of the Bristol and Exeter divisions. In the days and weeks leading up to the final conversion, track gangers undertook preparatory work, greasing bolts which held the rail chairs to the sleepers so they could be undone easily, building sets of points and other complex trackwork which would otherwise take days to install alongside the railway, and cutting every third transverse sleeper to the correct length to speed the process. Standard gauge locomotives were dispersed across the remaining broad gauge network on broad gauge flat wagons so that services could be resumed quickly while all but the most essential broad gauge locomotives, carriages and wagons were hurried to Swindon Works where they lay in a gigantic loco-motive dump with more than 15 miles of tracks for conversion or scrapping. On Friday 20 May 1892 the preparations were complete.

That day dawned and broad gauge locomotives still departed Paddington on their way west, though goods traffic had ceased west of Exeter on 18 May, with some standard gauge trains using the LSWR route to access Plymouth. The last through-train to Penzance departed Paddington at 10:15, arriving at the West Cornwall terminus at 20:20. The last broad gauge departure of all was the 11:45 from Paddington, which terminated at Plymouth. In the opposite direction, the last scheduled service was the Night Mail to Paddington which departed at 17:00, followed at 21:45 by another train hauling the remaining broad gauge stock through Cornwall and Devon. As it cleared each section of broad gauge track, the gangers could begin work as soon as it got light.

As dawn broke on Saturday 21 May, work began. More than 4,200 track gangers and platelayers were ready, and many had been drafted in from across the Great Western network in special trains. They were allocated worksites in advance and as soon as they could they began work. It must have been a busy, pressured time for all involved, particularly as on the Sunday evening standard gauge trains were scheduled to depart Paddington for Plymouth and Penzance.

Working furiously in the sun until it got too dark to see, and again on the Sunday morning, sleepers were cut, rails lifted and shifted to standard gauge, pointwork installed and the gauge carefully checked to ensure it was accurate. Such was the exceptional planning and organisation behind the changeover, that progress went to plan and the entire 177 route miles of main line between Bristol and Truro were handed back to the railway as planned at 04:04 on Monday 23 May 1892 and the previous evening's Night Mail from London travelled serenely through all the way to Penzance.

When, on today's railway, routes are closed for weeks for track replacement or other engineering works, the last conversion from broad to standard gauge is invariably held up as an example of how such tasks can be done with minimal disruption. That view may overlook the fact that the Great Western's approach in this instance was only possible because of the huge reserves of manpower the railway could throw at the project, but there's no question that it was a remarkable piece of planning, organisation and manual labour.

So the broad gauge finally died, fifty years after the Great Western's first train ran, and for a long time afterwards, its passing was mourned by some railwaymen who felt that a distinguishing feature of the company had been irretrievably lost. Others argued that had it lasted longer it would have shown its potential by hosting bigger, more powerful locomotives, and more spacious carriages and wagons than standard gauge, but they were grasping at straws. The hard fact was that Brunel had come to the railways too late for his arguments to prevail. Had he made his loading gauge larger – say to North American standards – the broad gauge might just have found its niche, but of course he didn't and even with the slightly greater clearances under bridges and tunnels of the Great Western the standard gauge was more than able to cope.

The Great Western's broad gauge was, in the end, an expensive and disruptive misjudgement and no amount of ifs, buts and maybes will ever make a compelling case that eliminating it wasn't the best thing to do for the railway itself and the country as a whole.

*

Freed of the broad gauge, the Great Western now turned its attention to shortening some of its key routes, while Dean and Churchward of the Locomotive, Carriage & Wagon department began experimenting in a bid to provide locomotives of greater power and speed that would soon be needed. With the Severn Tunnel complete and the company now extremely profitable – dividends of around 7 per cent were typically paid to shareholders in this period – funds were available and used to usher in a bold new era.

In 1892, the senior management of the Great Western faced two related challenges. The first was that traffic was growing on its key routes to Wales and the West Country to a point where the network at Bristol, through which everything had to pass, was bursting at the seams. The second was that its route to the West Country was still rather longer than it needed to be, and if a way could be found to shorten it, not only would capacity be released at Bristol; journey times to Taunton, Devon and Cornwall could be shortened too.

The plans were threefold: to construct a new line from Wootton Bassett, west of Swindon, to Patchway on the northern edge of Bristol to connect with the line to the Severn Tunnel; and also to link the Berks & Hants with Westbury and then from Castle Cary to the Bristol & Exeter's Yeovil branch west of Langport. In addition, a later three-mile line between Athelney and Cogload was envisaged to speed things further, as the initial junction near Taunton was approached by an extremely sharp curve that trains would have to slow right down for.

Construction of the 30-mile Wootton Basset to Patchway line was by far the most important improvement, as it would finally allow the Severn Tunnel to be used at something approaching its potential and would also avoid some quite steep gradients which were causing operating headaches with the low-powered locomotives of the time. At Chipping Sodbury a 4,444yd long tunnel would be built, and east of Patchway at Stoke Gifford, a new marshalling yard would be built. The bill passed through Parliament with relatively few problems and the Dowager Duchess of Beaufort cut the first sod at Old Sodbury in November 1897.

Work also began on the first phase of the Berks & Hants extension that year – it was an obvious way of shortening the route to the South-West and Brunel had said in 1847 that he envisaged it would become the main route to the region. Fourteen and a half miles of new railway had to be built between Patney and Westbury and another 15½ miles later on between Westbury and the Yeovil line, at a place which became known as Curry Rivel Junction.

Much of the inspiration for these vital engineering works came from the railway's Chief Engineer from 1892, James Inglis, another name who would loom large in Great Western history, and the railway's highly capable General Manager, Sir Joseph Wilkinson. Together they planned and developed these new routes, which were engineered to genuinely high-speed specifications. The minimum curve radius on these new sections was to be one mile and gradients were to be limited to as little as possible. It was as if the spirit of Brunel's original main line had been reincarnated.

Another obstacle to progress was cleared in 1895, when at a cost of £100,000 the ninety-nine-year lease on Swindon station's refreshment rooms signed in 1841 was bought out. Attempts at evading the clause in the lease that mandated a ten-minute stop there had been made in the past and failed, and the enforced stop was a major headache in operational terms that needed to be eliminated in order to accelerate services. The reputation of the refreshment rooms was awful – Brunel had complained about the standard of the coffee very early on – and probably had much to do with the notoriety that railway catering retains to this day (though these days it is largely undeserved). It was a huge amount to pay, but it helped give the Great Western control over its destiny.

Then in 1896 with the death of the Works Manager Samuel Carlton, Dean promoted Churchward, who had gradually been moving up the career ladder, to the post of Assistant Locomotive Works Manager – his second-in-command in all but name. Many improvements were to be introduced over the next decade: in 1896, dining cars began operating between Paddington and Plymouth/Cardiff, in March 1902 the company began operating full corridor trains with lavatories, and the following year steam heating was introduced. With the cut-off routes soon to begin construction and train weights starting to rise due to demand, it was possible to see the existing locomotive fleet being stretched beyond its abilities before too long. More powerful locomotives would soon be needed and Dean and Churchward began examining what the best way of meeting that need would be.

The process started in the late 1890s, with Dean and Churchward considering very carefully how the Great Western locomotive fleet should develop. In almost every text of the period it is Churchward who is given credit for the technical developments and experimentation about to take place. He was given a free hand to do what he liked – so the legend goes –as Dean was going senile and was unable to take big decisions for himself. There is little evidence to prove this assertion, which has been repeated so often it is generally regarded as historical fact.

There is no question that Dean was slowing down – he was fifty-eight, after all – but to seriously suggest that he was going senile seems wide of the mark. He was starting to become forgetful and absent-minded at times, but that comes to almost all of us, and he had borne a heavy burden with his first wife dying after his third child was born. Dean had remarried in 1878 but his second wife died in 1889 and worse still, one daughter died in childhood, then another in 1893. Given the intensity of work he had on his plate throughout this period, it is hardly surprising he was forgetful at times.

It wasn't much of a leap of imagination for Churchward to see that he was likely to succeed Dean on his retirement in 1902, and as one of the most capable railway engineers in the country, it's quite probable the directors had assured him that the top job was his if he wanted it (barring any massive cock-ups). His promotion was essentially secure. The assurance by the directors to Churchward of his promotion would have made a lot of sense as it would retain his services at Swindon should any other railways approach him. It seems that some commentators have read between the lines and inferred that assuring Churchward of his succession left him in charge of the Locomotive Department. This is nonsense: if Dean had been seriously ill he would have retired early and Churchward's promotion made earlier. The only conclusion borne out by the facts is that Dean and Churchward collaborated very closely on a series of experiments and developments that would later provide Churchward with the means to develop his own locomotives.

When Churchward became Assistant Locomotive Works Manager, the fastest express services were worked by Dean's beautiful '3031' class 4-2-2s, increasingly supplemented on slower trains by the 'Duke' class 4-4-0s. These locomotives offered double the grip of the '3031s' and had smaller driving wheels, which limited their top speed but gave them better acceleration – useful on the steep gradients of Devon and Cornwall where top speed was limited by the route itself.

At the time, virtually all steam locomotives in Britain had rounded fireboxes of slightly wider diameter than the boiler, with the curve following the line of the boiler, narrowing to fit between the frames. A firebox has two skins. The inner contains the fire itself and the tubes that convey the fire's heat through the boiler. Surrounding this is an outer layer separated from it by metal bolts known as stays to allow water to circulate around it. Although there have been occasional attempts to deviate from this formula, nothing better has ever been found.

These round fireboxes worked reasonably well but were difficult and fiddly to manufacture. A Belgian called Alfred Belpaire had invented a new design with straight sides and top, which was simpler to manufacture because keeping two parallel sides separated is much easier than two curves of differing radii. It also offered greater space for the water to circulate and boil at the top, and this was also useful as it didn't restrict the amount of steam generated.

The experiments with different types of boiler started in 1896 when Dean produced a prototype goods locomotive of the then rare 4-6-0 configuration, No. 36. It was a typical Dean locomotive with outside frames, and it was soon followed by another, No. 2601, which had a Belpaire firebox extended forward to form a combustion chamber in a bid to ensure that all the combustible gases released from the coal burnt properly. It was also the first of the new wave of Great Western locomotives with piston valves, and although this installation wasn't particularly successful, it led to developments on passenger loco-motives. No. 2601 was followed in turn by nine others built as 2-6-0s and although these weren't successful either, they were developed into the 'Aberdare' 2-6-0s which led long, if unpopular, lives on the South Wales coal trains.

Churchward was keen to use the Belpaire firebox and five of the final batch of 'Dukes' were fitted with them. Another, No. 3212 *Bulldog*, was fitted with a prototype boiler that was intended to be one of a series of standardised designs for future locomotives. The aim was to assess which features worked and which didn't, so it made sense to use the 'Duke' chassis as the basis for these experiments.

Investigations were also taking place into the cylinder valves, again with bigger locomotives in mind. It was clear that if more powerful locomotives were to be introduced, they would need bigger cylinders and that if these were retained between the frames as was convention at the time, the slide valves used on most other designs would be inadequate. It wasn't so much that there was anything wrong in principle with slide valves, it was simply that to cope with much larger cylinders there wasn't enough space for them. The only option was to use piston valves which, as their name suggests, run back and forth inside a cylinder, and these were far from proven in British service. A small stationary engine was set up in Swindon to allow experiments to take place on the proportioning of the valves, as this was something of an unknown.

Gradually the elements of a new wave of locomotive design were coming together and, by the turn of the century, this was timely because the Wootton Basset–Patchway and Berks & Hants cut-offs were due to be open by the middle of the next decade. The new generation of locomotives would be needed quickly.

It began cautiously with Dean and Churchward using Dean's 4-4-0 chassis as the basis for a series of passenger locomotives, starting with the 'Bulldogs' of 1899 which had a new design of boiler but were otherwise identical to the 'Dukes'. Then, in 1900, they were followed by the 'Atbara' class, which differed in having 6ft 8½in driving wheels (as opposed to the 5ft 8in of the 'Bulldogs') and were better suited to sustained high-speed running.

In preparation for a major expansion of the locomotive building programme, improvements were progressively made to Swindon Works as there had been no major extensions to its capabilities since 1876. The locomotive repair shops – known collectively as 'B' shop – were upgraded and modernised and, in 1896, the familiar Pattern Store was built, complete with a 225,000-gallon water tank on its roof. New machine tools were ordered to allow the works to improve its capabilities, and in view of rapidly developing aspirations for a much larger series of locomotives, plans were developed for a massive new workshop in which these could be built. Construction of the first part of the famous 'A shop' was authorised in June 1900 at a cost of £33,000. A single building 480ft long, 486ft wide was designed and built entirely by Swindon staff. Extensive attention was paid to ensuring that natural light could enter, and it was soon followed by approval for a 480ft long, 165ft wide lighting and machine shop. They were a giant investment at the time but would more than prove their worth.

The experiments in boilers and valves were being conducted in anticipation of a major rethink of how Great Western locomotives were configured. When, in 1901, one of the Dean 'singles', 3021 *Wigmore*

Castle, was spied at Wolverhampton Stafford Road shed with wooden templates outside the frames looking rather like outside cylinders, the never-silent railway grapevine started buzzing with rumours of what would emerge next from Swindon. Further sightings of the modified locomotive at other locations on the Great Western's principal routes further solidified expectations that Dean and Churchward were about to make a sudden break with tradition.

As Dean neared retirement, a startling new locomotive emerged from Swindon Works. It retained the cast numberplate, brass safety-valve bonnet and copper-capped chimney so distinctive of Great Western locomotives, but in every other respect it was completely different. No. 100 was a 4-6-0 locomotive with outside cylinders, a large Belpaire firebox, a 14ft 8in-long, 5ft-wide domeless boiler (a giant for the time), working at a pressure of 200 pounds per square inch (psi) and none of the graceful curves and flourishes which characterised passenger locomotives of the era. It was at least 25 per cent more powerful than any other passenger locomotive in Britain at the time.

No. 100's origins lay firmly in North America, where outside-cylindered 4-6-0s were hauling the country's fastest and heaviest express trains. The Americans had long-favoured simplicity over elegance and Churchward wanted to bring this configuration and approach to Swindon. It was the last major locomotive design under Dean's aegis and he would have had to have approved the locomotive's design and construction, even if Churchward had done most of the work. William Dean might have been ageing and forgetful – and for the past couple of years not in great health – but he was no fool and if he had any doubt about the merits of No. 100's design he would not have signed it off.

Dean retired in June 1902 after a career spent working for the Great Western. The company bought him a house in Folkestone and a collection from engineering staff across the Great Western raised £400, which was used to buy him a chiming grandfather clock. That Churchward held him in the highest regard is clear from his speech made at the presentation to Dean on his retirement:

Those who had been more particularly employed at Swindon, and especially the older men amongst them, remembered the very great work which had been done by Mr Dean in bringing their works to this present magnificent size and condition. Their admiration was further drawn forth when they saw the latest addition to those Works. The whole of that – practically in every detail – was designed by Mr Dean himself.

When they looked back on the long series of years during which Mr Dean had so ably discharged the duties of his office, and when they realised the fact that during the past two or three years he had not unfortunately, enjoyed the good health which a man must have to perform those duties they could only feel pleasure that the time had arrived when he could enjoy that richly deserved rest and ease which he was now about to take.

It was a warm and affectionate tribute from a man who owed Dean a great deal. It was now time for the Great Western's rising star to shine in his own right. Dean died in 1905 in Folkestone.

Chapter 13
The Modern Railway

With Churchward in charge of the Great Western's locomotive fleet, change was inevitable and rapid. No. 100 was rapidly named *Dean* and later *William Dean* in honour of his predecessor, but Churchward knew that the design wasn't quite right. The valves weren't properly dimensioned and were between the frames, making construction and maintenance more difficult than he would have liked.

He must have been already thinking about remedying these defects as soon as No. 100 emerged from Swindon, because between then and March 1903, he had designed a small family of locomotives that would be able to handle the full range of Great Western duties between them. After careful evaluation, he decided on three driving-wheel diameters – 4ft 7½in for heavy freight or slow-speed passenger duties, 5ft 8in for general purpose locomotives which might find themselves working freight and passenger trains, and 6ft 8½in for high-speed passenger engines. The other smaller wheels that would, depending on the locomotive's configuration, support the front or both ends, were all the same diameter. The driving wheels would be connected in varying configurations to standard cylinder blocks with a bore of 18in diameter and 30in length. The latter was far longer than orthodox practice but Churchward was convinced that by giving the steam in the cylinders more space to expand, less would be exhausted to the atmosphere and thus wasted. On top of the chassis would be mounted one of a few standard boilers, all of which would steam freely and efficiently, and again would be interchangeable with locomotives of the same size – so when the boiler of a heavy freight locomotive was replaced, it could receive an overhauled one which was first installed on an express passenger locomotive. Such was the interchangeability of parts that Churchward had in mind.

The designs he planned were a heavy freight 2-8-0 (the first time such a wheel arrangement had been used in Britain), a versatile 2-6-2T – the 'T' stands for 'water tank' – suitable for short-distance passenger and freight work, a general purpose 4-6-0 with the intermediate size of driving wheels, a 4-4-2T suitable for fast short-distance passenger trains, a 4-4-0 equivalent for light passenger trains over longer distances, and most significantly of all a new design of express passenger 4-6-0 for the Great Western's heaviest and fastest trains.

He wanted the latter locomotives to be able to sustain a high average speed of 70mph for long distances, and with maximum efficiency in material used in construction and consumption of coal and water in operation. To Churchward, efficiency was God.

In March 1903, he put his thoughts into action in spectacular fashion, with what we would recognise today as the country's first modern steam locomotive, No. 98. Its configuration was a refinement of No. 100's, retaining the 4-6-0 wheel arrangement with 6ft 8½in driving wheels but with a modified and more efficient boiler with a cone connecting the smokebox with the firebox, and outside cylinders and valves. It was a massive leap forward even from No. 100 and when W.A. Tuplin wrote many years later that it was perhaps the greatest single steam locomotive since *Rocket,* he was telling no more than the truth. For a prototype, it was extremely close to later production versions – and incredibly, it would exert an influence on British steam locomotive design until the 1950s. If *Rocket* was the genesis of the typical Victorian steam locomotive, Churchward's first masterpiece was an equally important moment. In every sense it was a watershed.

And it was followed by two more locomotives – No. 97, a heavy 2-8-0 freight locomotive using an identical boiler and cylinders to No. 98, and No. 99, a 2-6-2T which shared the same cylinders but had a smaller boiler and 5ft 8in-diameter driving wheels. The cab fittings were identical; the cylinders were made in one-piece castings that were bolted together under the smoke box and formed a saddle to support the boiler. Even the valve gear was largely identical. In one year Churchward had established the template for Great Western locomotive design that would serve the company well until the very end.

The benefits of sharing so many parts were obvious: construction would be simpler and cheaper because so many designs were common and there would be less need to retool production lines for different locomotives; maintenance would be simpler as shed staff would have fewer different designs to maintain, and the familiar footplates would make driving and firing different types of locomotive more predictable. It would inevitably take a long time for the new designs to become the majority but they would eventually spread all over the Great Western system.

Churchward did have one concern and that was that compound locomotives, which passed the exhaust steam from one set of cylinders to another larger set in order to extract maximum power, could be far more efficient than his simple expansion designs. So, in the year he introduced the prototypes of his first three standard locomotives, he ordered a 4-4-2 ('Atlantic') compound locomotive from Societé Alscacienne in Belfort, France. He would compare it with a follow-on to No. 98, No. 171 *Albion*, which would be built with the same wheel arrangement as the French locomotive to ensure the comparison was fair. Churchward was confident enough in his locomotives to believe there would be little in it but it is a mark of his open-minded nature that he was prepared to modify his designs should it prove otherwise.

Suddenly the Great Western was blossoming. The Wootton Basset to Patchway cut-off opened on 1 July 1903 throughout to passenger trains, shaving 25 miles off the main route via Gloucester and allowing journey times between Paddington and Cardiff to be cut to 2hrs 55mins from 3hrs 17mins. The shallow gradients allowed the weight of freight trains to be heavier without resorting to expensive double-heading and banking – and they could avoid the congested Bristol network.

In the West Country, the first part of the direct line to Taunton as far as Westbury had opened in July 1900, allowing an acceleration of services to Weymouth and work was now underway on the remaining section from Westbury to Cogload Junction near Taunton. This would open in May 1906. The Great Western was rampant and in 1904 it once again added speed to its repertoire with the astonishing journey from Plymouth to London by *City of Truro* in 1904.

That year, competition between the Great Western Railway (GWR) and London & South Western Railway (LSWR) for the lucrative transatlantic mail to and from Plymouth was hotting up. Sending the mail bags from London via Plymouth was the fastest way for letters to cross the Atlantic and although public opinion had firmly turned against railway 'racing' following the Great Races to the North of the nineteenth century, drivers from both companies were starting to ignore the schedules.

It was a matter that was giving George Jackson Churchward, the Great Western's forty-seven-year-old Locomotive, Carriage & Wagon Superintendent, some niggling headaches. He was keen that the Great Western shouldn't be seen to be slower than the LSWR and when he heard that his opposite number Dugald Drummond was taking an interest in the trains it became personal. Churchward felt, probably correctly, that his locomotives were far superior to the LSWR's and was damned if he was going to be beaten. For a hunting, shooting and fishing sportsman as he was, this contest – because that's what it was – was one of professional pride and demanded some serious thought if it were to be won. He leaned back in his chair at Swindon Works and stroked his bushy moustache – he was bald so he couldn't ruffle his hair – trying to decide how the Great Western could do something so dramatic the LSWR would be forced to concede defeat.

Churchward summoned a young locomotive inspector from Newton Abbot, G.H. Flewellyn, into his office and outlined his thinking about the Ocean Mails. Flewellyn was charged with supervising the running of the trains and ordered to ride on the footplate of each one. As a locomotive inspector, it would be Flewellyn's job to encourage the driver and fireman to make good time and to intervene if necessary either to speed up or slow down. Churchward spoke to Flewellyn with calm authority: his experience on the running sheds of the South Devon Railway and on the Great Western meant he knew what he was talking about, as did the young locomotive inspector. The emphasis should be on speed, Churchward said, but not at the price of safety – he would decide when and how far the risks should be stretched. 'Withhold all attempts at a maximum speed until I give you the word: then you can go and break your bloody neck,' he concluded. The profanity was for emphasis – something he used often. Flewellyn would not have been surprised or offended by Churchward's swearing.

In early May 1904, Churchward sent word to Flewellyn to prepare for a really fast run from Plymouth to London. The locomotive selected was No. 3440 *City of Truro*, one of the Great Western's most modern passenger locomotives. It had been built in May 1903 at Swindon Works and was of the right age to attempt something out of the ordinary: old enough to run smoothly and have any glitches solved but young enough for everything to still be nice and tight. The date was set for 9 May.

The driver selected was Moses Clements, a man who, to borrow from automotive parlance, liked to put his foot down – or to be more exact, put his regulator arm up. Clements' reputation was known from Devon to London as one of pushing the free-steaming Great Western locomotives to the very limit. His fireman (who after all would be doing most of the work) sadly is unrecorded.

When the guard's whistle blew at 09:23 Clements released the brakes at the now long-closed Plymouth Millbay station and put *City of Truro* to work with the light train of 148 tons. Three minutes later, it had passed Plymouth North Road (today's main station) and flew up Hemerdon Bank immediately outside Plymouth at speeds rarely if ever seen before. Between there and Totnes, she made short work of the stiff Devon banks that were the legacy of Isambard Kingdom Brunel's failed attempt at finding an alternative to the steam locomotive in the 1840s and which to this day test the fastest and most powerful trains. The fireman was working like a demon, shovelling coal furiously but precisely in a bid to keep pace with *City of Truro*'s demand for steam and Clements was using his intimate knowledge of the route to the full, gaining as much speed as possible down the banks and braking as late as he dared. Flewellyn and the men working in the mail coaches behind were being given a good shaking and with no intervention forthcoming, Clements realised that very high speeds really were there for the taking. It was entirely up to him as to when to slow down.

The spectacular sea wall section between Teignmouth and Dawlish limited speeds and perhaps holidaymakers gave the train a wave as it hared past, the safety valves simmering with pent-up pressure. With the characteristic bark of a Great Western locomotive, *City of Truro* was in its natural environment, green paintwork complemented by burnished copper-capped chimney and brass safety-valve bonnet with an almost mirror finish. This relatively slow section allowed the fireman to build up his fire and once past Exeter, Clements opened *City of Truro* up once more. They tore up towards Whiteball, a distance of 20 miles, and when she nosed over the summit at something like 50mph, Clements really went for it and something magical happened.

Speed gathered rapidly on the downhill section, the coupling rods whirring round the outside frames in a blur, the fire dancing white-hot and the exhaust beats merging together to form a single continuous roar. They emerged from Whiteball Tunnel at 80mph, according to the railway journalist Charles Rous-Marten, who was onboard timing the train with a pair of stopwatches. The quarter-mile posts flashed by at an ever-greater rate, the time interval between them falling over the course of a mile and a half to 8.8 seconds.

City of Truro was swaying and bucking with ever-greater force and still accelerating. Still Flewellyn remained in his position, not ordering a slowdown. Rous-Marten was furiously doing calculations in his head to work out the speed of the train, and his heartbeat quickened further when he realised the train was travelling at more than a hundred miles per hour – 102.3mph, to be precise. Clements must have also been working out how fast the train was going and he decided that the delicate balance of risk and reward had tipped against the train at last. He saw a track gang working ahead and whistled to alert them before slamming on the brakes. The speed came down to 80mph at Taunton and, presumably feeling he had proved his point, Clements kept it down to 75mph to Bristol, arriving at 11:26.

At Bristol, *City of Truro* was replaced by one of Dean's beautiful and elegant 'singles', No. 3065 *Duke of Connaught,* which was to take the train forward. The Bristol mail coach was detached and the train set off at 11:30 – smart work indeed from a crew that knew exactly what they were doing. Despite only having a single pair of driving wheels to grip the rails, *Duke of Connaught* got hold of its train quickly and accelerated with the grace only one of these fine machines could.

Through elegant Bath the train went, locomotive, carriages and railway blending into this beautiful city, and then it blazed into Box Tunnel at around 70mph. Speed only dropped to 60mph at the summit at Corsham and this remarkable run would soon get even better. After observing a niggling speed restriction at Cricklade Bridge, Driver Underhill opened out *Duke of Connaught* once more past Swindon Works, hitting 80mph with ease for mile after mile on the remaining stretch to London on Brunel's almost perfectly flat railway line. Underhill judged the final braking finely and the Ocean Mails came to a stand at the buffer stops in London Paddington at 13:09:58 exactly, covering a distance of 245¾ miles between Plymouth North Road and Paddington in just 223 minutes, a journey time today's railway would struggle to match.

The following morning, a newspaper carried an illustration of *City of Truro,* claiming the locomotive was averaging 99 to 100mph. Rous-Marten's more precise figure was kept secret and he headlined his article for *The Railway Magazine* of June 1904 'The Great Western's Record of Records' without saying what that was and leaving nothing for readers to guess what the actual top speed was.

Did *City of Truro* really hit 102.3mph, or was Rous-Marten's timing slightly inaccurate? Nobody will ever know for certain, and arguments raged almost from the day after the run about what exactly happened on 9 May 1904. One thing is certain: Clements, his firemen, the locomotive inspector and staff in the coaches behind were the fastest people in the world for a brief moment on 9 May 1904. The Great Western had recaptured its reputation for speed that it won so proudly on the broad gauge railway of the 1840s.

This was one of the more remarkable tales told of a company which has had more material published about it than any other railway — perhaps any company full-stop — in the world. The Great Western Railway, even sixty-two years after it was nationalised, is revered and adored by millions all over the world who are smitten by its spectacle, its ethos, and its achievements.

*

While the spotlight was shining on Churchward's locomotives, the Great Western was girding its loins to revitalise its long-distance traffic to the west. The Berks & Hants cut-off was going to be ready for passenger service in 1906 and would make a big difference.

To conclude the story of the major cut-off routes, two others were being planned at the time. The first was a 23-mile line between Old Oak Common, just outside Paddington, and High Wycombe, which joined the former Wycombe Railway from Maidenhead to Aylesbury. The Great Western also won approval for a link from Ashendon Junction, four miles north west of Haddenham, Oxfordshire, to Aynho Junction on the Oxford to Banbury stretch of the main line to Birmingham. It would share much of the route to High Wycombe with the Great Central Railway, which was seeking an alternative route into London in order to avoid the Metropolitan Railway (with which it shared tracks and which was also continuing its obstructive practice). The combined effect was to give the Great Western a new and more direct route to Birmingham from London, and new sources of local traffic too. The Old Oak Common to High Wycombe (and effectively Princes Risborough) opened to passenger traffic in April 1906.

The final cut-off was designed to shorten the route between South Wales, the West Country and Birmingham, and involved improvements to the Honeybourne to Stratford-upon-Avon branch and a new 21-mile line from Honeybourne to Cheltenham. The latter section opened first, on 1 August 1906, with the improved Stratford line opening to passenger traffic two years later.

The inspiration behind all of these was the new General Manager, James Inglis, who succeeded Joseph Wilkinson after he died in 1902. Inglis was a remarkable man, the unsung hero of the Edwardian Great Western. Born in Aberdeen in 1851, he was consulting engineer to the Alexandra (Newport) Dock Company in 1875 and then moved to Plymouth to help construct the deep-water quays and other infrastructure at Millbay Docks for the South Devon Railway. When that company was amalgamated with the Great Western in 1876, Inglis resigned and became a consulting engineer in Plymouth where he helped the GWR build the Bodmin Road to Bodmin branch and rebuild some of Brunel's timber viaducts with more robust materials.

Inglis's work with the Great Western had impressed many and he was appointed Chief Engineer in October 1892. He was responsible for the tracks, structures and civil engineering across the whole company and his department planned the bold cut-off lines which would help slash journey times in the future. His drive and ability duly noted, he was the logical choice to succeed Wilkinson on his death in May 1902 and then as General Manager.

Churchward was responsible for providing the locomotives, carriages and wagons to run the Great Western's services but it was Inglis who decided the direction of the company, how fast its trains would run, whether to sanction capacity improvements – and what customers should expect. Churchward provided the tools, but it was Inglis who decided how they should be used.

He set to work quickly, ordering Churchward to develop a new range of coaches for the London to Penzance services which he intended to speed up, and one of his most daring acts was to extend the non-stop run of a London to Penzance train known colloquially but unofficially as 'The Cornishman' from London to Plymouth rather than Exeter, a distance of 245½ miles. It was the longest non-stop train journey in the world at the time and it was only possible through the use of strategically placed water troughs between the rails from which locomotives could lower a scoop in the tender and pick up fresh supplies. The commercial value of saving a few minutes on the journey time by eliminating water stops might have been marginal (though to some passengers it would doubtless have been extremely important) but the publicity which resulted was extremely positive.

Inglis realised that the old practice of giving specific train services names (such as the old broad gauge 'Flying Dutchman' from London to Exeter) was an easy and effective way of promoting services and making them easier for the public to remember. It also made them more attractive – how much nicer it is to say that you're catching the 'Flying Dutchman' on the way west rather than a mere time of departure) so he asked readers of *The Railway Magazine* to help give 'The Cornishman' an official name.

The winning entry was 'Riviera Express', soon modified to 'The Cornish Riviera Express' and finally 'The Cornish Riviera Limited'. What a marvellous, evocative name that final choice was, and what a stroke of genius from Inglis to accept it. That name instantly conjures up a vision of lush green farmland, long golden beaches, endless warm summers and a just a soupçon of the glamour of the French Riviera. It was brilliant and the service began running under that name in 1905.

The image invoked by the name was backed up by the carriages that Churchward provided for the train. Leaving Paddington at 10:10 every day in the summer, seven of his mighty 'Dreadnought' carriages headed non-stop to Plymouth and then beyond. The coaches were giant by the standards of the day. They were 70ft long and 9ft 6in wide, carried on two four-wheel bogies. They broke with convention by ditching the fussy clerestory roof in favour of a simple all-over ellipse which made them much more spacious, and also by only having doors at the ends and middle rather than to each compartment. The Great Western was able to build these remarkable vehicles, which were longer than almost any in front-line service until the advent of British Rail's iconic Mk 3 coaches in the 1970s because of the greater clearances provided for the broad gauge. The 'Dreadnoughts' wouldn't be able to run over the entire Great Western network, and certainly not over many other companies' lines, but they were able to provide the newly named 'Cornish Riviera' with a distinctive and roomy set of coaches that should have proved popular. Alas, the travelling public disliked not having an exterior door to each compartment, and no further coaches would be built without them until the 1930s.

When the Berks & Hants cut-off opened in 1906, the 'Cornish Riviera' was immediately placed on that route and allowed the journey to Plymouth to be cut by 15mins to 4hrs 10mins and in time this would come down to an even 4hrs.

One feature of the 'Cornish Riviera' that definitely wouldn't be allowed today was the use of slip coaches to provide direct services to stations without the main train stopping. These coaches were coupled to the main train and to each other with a special coupling device which could be detached while the train was in motion. As the 'Cornish Riviera' neared the drop-off points for coaches to Weymouth, Minehead and Exeter (Westbury, Taunton and the approaches to Exeter St David's correspondently), a guard in the slip coach would release the coupling, separating it from the train. A vacuum reservoir on the coach kept the brakes from applying once it was coasting and the aim was to let the slip coach coast to a stand at the station it served, or where it would be added to another train to take it to its destination. It was a neat way of serving places while keeping journey times as short as possible, though of course in the opposite direction, the 'Cornish Riviera' had to stop at each calling point for the slip coaches to be added to it.

Slip coaches sound horribly risky today, but they were protected at the rear by signals at danger and obviously could not run into the train they had split from. Sometimes the guards on slip coaches misjudged their braking and stalled before they wanted to, and when this happened, a locomotive had to be sent to reel them in, but generally speaking, slip coaches were a resounding if compromised success. No less than seventy-four daily slip coach services were operating before 1914.

A further addition to the Great Western's network opened in 1906, an extension of the South Wales Railway from Clarbeston Road to Fishguard, very much as Brunel had anticipated when he planned the route in the 1850s. The aim of this was to serve the redeveloped port of Fishguard, which offered a shorter route to Rosslare, Ireland, than any other port and also to serve ocean liners. The Great Western acquired ships to provide a service over the Irish Sea and had a day and night crossing in each direction, all, of course, served by trains. These trains were run smartly, arriving in Fishguard no more than 15 minutes before the ships sailed, and departing no more than 15 minutes after they arrived, such was the attention paid to moving passengers, baggage and mails between these two very different modes of transport. Waterford and Cork were also served from Fishguard from August 1906.

The Great Western wasted no time in promoting its revitalised services, and thanks to a young man in the General Manager's office, Felix Pole, the hitherto scatter-gun approach to publicity was replaced with a modern, persuasive range of communication materials. Mindful that it was only the middle classes who could afford decent holidays, GWR targeted them in a way that companies today could still learn from. A full-page advert illustrating the merits of travelling Great Western was inserted in the *Daily Mail* in 1904 and was followed almost immediately by a book called *The Cornish Riviera Express*, written by A.M. Broadley. The book was a thinly veiled promotion of the Great Western's flagship train but it was well written and sold not in the thousands, but hundreds of thousands. The first edition alone sold 250,000 copies and this was followed by four more!

In 1906, Felix Pole went one better, and encouraged the Great Western to publish a radical new book called *Holiday Haunts*. This was a giant publication, containing page after page of advertisements for holiday accommodation, and editorial articles about what holiday-makers could do when they reached their destinations. Needless to say, the Great Western took full advantage of the opportunity to promote its new, faster services too. The underlying tag-line of all of this tourist-oriented publicity was simple: why holiday abroad when you can holiday at home in England and Wales, and travel in comfort, safety and style with the Great Western Railway? With the company's gorgeous green locomotives hauling chocolate-and-cream coloured coaches in gorgeous scenery, it was irresistible to the growing middle classes.

James Inglis was driving himself hard too, doing his utmost to improve the Great Western and in 1906 won approval for a major expansion of London Paddington. The plan was to build three new platforms on the arrival side under a 190ft wide, 700ft long steel and glass roof carefully designed to complement Brunel's original train shed. Development of Paddington would continue for another thirty years but it was Inglis who kick-started it.

Chapter 14
The Safest Way

The introduction of continuous braking and absolute block signalling had vastly improved railway safety from the dangerous days of time interval operating but it wasn't foolproof. There was nothing stopping a driver from ignoring a signal at danger and continuing at full speed into either a rear-end or, worse still, a head-on collision. Passing signals at danger happened far more often than accident statistics suggested, and often because drivers simply saw them too late in bad weather or fog.

Britain's towns and cities relied almost exclusively on coal to provide heat and power, and in cold weather when all the fires were burning, the smoke could add dangerously to fog, thickening it into an impenetrable murk. The signals were of the semaphore type, which on the Great Western meant that when the arm was pointing downwards, the route was clear and when horizontal at danger; they also had red and green lenses that shaded an oil lamp to indicate their aspect at night and in poor visibility. In foggy weather, the traditional method of alerting a driver to signals at danger was to use track gangers as fogmen, who placed two explosive detonators on the rails. When the train ran over them, the driver heard two loud bangs and knew it was time to brake. This was labour-intensive and fallible, as there was no positive indication to the enginemen that the route ahead was clear. In effect, they relied on the absence of noise to tell them it was okay but if the fogman hadn't turned up, or if he hadn't been quick enough off the mark in placing his detonators then disaster could result. To the Great Western this wasn't good enough.

The signalling and locomotive departments put their heads together in a bid to devise a system which would let the driver know not only that the line ahead was blocked but also that it was clear as far as the next signal; what they came up with was a method that in its principles forms the bedrock of the railway's first line of defence against passing signals at danger to this day.

At so-called Distant signals, which were yellow, the rule was that when the arm was down, the section immediately in front and the one beyond that were both clear, allowing the train to proceed at its scheduled speed. When the arm was up at danger, it alerted the driver that while the section ahead was clear the next signal along the line was at danger, giving him time to slow down in anticipation of stopping.

The Great Western's plan was to install ramps between the rails connected to these Distant signals electrically. When the route was clear it would be energised, and when the route wasn't clear, the ramp would be electrically dead. Locomotives were fitted with a plunger underneath the buffer beam. When this plunger made contact with the ramp, it was lifted and opened an air valve on the locomotive. When the ramp was dead, the air passing through the valve would sound a warning siren to let the driver know the route ahead was occupied. When the ramp was energised, meanwhile, electro-magnets on the locomotive would close the valve immediately to prevent the horn sounding, and sound a bell in the cab instead to give drivers an audible indication the route was clear. The idea was first tested on the Henley branch in 1906 and very quickly developed so that the air valve automatically admitted air into the braking system to stop the train unless the driver intervened to cancel it.

The system was called Automatic Train Control (ATC) and it was a brilliant innovation. Should some calamity have befallen the footplate crew, it could stop the train before it reached a stop signal, while in poor visibility it provided the drivers with positive assurance that they could continue at line speed in safety. It was possible for a driver to cancel a warning and continue blithely on but in practice this seldom happened. Passengers were safer and trains more punctual. The Great Western had a winning design that put it far ahead of any other railway in Britain – and possibly the world – in terms of safety and it began to install ATC on its key routes.

Churchward's new range of standard locomotives was beginning to filter into service as development of ATC neared its conclusion, but he was still continuing to build the 'Bulldog' outside-framed 4-4-0s for service on secondary routes. Fitted with his standard boilers, they were good machines for the job and while he was in some senses reinventing the wheel, he had the good sense not to do so just for the sake of it. The same applied to the small shunting locomotives used on local trains and in goods yards across the Great Western network – they were good enough to do their jobs, so why bother replacing them?

His big 4-6-0s, collectively known as 'Saints' because many were named after them, were entering traffic too. Some were built as 4-4-2s as there was still some doubt as to whether the extra traction gained by six driving wheels offset the frictional losses incurred by the extra coupling rods (it more than did so), but others were built as he intended. In comparisons against the French 'Atlantics' they had proved that there was little difference in efficiency and they were far simpler. However, the French locomotives had four cylinders – two outside and two between the frames – and this meant they were much smoother riding than the two-cylinder 'Saints'.

The reason was that because the tractive forces on the French locomotives were divided four times rather than two there was less stress imposed on the coupling rods and axle boxes, and in turn this might mean that maintenance intervals could be extended.

He was keen to further explore the possibilities the French compounds seem to offer and in 1905 ordered another pair, which were slightly more powerful than the 1902 locomotives. Again, they proved little more efficient than his two-cylinder 4-6-0s, and again the ride was far superior. Furthermore, there was none of the rough riding that developed in his designs as components began to wear. On long-distance expresses such as the 'Cornish Riviera' this rough riding made life uncomfortable and difficult for the enginemen, and when they altered the regulator and cut-off (analogous to a car's gears) settings to make the ride smoother, they used far more steam, defeating Churchward's fundamental aim of making his locomotives as efficient as possible.

Churchward decided to build a prototype locomotive using the same standard No. 1 boiler as the 'Saints', and as many other components as possible but with four cylinders rather than two. It was released from Swindon Works in April 1906 as an 'Atlantic' for comparison with the new French compounds, and in view of the leap forward Churchward thought it represented, named *North Star* after the first truly successful locomotive the Great Western ever had.

North Star wasn't just different in its configuration. Successive developments of the No. 1 boiler had finally evolved into a rather elegant design. In order to match a small drumhead smoke box calculated to provide the freest-possible draughting with a large firebox, it was tapered continuously upwards from front to back. It was a small difference in functional terms that took great skill in manufacture as the bottom of the boiler is straight and horizontal: one thing a Churchward taper boiler *isn't* is coned.

So far, Churchward's rationale for *North Star* was perfectly sound, but he did make a rather surprising decision when it came to the positioning of the cylinders. He decided to copy the French layout, with the two outside cylinders hanging to the sides of the bogie's rear wheels and the two inside cylinders forwards, lying in line with the bogie's front wheels. The issue came with the outside cylinders, which were attached to the locomotive's frames just where there is a semi-circular cut-out to provide clearance for the rear bogie wheels when the locomotive goes around curves. Churchward evidently recognised this problem at the design stage, because he installed a massive bracket running between the frames to provide extra strength. At a stroke, this made it almost impossible for a driver built any larger than a whippet to go between the frames and oil the valve gear and on some occasions, trains were delayed because of the difficulty in oiling a 'Star' thoroughly. Gallingly, a solution was staring Churchward right in the face – place all the cylinders in line with the space between the two axles of the bogie – but as he had never seen that configuration used successfully on a four-cylinder locomotive he refused to consider it.

This small but significant issue with the design of *North Star* highlights one of Churchward's most surprising characteristics – he was willing to bring ideas from the other side of the world for use on the Great Western yet curiously reluctant to develop his own new thinking. There's nothing wrong with this but given his undoubted stature and ability it is curious.

North Star entered traffic and quickly demonstrated that she was a remarkably free-running and very powerful machine for the time. Charles Rous-Marten (who had timed *City of Truro*'s epic run two years before) travelled behind the locomotive on a westbound 'Cornish Riviera' and although it put in a respectable performance, he thought that it didn't have enough grip, something borne out by the fact that *North Star* didn't have anything in hand over a 'Saint.'

Churchward was impressed enough by *North Star*'s early per-formances, however, to order a production batch of ten follow-on locomotives, all to be built as 4-6-os. On 8 August 1906, No. 4001 *Dog Star* emerged glistening from Swindon. In February 1907, Churchward made one significant change in *Dog Star*, changing the valve gear between the frames to a variant of Walschaerts-type motion, which was expected to give better performance. As 4-6-os, Churchward's four-cylinder locomotives looked far better than *North Star*. The smaller rear wheels of the latter gave it an oddly unbalanced appearance, which the 4-6-os corrected. The large distance between the front of the outside cylinders and the buffers has always looked a little odd to my eyes but without doubt, *Dog Star* and its sisters were attractive engines.

Churchward finally added some small embellishments to his locomotives, inserting curved sections between the different horizontal levels of the footplating around the front and sides of *Dog Star*, and lowering this under the cab to give the impression that it wasn't simply perched on top of the frames, though of course, in reality, it was.

The last of this first batch of locomotives, No. 4010 *Western Star*, also incorporated the final element in Churchward's quest to make his simple expansion engines as efficient as compounds – the superheater. The superheater is simple to describe but it was much harder to manufacture. It is a series of pipes which take the steam from the boiler and pass through the large boiler tubes in order to dry the steam out properly and give it as much potential energy as possible: the hotter the gas, the more it will expand in the cylinders so less water and coal are consumed to get the same amount of work out of a locomotive.

It took Churchward and Swindon some time to refine the super-heater design just right for their applications but with this development the Great Western's 'Stars' and 'Saints' were – and by a very wide margin – the finest express passenger locomotives in Britain, as well as quite possibly in all of Europe, so it was surprising that in 1908 the Great Western built a giant locomotive that in terms of size at least eclipsed even these.

Still looking abroad for ideas, Churchward noticed the introduction of 4-6-2 (or 'Pacific') locomotives in North America and France and having made such strides in locomotive development, it appears he concluded the Great Western ought to have one too. His suggestion of a 'super locomotive' was approved by the board in January 1907 and £4,400 was allocated for its construction.

It's likely that Churchward was being far-sighted in trying to identify how best to augment the existing fleet should trainloads increase significantly. A 'Pacific' appeared to offer the best solution because it could have a larger firebox over the small trailing axle that would mean the grate area – which ultimately dictates how much coal can be burned – could be increased without having a really long firebox that would stress the fireman. In fact, Churchward's new 'Pacific' would have a grate area of 41.9 square feet compared with the 27 of the 'Stars', 'Saints' and '28xx' 2-8-os.

The boiler was to be much larger than the Standard No. 1 too, with the boiler barrel itself coming out at a whopping 23ft long, far bigger than most steam locomotives ever built in Britain. Where, with hindsight, the design team made a mistake was in not making the heating surface of the boiler – the surface area of the firebox and outside of the tubes – commensurately larger than that of the Standard No. 1 boiler. It meant that the fireman could shovel as hard as he liked: there was no guarantee his efforts would translate into extra heat added to the boiler water.

Designing the Great Western 'Pacific' was a demanding and difficult task and for once there were no prototypes Churchward could readily draw inspiration from. But when it made its first trial run on 4 February 1908, it certainly made an impression. Numbered 111 and named *The Great Bear*, the Great Western had built a giant of a locomotive. (Presumably it was felt that after the 'Stars', the next step up was 'Constellations'.) It was long, had a massive boiler and an imperious, superior presence, although the odd eight-wheel tender coupled behind looked like something of an afterthought. If the Great Western wanted its new locomotive to make a splash, it certainly achieved it.

It very quickly became apparent, however, that something wasn't quite right with *The Great Bear*. Its weight caused the Civil Engineer to bar it from everywhere except the London to Bristol Main Line but as a prototype locomotive this wasn't necessarily a bad thing. However, what *was* bad and for firemen particularly, was that the locomotive struggled for steam. Some of this can be attributed to the fact that *The Great Bear* was the first Great Western locomotive to have a wide firebox, and this does require a quite different technique to what they were used to, but it doesn't excuse the relative lack of heating surfaces for such a big boiler, and without a fundamental redesign which wasn't likely to come given that the 'Stars' and 'Saints' were well on top of their duties: *The Great Bear* was always going to be a white elephant. When Nigel Gresley of the Great Northern Railway started building a 'Pacific' at Doncaster in the early 1920s, Churchward remarked: 'What did that young man want to build it for? We could have sold him ours!'

Churchward's other designs were generally extremely successful, however. The 'County' 4-4-0s were designed as a pint-sized 'Saint' and although they gave their crews a jolting ride they were fast and lively performers. The '28xx' freight locomotives, meanwhile, used the same boiler as the 'Saints' and 'Stars' on a 2-8-0 chassis optimised for heavy freight trains and proved extremely successful and durable, lasting until the end of Great Western steam. A 2-8-0 freight design which was not in Churchward's original plan but was developed using his standardised components was the '42xx' tank locomotives, which were designed for short-distance but heavy goods trains, while general duties were taken care of by the '43xx' 2-6-os, a surprisingly late addition to the Great Western's stable, the first entering service in 1911. Although the '43xxs' were quite small locomotives, they packed a surprising punch and when they occasionally found themselves substituted onto express passenger trains could in the right circumstances keep pace with timings designed for the 'Saints' and 'Stars'.

The remaining types of Churchward standard locomotive which entered service in the first fifteen years of the century were the '44xx' and '45xx' 2-6-2Ts (known generally as 'Small Prairies', and '5101' class 'Large Prairies'. The former were designed for the hilly branch lines of Devon, Cornwall and South Wales and were a development of the 'large prairies'. These spread all over the Great Western on short-haul passenger and goods duties.

In fairly short order, Churchward had provided the Great Western with designs that, with the exception of the 'Counties' and *The Great Bear,* would set it fair for years to come. They weren't cheap but they were the best in the country, and when one director asked Churchward why his locomotives were more expensive to build than those of the LNWR he replied in the only way he knew how: 'Because one of mine can pull two of their bloody things backwards!'

To prove his point, in 1910 Churchward offered to send No. 4005 *Polar Star* to the LNWR to be tested against one of that company's most recent comparable passenger locomotives, the 'Experiment' 4-6-os, while an 'Experiment' would be sent to the Great Western to make things fair. The results were decisive: the 'Star' was much more power-ful and efficient than the LNWR design, and could keep time on the heaviest trains. When an 'Experiment' was tried on some of the Great Western's most demanding duties, it struggled to keep time and burned a lot more coal in doing even this.

The average difference in cost between the LNWR locomotives and those on the GWR was slight – the former cost around £975 per engine a year, and the Great Western's £1,003. On a power to price ratio however, Churchward's designs were far ahead of the LNWR's. The directors' concerns were allayed and Churchward was vindicated.

The Great Western suffered a devastating loss in 1911 when James Inglis died aged sixty-one. He had been knighted in the New Year Honours that year in recognition of the transformation he had wrought on the Great Western. In addition, he was a governor of the London School of Economics and a member of the Royal Commission on Canals & Inland Waterways. He was so highly regarded, he was elected not once but twice as President of the Institution of Civil Engineers, a rare and distinguished honour.

His obituary in the Institution of Civil Engineers Minutes of Proceedings included this passage:

> In personal character Sir James was eminently practical with a mechanic's instinct to recognise that which rang true. He was thorough, broad in his views, alike in engineering and his more private opinions. A Liberal-Unionist in politics, he was an Imperialist in the highest sense of the word. Kindly and warm-hearted, he did much to encourage others both in business and in private life.

The Great Western had lost a truly inspirational leader but Inglis's foresight in expanding capacity and providing more direct routes to the north and west, as well as that of Churchward with his new locomotives would soon be stretched to the limit as the final years of peace in the twentieth century ticked away.

*

The rapid-fire revitalisation of the Great Western Railway in the first decade of the twentieth century might have singled the company out in narrow technical and operational terms but the abolition of the broad gauge and shortening of its routes emphasised the profound changes that railways all over Britain were priming.

While many writers have pinned successive decades – the 1920s, 1930s and 1950s in particular – as so-called golden ages for the steam railway, the reality is that if there ever was such a thing, it lasted from the early 1900s to the Great War. It is untrue to say that railways had a monopoly then – canals were generally still profitable even if their viability was declining, while trams were increasingly popular in towns and cities for passengers. Horse-drawn traffic inevitably predominated on the roads too – but the railways' position as the fastest and often the cheapest way of moving goods and people was in no doubt.

It is difficult to comprehend the scale of the changes wrought by the railways. Perhaps the only modern equivalent is the rise of computers and the internet, but even they haven't yet had quite the same impact. The most obvious effect the railways first had, of course, was on the landscape. With vast earthworks and structures spreading all over Britain it could hardly be otherwise, but they changed our geography in other more subtle ways. Towns and cities were split by the new form of transport, changing not only their appearance but also their complexion. The phrase 'from the wrong side of the tracks' reflects the fact that railways formed an effective barrier between different areas, relieved only by bridges and level crossings. In many places, the early railways blended in quite well with their settings (though how much of this is viewed through the lens of later development is difficult to say) but when they were being built, there were plenty of voices criticising their appearance: not all engineers were as careful as Brunel to ensure elegance.

Away from the towns there were more subtle changes, but these too all had their impact. Fields worked for generations were sometimes divided by the new railways and, while there were occupation crossings and cattle creeps, in many cases the farmers simply had to get on with it. When you see a small irregular-shaped field on the side of a railway, there's a good chance there'll be another directly opposite. Ancients rights of way were severed too, so in some cases the railway inadvertently created a 'great way round' road for those unfortunate to live in the area. There are still, occasionally, calls for these rights of way to be re-established over railway lines, though only in a very few cases has this happened: the costs of providing a bridge or level crossing are too great for the few people that road reinstatement would benefit.

Agriculture was one of the main beneficiaries of the railways from the very earliest days. We have already seen how farmers near London feared the arrival of the Great Western Railway, because it could bring cheaper produce from further away, lowering food prices – and their fears did indeed come to pass. Yet the diet of many in the cities was transformed for the good by the railways. Fresh produce became much more readily available once the rail network was largely complete, as it was possible for growers to send their fruit and vegetables to market in a matter of hours, and for farmers in faraway areas such as Devon, Cornwall and West Wales, it transformed the economics of farming for good. It wasn't just fruit and vegetables: trains carrying milk by the churn were sent to their destinations at express speeds (though, in the process, making redundant dairy cows kept in cities for providing milk locally), while farmers who could previously expect their livestock to lose hefty amounts of weight being walked long distances to market could simply load them onto a train and recoup the full value.

Manufacturers could not only distribute their goods more effectively than before – a rail link to their factory meant that raw materials could be acquired more cheaply too (there were thousands upon thousands of rail-connected businesses, many with their own internal rail networks). It became possible for a company based in, say, Taunton, to compete on a much more level playing field with its counterparts in key markets such as London and the Midlands than ever before, retaining expertise in remote areas and generating income.

Railways were inevitably a key factor in Britain's vast export trade: the competitive advantage provided to British companies often meant that they could export all the way round the world at relatively low cost. It's not surprising that ports on the South Coast in particular boomed, almost entirely thanks to the railways being able to supply them, and vast dock railway systems were needed to cope with the volumes of goods being transhipped.

This process worked both ways, however. In some areas, local firms were simply unable to compete against distant rivals, while the ability of the railways to carry bulk loads also ultimately worked against some sectors, as imported raw materials could be much cheaper than indigenous equivalents. Foreign imports of copper and tin lowered prices to such an extent that Cornwall's once extensive mining industry entered a rapid decline from which it never recovered. The same railways that brought tourists to the region, also inadvertently removed the lifeblood of many communities who depended on the mines.

The railways gave vast numbers of people stable and relatively secure (if at times highly dangerous) employment and, in rural areas, it was hardly surprising that they drew many of their staff from the ranks of poorly paid farm labourers. After all, for a man used to hard physical work, being on a track gang was unlikely to be much worse and offered the bonus of a stable wage. So companies like the Great Western could by and large take their pick of the working classes – and they did so, particularly for engine cleaners, the first rung on the long career ladder to being an engine driver. One of the reasons the trains were so smart and the railway so revered in the early twentieth century was that the railways employed many of the most capable people.

Most of all though, the railways affected people by giving them the opportunity to travel further than ever before. It wasn't unusual in the nineteenth century for people to be born, live their whole lives and die within a 10-mile radius, which they seldom if ever ventured outside. As train fares became cheaper and the services faster, this began to change. Not only did the railways change our physical geography, they changed our perceptions of it. Bristol changed from being a key port quite a long way from London and requiring a lengthy journey, to a place which people could travel to and from in a day. As the distances increased, so that perception was amplified. By the First World War, travelling to the very extremities of Britain was a feasible journey rather than a lengthy adventure. In a sense, Britain became smaller with the advent of the railways.

With a more mobile and increasingly wealthy population, some took the opportunity to live better than before. Whereas the professions had tended to live in the towns they worked in, the railways allowed them to be a little more selective: 'Nice villa in the countryside, sir?' 'That'll do nicely.' Despite this trend, the Great Western never pursued the commuter market as much as other railways. This was partially because by the 1900s, the competition with tram systems and omnibuses in towns and cities was intense, but also because it recognised that going full bore for this traffic would have required a lot of locomotives and coaches that might only be used for a few hours a day. Carrying huge volumes of commuters at peak times almost inevitably means carrying a lot of fresh air for the rest of the day, and that conundrum continues to the present day.

For much of the nineteenth century, large swathes of the South-West were rural backwaters; picturesque towns and villages on the coast were undeveloped and reliant on agriculture and fishing, except for the major ports like Plymouth, Falmouth and Weymouth. The GWR may not have been all that keen on carrying commuters but the railways gave people the means to travel, and those who could afford to, took full advantage of the opportunity, seeing many parts of the country for the first time. Many people in Britain had never seen the sea in 1810: a century later, many, if not most had – and when the weather got warmer, the Great Western had no equal in persuading the Great British Public that what they really needed was a trip to the seaside.

The development of seaside resorts from Weston-super-Mare to Minehead (where Billy Butlin established a holiday camp in the 1960s served by its own halt); Newquay and St Ives on the north coasts of Devon and Cornwall; and also of the likes of Dawlish, Torquay, Paignton, Looe, Falmouth and Penzance on the South coast, was largely driven by the GWR's alluring and insistent marketing. Some of the growth of these towns was astounding. Torquay was just a hamlet of 800 or so in the early 1800s, yet by 1901 it had grown to a bustling town of 35,000, the bulk of the growth occurring since the railway from Newton Abbot opened in 1848. This was only the resident population: on a busy summer Saturday, places like Torquay could easily receive an extra 20,000 tourists arriving by rail. To put this in context, Exeter Airport, the busiest in Devon and Cornwall, carried an average of just 3,696 passengers per day in August 2008, which at the time was claimed as its busiest ever month. And this was just Torquay – the numbers travelling by rail to tourist hotspots all over the South-West were vast and growing in the early years of the nineteenth century. Weston-super-Mare was another case in point – a village until the Bristol and Exeter Railway opened in 1841 – the railway spurred its development in similar fashion to Torquay. Better still, the town's proximity to Bristol gave the GWR a chance to run trains through Bristol and terminate them at Weston, relieving capacity in Bristol and providing Weston-super-Mare with a lavish passenger service that it otherwise would never have had.

While all of the rail-connected seaside towns grew with the advent of tourism, the growth of Torquay wasn't mirrored everywhere. Ilfracombe had a population of 1,801 in 1838 – more than Torquay at the turn of the century – but by 1901 it had only risen to 8,557. Despite being served by rail from 1865, Ilfracombe's railway was a lengthy connection to the LSWR at Barnstaple and the branch line from there to Exeter, making Ilfracombe's line more of a twig than a branch. Journey times were long and unsurprisingly, private car ownership saw passenger numbers collapse in the 1960s. Ilfracombe escaped the Beeching cuts but lost its passenger services in 1970.

As the first trickle of tourists travelling by rail became a torrent and then a flood (helped in no small measure by *Holiday Haunts*), hotels and other accommodation sprang up along with the amusements and facilities the tourists wanted. The tourist trade had a symbiotic relationship with the railways: the trains brought the tourists to the resorts, and in return the resorts developed their attractions to entice them. The hotels and piers, the beach huts and ice-cream stalls; the promenades and the donkeys . . . without the railways sending so many millions of people to seaside towns, the concept of a British seaside holiday might be very different.

A whole host of practices were started by the railway – the tradition of Saturdays becoming changeover days where one group of tourists departs and another arrives was started by them, as was that of a short concentrated tourist season in the summer. Initially it was simply because employers refused to let their staff take leave on weekdays, but it continued when paid holidays became the norm, becoming ingrained in the British culture. When you get stuck on roads heading to the South-West on a Saturday, it is as much as anything because that was how it always was rather than there being any particular need for it to be so today. Only the start of widespread automobile ownership from the 1960s began to change this and in the process, stretch the tourist season from April to late September.

These were all ongoing processes but having rid itself of its reputation for slow running, the inconvenience of the broad gauge and the 'Great Way Round' tag, the Great Western Railway was exploiting the growing affluence of Edwardian England to the full. It was establishing the basis of perhaps its territory's most important industry – the tourist trade – and even the First World War couldn't prevent people from taking seaside holidays.

Chapter 15
The Great War

On 5 August 1914, just a day after Britain declared war on Germany, the government took control of every railway in the country. Powers to do this had been granted under the Regulation of the Forces Act of 1871, in order for the government to deal with a national emergency.

The terms of the takeover were that the companies would be compensated based on the same amount as net receipts for 1913, the last full year before war, then divided proportionately amongst the railways. This not only gave the government control of the railways – it meant it could charter as many trains as it needed without paying extra for them and, of course, it could give priority to them over ordinary service trains.

For the Great Western the impact was immediate. In the first two weeks after war was declared, 632 troop trains were run over the company's metals, along with 41 coal trains for the Admiralty and 149 of petrol and oil. This demanding extra workload increased immediately and by the first week of September 1914, 376,787 officers and men had been transported, along with 33,101 horses, and 355 guns and limbers – in addition to all of the other stores the army and navy needed.

And it wasn't just extra traffic that stretched the Great Western: 4,500 of its own men had volunteered for active service by the end of August alone and many more were planning to do so. This drain on the railway's manpower was slowed by designating key railway jobs such as drivers and firemen as Reserved Occupations, which meant they were not liable for active service. Throughout the war, however, a steady stream of volunteers went to the services totalling 25,479 in 1918 – a third of the GWR workforce at the declaration of hostilities. One

move, which with hindsight strikes us as amusing, was the renaming of
'Star' No. 4017 *Knight of the Black Eagle* after somebody remembered
that this referred to a Prussian order of knights. It was hastily renamed
Knight of Liege in order to show some support for Belgium. It wasn't
much and it certainly wouldn't have bothered the Germans but in a very
small way, acts like this did their bit for morale, or at the very least
ensured that the Great Western wasn't seen to support the Germans in
any way.

With the focus of the war effort on the Western Front, it was always
likely the South Coast ports would be busier than ever. The Great
Western's north–south routes via Basingstoke were all jam-packed
with men and equipment, as were the Midland & South Western
Junction and Didcot, Newbury & Southampton railways (which the
Great Western had operating powers over), and all lines to Weymouth,
Plymouth and the Cornish ports.

It was the Navy, however, which demanded much of the Great
Western's war effort. A strategic decision had been taken to base the
Grand Fleet of battleships at Scapa Flow in the Orkneys to prevent a
breakout of the North Sea by Germany's High Seas Fleet but Scapa was
a long way from anywhere and at the time the vast majority of the
Navy's Dreadnoughts were fired by coal – Welsh steam coal to be exact.

Immediately after war was declared, the Navy dispersed its fleet to
Scapa and set in motion plans to switch some of the supply of coal from
collier ships (which would be vulnerable to attack by submarines) to
rail. In preparation for war, the Navy had hired 4,000 coal wagons to
help keep the Grand Fleet supplied and in the course of the war would
lease many thousands more. The plan was for the Great Western to
haul lengthy 600-ton coal trains which became known as 'Jellicoe
specials' from Pontypool Road to Warrington via the 'North and West'
route through Hereford and Shrewsbury. From Warrington, the
LNWR would take the trains to Carlisle and then the North British and
Caledonian railways carried the cargo to Grangemouth, which was the
closest port to Scapa Flow capable of loading huge quantities of coal.
The trains had to run around 375 miles (some trains were diverted on

other routes as the rail network's capacity was soaked up) and such was the urgency of these trains that it took just 48 hours to deliver the coal, an average speed of 7.8mph. That sounds like a very low speed but when you bear in mind the trains were formed of a locomotive, forty un-braked wagons and a brake van, and would be doing well if they got up to much more than 30mph at best, it was actually quite an achievement. (The trains invariably spent most of their time running far slower than their top speed as the trains could only be accelerated and braked gently to avoid breaking couplings or the weight of the train causing a runaway; there were at least two locomotive changes en route.)

The increase in military traffic had been predicted and was managed very well but what surprises us now is that ordinary passenger traffic continued largely as normal. In part, this was down to the government not wishing to cause public unrest by restricting travel, but much more was simply about people trying to live their lives as normally as possible despite events over the Channel. In 1916 the *Great Western Magazine* reported that the 'Cornish Riviera' left Paddington in three separate trains on 9 July 1916 (and on at least eight other occasions too), and on that day carried 2,027 passengers and their luggage. So great was the demand that other staff had to help move the luggage, which seems to have increased in volume dramatically in the war years.

Predictably, the war's start caused a degree of dislocation and chaos. The Great Western was alarmed by the numbers of its men volunteering to fight and ruled that they could only do so with permission. Anyone who broke this order saw their families penalised by not receiving any wages owed, but this only stemmed the flow rather than staunching it completely.

Concerns about German infiltration and sabotage of the rail network were rife. The Royal Albert Bridge and key tunnels including the Severn Tunnel were guarded by armed sentries who had orders to challenge anyone seen walking on the railway and if necessary shoot them. It made life risky for the track gangers who still had to walk their patch of track every day to check for defects and it was soon decided that where the railway was guarded, anyone who needed to be on the line should advise the military and wait for an armed escort. Even this didn't work: when the weather closed in or at night the sounds of footsteps approaching was bound to make the soldiers nervous and trigger-happy. After fourteen were hit by trains and another two shot their reliefs, the plan to post sentries was abandoned. It soon became clear that they were far more of a danger to their own side than the enemy.

The manpower drain affected every part of the Great Western and although initially replacement men were sought, it wasn't long before orders were sent out to recruit women where possible – it was felt they weren't as essential to the war effort and, in those discriminatory days, were cheaper to employ too. Needless to say, when the war ended the women were laid off, despite having proved themselves every bit the equal of the men they replaced.

As the war progressed and it became clear that it would last a long time, the demands on the railways increased. The introduction of a 'common user' policy for wagons in 1916, whereby all the open wagons across the country were placed in a single pool to be sent wherever they were needed helped ease the difficulties in running the freight trains but as the war effort expanded so too did railway traffic.

Take the supply of ammunition: there were 277 ammunition factories on the Great Western network alone and almost all needed their produce transporting by rail. The shell factory at Hayes produced enough shells to fill 3,800 wagons a month, while nitro-glycerine produced at a giant factory near Pembrey, Wales, had to be conveyed with extreme caution in sealed steam-heated vans to other plants in Kent and Surrey. This factory employed around 5,000 and all of these men and women had to be taken to and from their workplace by rail too.

The development of Swindon Works into a modern engineering facility had come just in time and, on the outbreak of war, coaches under construction were requisitioned by the government and converted into ambulance trains, with new vehicles being built specifically for this purpose. Another military order was for the conversion of a number of open wagons to make them suitable to transport horses. Of course, the wagons could be replaced but when 221 heavy draught horses were bought from the railway in 1914 *their* replacements were some of the few things Swindon Works couldn't manufacture!

All of the great railway factories soon found their comprehensive engineering and manufacturing capabilities put to use in military production and Swindon was quickly tasked with producing fabricated parts for howitzers and artillery guns. In order to gear up for a huge swathe of military production the government paid for the Great Western to buy new machine tools. Very quickly, the workshop which made the switches and crossings that allowed trains to cross from one line to another (appropriately named 'X' shop) was turned over to artillery-shell production and this was just one of the myriad tasks given to Swindon on top of its primary purpose of producing much of the equipment the Great Western needed to keep running safely.

With the railway system being pushed to its limits, in 1916 the weather then added to the difficulties and a two-day snowstorm that started on 27 March added to the chaos. The Newport to Gloucester, Newport to Hereford and Worcester, Gloucester to Birmingham, and Birmingham, Bicester and Oxford as far as Wellington (Salop) routes were almost completely closed by snow. Telegraph poles were blown down, destroying the signalling system and so the railway ground to a standstill. The time interval system was hurriedly reinstated in order to get trains moving again, at no faster than 15mph to give the enginemen a fighting chance of stopping before a collision and the Great Western sent every spare telegraph engineer to help repair the damage. The General Post Office and Royal Engineers were drafted in too but it took until 7 April for normality to resume. It was a system nearing breaking point.

The huge traffic volumes placed great pressure on the enginemen and signalmen in particular, with long shifts the norm. One driver from Reading, Dick Davey, worked to Plymouth on a journey that took twenty-four hours, then a day later worked back as far as Westbury where he finished exhausted. Another was away from home for nine days at a time working ambulance and war trains one after another. With such unpredictable duties sourcing food became a problem, and some crews even had to beg for sustenance from the soldiers in their trains. By and large the railwaymen were aware of the importance of what they were doing and strove to fulfil their duties but the strain took its toll, not helped by the fact that fit young men in civilian clothes were liable to be handed a white feather by women who believed they were cowards. The government refused even to give them armbands to denote that the railwaymen were doing their duty on the grounds that their work was *not* essential to the war effort.

In Britain, restrictions were finally placed on passenger travel from 1917, with many express trains cancelled, stops omitted, and the provision of restaurant, slip coaches and sleeping cars reduced. Some small stations were closed to release staff and some branch lines were even lifted to release track for use elsewhere.

The efforts of Great Western railwaymen even spread to France, where they were needed to operate trains for the British Expeditionary Force's Railway Operating Division (ROD). Here in France were sixty-two 'Dean Goods' and from 1917, eleven '43xxs' hauling trains of ammunition, men and supplies to the front, and wounded soldiers back. The agreement was that the ROD would take over much of the rail network behind the British front lines and it encompassed the full scope of railway operations, including dock shunting at Dieppe and Dunkirk: the variety of work was immense, and dangerous too, as the routes neared the front line coming within range of German artillery.

The Great Western's contribution to the war effort was vast. By the end of 1918, it had carried 33,615 extra troop trains, 13,676 coal trains for the Admiralty and 41,312 supply trains. It had also sent 95 locomotives, 105 tenders, 6,086 wagons, 15,000 tons of rails, 50,000 sleepers and 49 miles of complete railway abroad. There was inevitably a human price paid too: 2,524 Great Western Railway staff lost their lives in the Great War.

On a brighter note, in recognition of their services to munitions production, Churchward was awarded the CBE and his Works Manager, Charles Collett, an OBE in the Birthday Honours of 1918. Both deserved their awards.

*

The Great War had left Britain exhausted and indebted, and the railways had stretched themselves to the limit in dealing with the vast extra traffic the war generated. Equipment was worn, though by and large the Great Western had just about kept on top of maintenance requirements. More damagingly, however, its staff were worn out and increasingly dissatisfied with their lot.

The seeds of discontent began in the early years of the twentieth century as the cost of living started to rise while pay packets remained static. It created a tinderbox of unrest but for a while the railways were able to keep a lid on it, refusing to recognise trade unions and attempting to deal with grievances through 'conciliation committees'. In 1907, things began to simmer when short-time working was introduced at Swindon Works, in part thanks to the economies that had been generated by Churchward's new locomotives, whose inter-changeable parts meant the previously gigantic inventory could be scaled down.

The timing of the announcement came just before the annual 'trip' holiday, an annual event where Works employees were given free passes to a range of destinations on the company's network and much of the Works closed for a week. The holiday was unpaid but was a holiday nonetheless and was anticipated keenly almost from the moment people returned to Swindon from the previous year's trip. With the announcement of lay-offs and short-time working appearing just before the 1908 trip, petitions were signed, meetings held and the embryonic railway unions started to exert some influence. Needless to say, Churchward wasn't impressed: 'If you and those you represent are not satisfied with conditions in my department I shall be pleased to receive your notices,' he told one union representative.

Partial stoppages began across the country from then on, culminating in the 1911 railway strike that lasted several days and caused widespread disruption but it was only after the Great War that labour was sufficiently organised to bring the network to a complete standstill. The GWR marked the service records of the strikers with a 'D' for 'Disloyal' though it reluctantly let most return to work. Despite negotiations for an eight-hour day and a 5-shilling rise still dragging on into 1914, on the outbreak of war union negotiations were suspended and the men threw themselves into the war effort, even those the Great Western branded 'disloyal'.

Rapid inflation during the war had further eroded wages by 1918 to a point where the cost of living was 120 per cent higher than in 1913, and to many railwaymen, the privilege of working for the Great Western wasn't enough. In *Life in a Railway Factory,* Alfred Williams wrote of the horrendous conditions in Swindon Works in the early years of the century and little had improved. For many railway staff, being asked to do a difficult and sometimes dangerous job on a shrinking pay packet was too much to take.

In 1919, the railway unions forced through a series of demands which included eight-hour days and pay increases. The pay increases more than doubled the wage bill from £6 million to £14 million yet the rates for goods traffic were still at 1913 levels, and only a 50 per cent increase in passenger fares imposed in January 1917 had increased that source of revenue. The unions pressed for further improvements – a national pay scale and compensatory payments for the loss of war bonuses – and when the railways refused to meet them, railwaymen across the country downed tools at midnight on 26–7 September 1919.

The strike was extremely popular: 94 per cent of the Goods & Traffic Department men and 65 per cent of footplatemen all went on strike. Faced with such crippling increases in the cost of living, they felt they had little choice.

The new General Manager, Charles Aldington, who succeeded Frank Potter after his death in 1919, was contacted by the Prime Minister, David Lloyd George, who believed that the unions' demands had been met: 'No measures have been omitted which might have prevented the strike and I am convinced there is something more behind it than mere wages and conditions. Please instruct your Chief Officers to do everything in their power to carry on and break the strike.'

With revolution in Russia and the growing strength of the labour movement, Lloyd George was terrified that a strike could turn more serious. Volunteers were sought to keep some semblance of a service running, with many of the Great Western's salaried staff proving eager to have a go at operating the railway.

The strike affected everything – even some of the company's animals went unfed – while at Fishguard, the annual influx of Irish cattle had to be found grazing as there were no trains to take them onwards. Worse still were the attempts at sabotage. Between Wootton Basset and Swindon, one of the few trains running ploughed into a pile of sleepers placed across the track in a bid to derail it, though fortunately no damage was done.

Lloyd George intervened with an offer on the day of the strike that promised no adult railwayman would be paid less than 51 shillings per week unless the cost of living fell below 110 per cent of pre-war levels and that wages would remain at these levels until 30 September 1920. Standard wage rates were laid down which applied to all railways across the country. Suspicious of an apparently hostile government which had been waging an expensive and high-profile publicity war against them, the unions resisted until 5 October when services finally returned to normal.

The railway unions had got their members a good deal for the time being but the railway would pay a heavy price for this and other industrial actions. Army surplus lorries were plentiful and cheap, and where companies had been forced to find alternatives to rail they began to look seriously for the first time at the benefits offered by road transport. In those eight days in 1919 it was the roads that kept Britain moving rather than the rails.

Chapter 16
New Dawn?

The Great Western had seen a number of changes to its management following James Inglis' death in 1911. His successor, Frank Potter, had died in 1919, and his replacement Charles Aldington lasted little longer, resigning due to ill health in June 1921. His successor was a forty-four-year-old man called Felix Pole.

Born in Little Bedwyn, Wiltshire on 1 February 1877, Pole joined the Great Western at the age of fourteen as a telegraph lad clerk in Swindon. He was evidently a talented young man as he was promoted to the Telegraph Superintendent's office in Paddington, before being moved on to the Chief Engineer's office and finally to the then General Manager, James Inglis's department in 1904.

Pole flourished under Inglis, being heavily involved in developing the Great Western's sustained and remarkable publicity campaigns. This suited him as he had never made any pretence of being a technical guru: Pole's strength was as a communicator, both verbally and in print.

After reviving the *Great Western Magazine* and turning it into a genuinely insightful read for staff and the few enthusiasts of the time, he was also made head of the Staff and Labour department in 1912, where he played a key role on the 'conciliation boards' that tried to resolve disputes amicably. There were few men better suited for such a delicate and challenging role.

In 1919 Pole became Assistant General Manager before his now almost inevitable rise to the top non-boardroom role on the Great Western Railway as General Manager. He was paid £6,000 a year – a high wage that he would fully justify in the years ahead.

Locomotive development had naturally been curtailed by the war, although Churchward continued to experiment with minor improvements to his existing locomotives. In 1919 though, Churchward produced his final design and it presented some intriguing possibilities. No. 4700 was a 2-8-0 locomotive designed for freight use but rather than the 4ft 7 ½in driving wheels of the '28xxs', it had 5ft 6in driving wheels the same size as the all-purpose '43xx' 2-6-0s. A large new boiler was being designed for it but this wasn't ready in time so was instead fitted with the Standard No. 1 boiler used on the Great Western's biggest locomotives at the time in order to prove the concept. When the new boiler was designed it showed that Churchward and his design team had learned lessons from *The Great Bear* as it had a much larger heating surface than the No. 1 boilers and was capable of generating more steam.

No. 4700 and its eight sisters which were built by October 1923, were the largest production locomotives on the Great Western and they were immediately used on fast, heavy freight services. They were equally suitable on all but the fastest passenger duties though they were rarely given the chance to prove it. Churchward's intention was to fit this large new boiler to his 'Stars', 'Saints' and '28xxs' in order to increase their power further at relatively little cost but he was overruled by the Civil Engineer who continued to maintain they were too heavy for a large number of bridges on the Great Western's principal routes. It was Churchward's last act as Chief Mechanical Engineer (a title which came into being in 1916). James Inglis had tried and failed to bring the department under his remit (Churchward reported to the board of directors rather than the General Manager) but Felix Pole, having long seen the weaknesses of this structure, was determined to push through reform, possibly even before Churchward's retirement date of 3 March 1922.

Churchward was the product of a different era and found the increased assertiveness of his workforce difficult to deal with. The final straw came during a confrontation with a union representative; asked what he thought of the representative's position, Churchward sat back and replied: 'I think it is time the old man retired.' He did so at the end of 1921 before Pole could remove his power base.

The new Chief Mechanical Engineer was Charles Benjamin Collett OBE, the former Works Manager and, since 9 May 1919, Deputy CME. His appointment to the top locomotive job was controversial and remains so to this day because Collett didn't have a pure locomotive background – his was in civil engineering. More importantly, in W.H. Stanier's son William, the Great Western had a locomotive designer of brilliance who would surely have been a better choice for the job. Be that as it may, Collett was a year older than Stanier and because the Great Western still promoted largely on the basis of seniority, it was Collett who got the top job.

However, just because Collett wasn't an engineering innovator in Churchward's mould that didn't mean he was ineffective. In 1921 the Churchward standard locomotives had proved themselves beyond doubt and by and large were equal to the demands likely to be placed on them. Although their numbers had multiplied over the years, there were still a lot of non-standard Victorian locomotives running on the GWR, and it would be some time before the standardisation programme could be completed. The need wasn't, therefore, for the new CME to introduce further innovation, it was to continue Churchward's plans and ensure that the economic and operational benefits of standardisation could be reaped to the full.

Collett's strength was as what we would now term a production engineer – somebody who would fine-tune and optimise production and maintenance to the full, and in this he would prove quite remarkably able. In any case, Churchward's excellent design team was still largely in place so when new locomotives, carriages and wagons were needed, Collett had the backup to make it happen.

*

Whatever hardships the railways had faced in 1914–18, there is no doubt they worked effectively under government control. Having now seen the benefits of a coordinated national system there was a growing body of thought which believed the railways should remain under state control and if possible be brought into public hands. Amongst the more surprising supporters of this idea was Winston Churchill.

A vigorous debate took place with good arguments being made for nationalisation, retaining the pre-War status quo, or something in between. The government finally revealed its hand in 1920 and it was a classic compromise – merging railway companies geographically into seven companies, with London and Scotland both having their own networks. As the plans for this 'grouping' developed, it was finally decided to merge all but a handful of Britain's public railways into four companies. Almost all of the great pre-war railway names would disappear: The Midland, London & North Western, Lancashire & Yorkshire and North Staffordshire railways would form part of a giant called the London Midland & Scottish Railway (LMS); the Great Central, Great Eastern, Great Northern, North Eastern and North British railways would become the London & North Eastern Railway (LNER) with the western half of the Scottish network largely going to the LMS and the eastern to the LNER. The South Eastern, London Brighton & South Coast and London & South Western railways would become the Southern Railway (SR). All of the biggest names in Britain's railways would disappear except for the Great Western. Thanks to its dominance over a huge wedge of territory in England ranging from Birkenhead through Birmingham to London, and across to Bristol, South Devon and Cornwall, plus the South Wales main line, the Great Western alone was allowed to retain its identity.

Even so, the Great Western was still merged with other companies and it is a fallacy to suggest the grouping had little effect on it. The key companies that joined the Great Western were a number of proudly independent Welsh railways. The Alexandra (Newport & South Wales) Docks & Railway, and the Barry, Cambrian, Cardiff, Rhymney and Taff Vales all became part of the new, expanded Great Western and added 560 route miles to the network.

With the exception of the Cambrian Railway, which ran from the English borders through mid-Wales, the Welsh lines were mainly built to serve the collieries of South Wales, and they were highly profitable.

Welsh coal was valued highly by railways around the world and also by shipping companies because it burned hot and well, and formed little clinker — a hard substance formed when impurities and trace elements in the coal melt and fuse with the ash into a thick toffee-like substance which starves the fire of oxygen and, if not dealt with quickly, sets like concrete. On the face of it, bringing the South Wales railways into the Great Western was a good move as it provided even greater access to the black gold of the Valleys.

As well as the addition of the Welsh railways there were some English lines too: the Midland & South Western Junction linked Cheltenham with Andover via Cirencester, with lesser-known stations at Swindon and Marlborough. Another was the Cleobury Mortimer & Ditton Priors Railway in Shropshire — a wonderfully idiosyncratic railway which has since passed into legend. It was hopelessly unprofitable but wonderful nonetheless.

Other lines were nominally independent but in practice already worked by the Great Western, such as the Didcot, Newbury & Southampton, which ran for 42 ¾ miles and provided what would later become a key strategic link but for now was a beautiful, bucolic byway which served some of the prettiest countryside in England. It had hitherto been leased to the GWR but would now be owned outright. A similar case was the Liskeard & Looe railway, which runs switchback from a platform at right-angles to the Penzance–Plymouth line, and reverses twice to reach the pretty Cornish seaside resort.

And there were three marvellous little narrow gauge railways in Wales which came into Great Western hands: the Corris Railway from Machynlleth to Aberllefenni via Corris; the Vale of Rheidol railway from Aberystwyth to Devil's Bridge; and the Welshpool & Llanfair Light Railway, which provided a connection from the main line at Welshpool. Although the Vale of Rheidol was a popular tourist railway, the other two existed primarily for freight. All three are fascinating railways which still each operate at least part of their routes today, but the Great Western's focus would always be on its standard gauge routes.

The first of these railways came into the Great Western in 1921, and by 1923 the process was largely complete. While the other big companies immediately had to attempt to reorganise and restructure, the Great Western was able to bring the new arrivals into the fold smoothly and without erasing old traditions. The stage was set for the Great Western to sparkle.

Having negotiated the rapids of the Grouping, the Great Western was the first of the railways able to recover fully from the First World War and introduce service improvements. The first move was to speed up the 14:30 from Cheltenham to Paddington over the 77.3 miles from Swindon to London to a journey time of 75 minutes, an average speed of 61.8mph, giving the GWR instant superiority over the other railways' best average speeds; and on 9 July 1923, the first day of the new timetable, No. 2915 *Saint Bartholomew* even beat that, covering Swindon to Paddington in 72mins 3secs, an average speed of more than 64mph.

The Fishguard to Rosslare sailings were resumed in September 1923 after a hiatus caused by near civil war in Ireland. The Great Western's chairman, Viscount Churchill, (Winston's father) was able to persuade the government that its plans to build new routes on Great Western territory to relieve unemployment would prove hopelessly unremunerative and got them dropped. Plans for expanded facilities at key freight locations as well as rebuilding of stations at Newton Abbot, Bristol Temple Meads and a new line from Wolverhampton to Kingswinford all got the go ahead, however.

Best of all these improvements was the appearance in 1923 of Collett's first new locomotive, *Caerphilly Castle*, and a return to the pre-war gloss and glamour for the passenger coaches from their drab wartime colours; they were again painted in that gorgeous chocolate-and-cream scheme which complemented the beautiful scenery of the Great Western so well. Collett's new design would result in one of the finest steam locomotives ever to take to the rails, and its success was all the more remarkable because from the start he was forced to compromise between what he wanted and what he was allowed to do.

Originally Collett simply intended to follow Churchward's plan of installing a '47xx' type boiler on a slightly modified 'Star' chassis but like his predecessor was blocked by the civil engineer who ruled that such a locomotive would be too heavy. So Collett took the 'Star' as the basis for the new locomotive as it retained some scope for development and would need little all-new design undertaking. By adding 1ft in length to the rear of the chassis, a longer firebox could be included, as well as a more protective cab for the crews (Churchward's locomotives were always appalling in this respect). With a bigger boiler in mind than the Standard No.1, it was decided to make the cylinders wider than the 'Stars', and by paying close attention to clearances and tyre thickness, it was just about possible to make the cylinders 16 inches in diameter rather than the 'Star's' 15 inches. Otherwise, the chassis was largely identical, with many of the alterations made on the original drawings for the 'Stars'. One thing Collett and his team didn't do was to change the size of the piston valves to match the new cylinders. A small change in the valve settings was felt to be enough to compensate.

The boiler was an all-new design with a firebox 1ft longer than the 'Stars' at 10ft, and this helped increase the grate area by 12 per cent. The boiler barrel was 3 inches wider than the Standard No. 1, but generally very similar to the Churchward boilers. On the exterior of the locomotive, steam was fed to the outside cylinders by pipes emerging from the side of the smoke box; this freed more space between the frames and also removed some clutter from the inside of the smoke box which had hitherto partially covered some of the smoke tubes. Finally the copper band around the chimney and brass safety bonnet were allowed to shine after the drabness of the war years when chimneys were made from plain cast iron; the brass beading around the splashers above the driving wheels was reinstated, and the plain green colour scheme of the war years was replaced by a glossy lined-out livery. Collett had designed a locomotive which was potentially 14 per cent more powerful than a 'Star' but only 6 per cent heavier, with much of this weight placed over the driving wheels to give the engine better grip. The question was – could this unquestioned compromise of a locomotive perform as well as predicted?

No. 4073 *Caerphilly Castle* was built at Swindon Works in August 1923, just in time for the Great Western to enter something of a steam locomotive arms race which was taking place at the time. From 1906 to 1921, the 'Stars' were undoubtedly the most powerful express passenger locomotives in Britain but in 1921, George Hughes of the Lancashire & Yorkshire Railway had introduced his design of the four-cylinder 4-6-0 which was in theory at least more powerful. Then, in 1922 Nigel Gresley of the Great Northern and Vincent Raven of the North Eastern had surpassed the 'Stars' with their 'Pacific' designs. *Caerphilly Castle* (for which all of its sisters were designated 'Castles' even if they weren't named after one) reasserted the Great Western's superiority, because its tractive effort of 31,625 pounds was higher than anything else in Britain.

Unsurprisingly, Felix Pole and the Great Western's Publicity Department trumpeted *Caerphilly Castle* to the full, describing it as a 'super locomotive' and claiming that it was the most powerful in Britain. A book about the locomotive sold 10,000 copies right away and soon after, another 30,000 were sold. There may not have been many trainspotters about then but there were certainly a lot of people interested in and enthusiastic about the railways.

All of these arguments about power were something of a red herring, however. All the term 'tractive effort' refers to is a locomotive's pulling ability to get a train moving, but it doesn't necessarily correlate to a locomotive's ability to sustain effort or to reach high speeds; it was all theoretical anyway, based on a locomotive's dimensions and potential capabilities rather than anything proved in service. The most powerful locomotives in Britain would be the ones able to haul the heaviest loads at the highest speed for longest, and tractive effort figures cannot provide a complete picture of this ability.

That did not stop the Great Western from crowing about its newest additions though, and nine more 'Castles' were built between December 1923 and April 1924. The last, No. 4082 *Windsor Castle* was even driven by King George V when he and Queen Mary visited

Swindon Works in 1924. Not surprisingly, *Windsor Castle* became the Great Western's preferred locomotive for Royal Trains. Brass plates fitted to the cabs to commemorate the short royal enginemanship said:

No. 4082 'Windsor Castle' was built at Swindon in April 1924 and driven from the works to the station by His Majesty King George V accompanied by Queen Mary on the occasion of the visit by Their Majesties to the Great Western Railway Works at Swindon on 28 April 1924. With Their Majesties on the footplate were Viscount Churchill, Chairman; Sir Felix Pole, General Manager; Locomotive Inspector G.H. Flewellyn; Engine Driver E.R.B. Rowe; Fireman A.W. Cooke.

Having been on the footplate of a 'Castle', with seven people there it would have been extremely cosy. The presence of Flewellyn on the footplate is intriguing too: presumably the same man who had encouraged *City of Truro* to 100mph had become extremely highly regarded by the Great Western hierarchy.

The Great Western then undertook detailed tests with No. 4074 *Caldicot Castle* to find out just how capable the new locomotives were. A series of runs were made in both directions between Swindon and Taunton, Taunton and Newton Abbot, and Newton Abbot and Plymouth with the maximum permitted load attached behind, including a dynamometer car which could measure the amount of power the locomotive was generating. *Caldicot Castle* did everything asked of it and more, because when the coal consumption was studied, it was found to be 2.83lbs per drawbar horsepower hour, the standard measurement of steam locomotive efficiency.

Locomotive designers across Britain and beyond were stunned, and some even believed the results of the tests were inaccurate. The best efficiency the Great Western had recorded before this was 3½ lbs per drawbar horsepower hour but few if any non-Great Western locomotives could even approach this, the best of the rest averaging somewhere between 4½ and 6lb per drawbar horsepower hour. There was only one conclusion to be drawn from the Great Western's experiments: the 'Castles' were far more efficient than any other steam locomotives in Britain.

Collett's compromise design had somehow been one of those occasions where the designers get it absolutely right: to reverse the famous aphorism about camels, the 'Castles' were thoroughbreds designed by committee. They were beautiful too, with a delicateness of feature and cleanliness of design that gave the impression of a solid reliable machine that was built to go fast. It is a very highly subjective opinion, but to my eyes at least, the 'Castles' are the most beautiful steam locomotives ever to run.

*

The marvellous performance of *Caldicot Castle* under test was matched by the Great Western's own commercial performance – in the Annual General Meeting of 27 February 1924, the Chairman, Viscount Churchill, announced a dividend of 8 per cent on ordinary shares. To add to the good news, Felix Pole had been knighted, and Churchill paid tribute to him:

> I can assure it is an honour of which we all of the Great Western are justly proud, as we knew that the recipient of it has, by sheer hard work, perseverance and outstanding ability, thoroughly earned it, and we wish him many years of health and happiness to enjoy it. We also hope that his working life may always be associated with the Great Western Railway.

Churchill wasn't alone and many Great Western shareholders were equally enthusiastic about Pole's stewardship of the company. They were right to be because although passenger and freight fares had been reduced in 1923, the railway carried 12,600,000 more passengers and 7,800, 000 tons more freight – a remarkable performance given that the national economy was still somewhat in the doldrums. Much of this increased freight was undoubtedly down to the grouping, but the passenger figures were surely attributable to Pole's efforts to make services more attractive.

Expertise from some of the Welsh railways was also being brought to bear: The Barry Railway's Locomotive Superintendent, John Auld, was made Docks and Personal Assistant to the Chief Mechanical Engineer, third in command at Swindon after Collett and William Stanier: it was a good move that proved the Great Western wouldn't simply run riot over the Welsh companies.

It was Pole who was at the fore during the early 1920s. He exhaustively evaluated the passenger services that Great Western was running and actually cut some services from 5 May 1924. Some thought this heralded a wave of economy measures, but Pole was simply ensuring that the services the Great Western did run were not wildly unprofitable, though many trains which undoubtedly ran at a loss were retained in order to provide a service people could depend on. He also looked at rolling stock utilisation in order to avoid, as far as possible, trains carrying little more than fresh air and, worse still, spending most of their time in sidings not earning any money. Some services were combined as far as possible – it makes more sense to run one long train from, say, London to Taunton if the loadings don't justify two separate trains, and then coaches can then be split off the combined train for further alternate destinations.

Some of the tweaks involved retiming trains slightly, by perhaps 15 minutes or so, in order to provide better connections but also to allow the rolling stock to make two journeys rather than one. A comprehensive re-cast of the timetable was launched in July 1924. Pole's guiding principle was that passengers upset by changes in timings would generally be balanced by those for whom it improved things and that if a change could save the use of a set of coaches it was worth doing regardless.

This new timetable regularised many departure times, so trains left Paddington for Birmingham at ten minutes past the hour, to Bristol at quarter past, the West Country at half past, the West Midlands at quarter to, and South Wales at five minutes to. It didn't mean that passengers could throw away the timetable but it did eliminate many of the peculiarities which had remained for years.

Thoroughly resurgent, Sir Felix, it seems, then engaged the Great Western in a remarkable publicity war with the LNER about whose locomotives were more powerful. At the Empire Exhibition in Wembley in 1924, *Caerphilly Castle* stood next to the LNER's soon to be famous 'A1' No. 1472 *Flying Scotsman*, which had been specially named for the show. Although the LNER's locomotive was much bigger than the 'Castle', it didn't stop the Great Western from boldly proclaiming it as the most powerful passenger locomotive in Britain.

Then Pole, having tweaked the LNER's tail, went further still and suggested comparative tests should be made on the principal routes of both companies to see which design really was best. I wrote about these locomotive exchanges in detail in *Flying Scotsman: The Extraordinary Story of the World's Most Famous Train*, and there is no question that in the end they were far more useful to the LNER than the Great Western. Despite being much smaller than the 'A1s', the locomotive the Great Western sent in competition in April 1925, No. 4079 *Pendennis Castle*, hauled heavy trains on the surprisingly steep line out of London King's Cross at speeds the LNER's larger locomotives couldn't begin to approach. The crowds of onlookers expecting the 'Castle' to struggle were consistently surprised by its sure-footed starts from the LNER's main London terminus, and not only was *Pendennis Castle* faster than the 'A1s' – it was much more efficient too.

On the Great Western routes it was slightly different, because the LNER's locomotive crew was rather more positive than the driver involved in the London trials and showed the 'A1s' could easily keep to time between London and Plymouth and, what's more, show even a 'Castle' a clean pair of heels on the steep Devon Banks from Newton Abbot to Plymouth. All things considered though, the Great Western's 'Castles' were at the time much better locomotives than the 'A1s' and that was largely thanks to Churchward's experiments into valve settings, which allowed the 'Castles' to make better use of the steam generated than the 'A1s'. Only when the LNER's big 'Pacifics' eventually had their valves modified to conform with Swindon practice did they really show what they were capable of.

These events all suggested that the Great Western was the most effective of the 'Big Four' railways at the time; however, problems in an industry all the railways depended on would soon savagely affect them and open the door to effective competition from the roads.

Chapter 17
The General Strike

Morale on the Great Western was high in 1925, and extensive efforts had been made to integrate the Welsh railways and modernise the movement of the gigantic amounts of coal from the valleys. Key to this was the Great Western's sales push to encourage companies to send coal in new wagons able to hold 20 tons of cargo. Generally most coal was transported in small wooden-bodied wagons with a maximum load of 10 tons. Using the GWR's new design was more efficient and discounts were offered to customers who agreed to send their coal in them.

There were problems within the mining industry, however. Little investment had been made in years and the miners were agitating for better pay and conditions, as well as long overdue safety improvements. Given that many mines were unprofitable, many mine owners sought pay cuts and longer hours from their workers. Industrial action started to disrupt coal supplies and the Great Western's coal traffic began to fall to the point where redundancies and pay cuts were considered. Negotiations between the Great Western and the railway unions saw both sides recognise the severity of the situation. The dividend paid in 1924 was 7.5 per cent, the bulk of which came from reserves as in 1924 revenue only equated to a 3 per cent dividend. By drawing on reserves, the GWR expected the downturn to be only temporary. The railway unions agreed that should cuts need to be made, temporary staff should go first, and then juniors, with permanent staff given the option of lower paid work if positions were available.

The miners' dispute escalated throughout 1925. The Prime Minister, Stanley Baldwin, extended subsidies to the mines in order to quell the discontent and set up a Royal Commission to look at the organisation of the mining industry. Baldwin thought he had solved it but the mining unions had already promised that when the latest period of subsidy ended they would call their men out.

The railway unions had given a clear signal that they would back their counterparts in the mining industry and as 1925 turned to 1926, the mood was getting uglier by the day. A General Strike was called for early May and the National Union of Railwaymen (NUR) and Associated Society of Locomotive Enginemen & Footplatemen (ASLEF) threw in their support. The results were catastrophic for the railways. The timing of the General Strike meant that the public could generally manage with far less coal than in the winter, so the people whose support the unions would really need were from the start less likely to be bothered.

With the strike timed to start at midnight on 3 May 1926, Sir Felix Pole sent a message to his staff:

The National Union of Railwaymen have intimated that railwaymen have been asked to strike without notice tomorrow night. Each Great Western man has to decide his course of action, but I appeal to all of you to hesitate before you break your contracts of service with the old company, before you inflict grave injury upon the railway industry and before you arouse ill-feeling in the railway service which will take years to remove. Railway companies and railwaymen have demonstrated that they can settle their disputes by direct negotiations. The mining industry should be advised to do the same.

Remember that your means of living and your personal interests are involved, and that Great Western men are trusted to be loyal to their conditions of service in the same manner as they expect the company to carry out their obligations and agreements.

Sir Felix was appealing to reason but sometimes events gain their own momentum beyond the reach of logic. The railway unions went on strike and for a short while it looked as if their secondary action would cause widespread and long disruption. They had, however, reckoned without an army of volunteers who did their best to at least keep some trains running.

Even on the first morning of the strike, some stopping trains ran on the main line, while the Irish Mail left Fishguard at 03:20 and continued all the way to London. It may have been a General Strike but it wasn't the complete shutdown the unions hoped for. Soon, even branch-line trains were running in some places and, from 194 trains running on 4 May, the total increased to 500 by 9 May, and 1,025 by 11 May. As the volunteers from all walks of life gained experience, the services themselves even improved, and on the 11 May, Felix Pole was sufficiently confident to issue a circular congratulating those staff who had remained at work, as well as the volunteers. On that day, the strike was ruled illegal and Pole issued another circular which attacked trade union claims of victimisation, pointing out that it was the GWR who was the victim. The very idea defied all comprehension, he stated, adding that he thought the only explanation was a conspiracy against the state itself. The trade unions capitulated and ordered their men back to work but it wasn't until 14 May that terms were agreed.

Significantly, the unions had to admit they had 'committed a wrongful act against the company'. The terms illustrated the depth of the unions' defeat: staff were to be reinstated, 'as soon as traffic offers and work can be found for them', and they promised neither to strike before negotiations, nor to support unauthorised strikes.

So, the railways started getting back to normal but the miners didn't, and for those in South Wales it was commercial suicide. Organisations and companies that had depended on the high-quality Welsh coal found other sources and overseas markets evaporated. The figures tell their own story. From a high of 52 million tons of coal a year carried in 1913, volumes fell to 50 million tons in 1923, then 46 million in 1924, and 41 million tons in 1925. In 1926, volumes collapsed to 21 million tons. Nationwide the fall was from 194 million tons to 114 million in 1926.

The railwaymen hadn't helped. The coal strike in itself was disruptive but nothing compared with the disruption caused to the train service. Britain depended very largely on its railways for goods movement, whether a box of racing pigeons or a machine tool, so much so that the railways were *obliged* to accept any traffic offered to them for carriage. They were a common carrier and freight rates had to be published by law at every location goods could be loaded. Now was the time for the road haulage industry to assert itself: it wasn't unionised so the drivers couldn't go on strike. Road companies could also deliver goods door-to-door, undercut the published railway rates and, even though roads were poor and lorries slow, they were often still faster than the railways.

It was a perfect storm that had been brewing for years and the railway companies' refusal – including the Great Western – to invest in continuous braking, faster wagons for goods trains and speedier journey times combined with the unions' illegal secondary action all presented a golden opportunity for road hauliers that few refused.

*

Road competition was undoubtedly mounting through the 1920s but the railways were still far and away the nation's most important goods movers and despite the loss of coal traffic during and after the General Strike, business continued to follow the economy's growth.

For a long time, passengers contributed most to GWR's revenue but by 1913, freight receipts were around £7.5 million against £6.95 million from passengers. Every town of significance had a goods yard, as did many villages. Mostly, goods were transported in four-wheel open wagons or vans. General goods were loaded and unloaded in special goods sheds; these had a covered platform from which porters could access the wagons for onwards movement by road, which were usually still horse-drawn carts in those days. While large industries such as coalmines and steelworks could send whole trains of produce much of the traffic was sent in mixed trains, with a variety of wagons carrying all sorts of traffic for their destinations.

Trains often had to be split into portions, with wagons heading to various destinations. This took place in marshalling yards all over the country, with little tank engines moving rakes of wagons back and forth to put them in the correct sidings for their trains, and shunters haring about on foot to couple and uncouple wagons, and apply handbrakes.

When goods trains were on the move, they generally ran very slowly. Sometimes this was simply because they were heavy but more often it was because the wagons' wheel bearings were lubricated with grease and would readily overheat at much over 30mph. Gradients were another consideration. At the top of particularly steep declines, trains were ordered to stop so the traincrew could apply the brakes on wagons to increase the stopping power of the locomotive and brake van at the back: trains could and did run out of control from time to time, with the locomotive being literally pushed along the track by the weight of the train behind. Driving these goods trains was long and arduous work that demanded even more skill on occasion than the fastest expresses. The speeds were slow but the drivers had to know the route intimately and anticipate how the train would behave. It was tricky enough on one gradient but there were places where a train could be on three or four different slopes simultaneously and each would affect the wagons differently. Driving a goods train was an art form.

Collective memory tells us that the railways were highly efficient at moving freight but often they weren't. The need to remarshall trains to release wagons for different destinations, and the slow speeds of many trains, meant it could take days for wagons to reach their destination; predicting arrival times for a consignment could be something of a lottery.

Not all goods trains were slow, though. Milk was carried in churns on vans and later in specially built tank wagons and was for obvious reasons sent to destinations as quickly as possible, often almost at passenger train speeds. Fish was a commodity with similar needs, again because of its perishable nature. Other seasonal crops such as broccoli from Cornwall, plums from Worcestershire and much else besides was sent by rail in vacuum-braked wagons; these could run at much higher speeds than their unbraked counterparts by virtue of their much better stopping power. The seasonal traffic took a lot of planning because weather conditions could dramatically affect the volume and timing of the crops. For Cornish broccoli, for example, there was no point in routinely sending wagons down to the Royal Duchy in say, February, as they would just clog up sidings – an informed view had to be taken about when the crops would be ready and how much capacity would be needed. It was a big and often finely judged effort.

Dealing with this piecemeal traffic was something the railways were obliged to do by virtue of their common carrier status and, in order to avoid soaking up all of their capacity with goods traffic, many goods trains ran at night when all bar a few overnight and sleeping car trains ran. From late evening, the freight railway experienced its own rush hours. Trains left goods yards across the Great Western at regular intervals in pulses, from London to just about everywhere, from the Midlands, Wales, Devon and Cornwall. It was a precision-planned operation and in a bid to attract business many of the goods trains – particularly the fastest vacuum-braked ones – were given names. Some were romantic and evocative such as 'The Moonraker' that ran from Westbury to Wolverhampton; others were more descriptive, like 'The Carpet' from Kidderminster to Paddington. As a mnemonic it helped, though whether the customers really appreciated all the names is unknown.

The heaviest freights were entrusted to Churchward's fine '28xx' 2-8-0s, and the fastest to the enigmatic '47xxs' (which were so rarely seen on trains in daylight enthusiasts later nicknamed them 'night owls'); other freights were hauled by '43xxs', 'Dean Goods' and even 'Saints' on occasion, not to mention the outside-framed 4-4-0s of the Dean and Churchward era.

Millions of people depended on the Great Western to deliver the goods and by and large it did. Unnoticed and unappreciated at the time, to have a rail-based distribution network of the size and scope of that in the 1920s would be a godsend today, but business simply wouldn't – and in the end didn't – stand for the unpredictable delivery times.

*

If the Great Western had hoped its trouncing of the LNER's 'A1s' would decisively end the locomotive arms race of the 1920s, one can only imagine the reaction in Swindon in particular when the Southern Railway announced it was building a four-cylinder 4-6-0 with a tractive effort of 33,510lbs, which was claimed to be more powerful than the 'Castles'.

Evidently the Great Western's pride took a hit with this announcement but as far as Collett or Pole knew, weight restrictions on certain bridges prevented the railway building anything much bigger. Ironically, a bridge-strengthening programme had been taking place since the early years of the twentieth century but the organisational structure of the Great Western combined with lack of communication between the Civil Engineer's, Chief Mechanical Engineer's and General Manager's offices had meant that neither Pole nor Collett was aware of this!

Pole asked the Civil Engineer, J.C. Lloyd, what the maximum axle load was; he replied that it was 22 tons for four-cylinder locomotives. When Pole found out that just four bridges needed to be strengthened between Paddington and Plymouth, he ordered the programme to be completed immediately, and told Collett to design a locomotive which would not just beat the Southern Railway but eclipse it. He set a target of 40,000lbs for the tractive effort.

On the face of it, the performance of the 'Castles' would seem to render this decision something of a publicity exercise but in fact on some schedules in 1926, they were losing time. A relatively small fleet of more powerful locomotives would be a useful addition to the locomotive stud, and would also release 'Castles' for other duties.

It was with this new locomotive that we see the first signs of Collett running out of ideas. He opted to use the same configuration of the 'Stars' and 'Castles' as the basis for the design and pushed it to the very limit of what was possible. Every possible millimetre of the Great Western's loading gauge was used to squeeze bigger cylinders and a larger boiler in. Churchward's carefully established standards had to be deviated from, and in order to meet Pole's target of 40,000lbs, the driving-wheel diameter was reduced from 6ft 8½ in to 6ft 6in, offering some evidence as to how absurd this tractive effort war really was.

The boiler was typical Swindon, with a narrow but 11ft-long firebox and a relatively short barrel pressurised to 250psi as opposed to the Swindon standard of 225psi; it was pretty much at the limit where even a good fireman could reach the front of. If you want to prove the point, take a shovelful of earth and try throwing it 11ft forward. Then try flinging it through a hole little bigger than a dinner plate and get it to land where you want and you'll see how difficult it was. It may have been difficult to fire but freed from the weight restrictions that compromised the 'Castles' boiler, the boiler's proportions were much nearer those of the superlative Standard No. 1. The 'Star' configuration also forced Collett to design a new bogie in order for the inside cylinders to leave enough room for the bearings, so one of his designers, A.W.J. Dymond, opted to place the front bearings outside the axles and the rear bearings inside, with the frame cranked halfway along.

Hitting Pole's target was awkward but the outcome was striking to say the least. It was originally intended to keep the building-themed names established on many GWR express locomotives by naming the new locomotives after cathedrals, and this was widely known in 1927. There was a change of heart after Felix Pole persuaded the President of the Baltimore & Ohio Railroad in the United States that a British locomotive ought to be present at the centenary celebrations in 1927. With this in mind, the Great Western approached King George V for permission to name the first new locomotive after him and he agreed readily. The new more powerful locomotives, would, therefore, be known as 'Kings'. It was too good an opportunity to pass up. This time the Great Western's victory was total. Modifications to the 'A1s' didn't approach the magic 40,000lbs figure, and neither did anything else for some years. In nominal terms at least, the Great Western had by far the most powerful passenger locomotive in Britain.

The new locomotive, No. 6000 *King George V*, was sent to the USA on 3 August 1927 following a series of publicity visits to locations across the Great Western network in early July. The Americans quickly took

King George V to their hearts. It was much smaller than the most advanced locomotives there but it was smoother running thanks to being lubricated by oil rather than grease – and with no clouds of black smoke from the chimney. At special run-pasts it was able to coast past crowds with the regulator shut and when a couple of American enginemen tried this with their own steeds, legend has it that they stalled embarrassingly.

King George V was presented with a ceremonial bell to mark its attendance at the Baltimore & Ohio's centenary, which it retains to this day. The bell was the subject of numerous practical jokes by engine cleaners assigned to it. The most popular prank was for a senior cleaner to ask a new hand to fling a shovel of coal into the firebox as hard as possible to ring the bell. Needless to say he failed, but with a little help from a piece of string the senior hand shovelled some coal into the firebox, lifted his leg and rang the bell, to the junior's amazement. I can't help but wonder whether a bit of string, or even cotton, might just have been noticed, but it's a lovely story nonetheless.

There were problems with the 'Kings' – a derailment at Midgham in August 1927 was blamed on poor springing of the bogies – and some firemen undoubtedly struggled but their introduction would allow them to haul heavier loads faster and ultimately, to allow the 'Cornish Riviera' to run non-stop from Paddington to Plymouth in four hours.

One thing the 'Kings' couldn't do was to run into Cornwall because of weight restrictions over the Royal Albert Bridge, and when the first portion of the 'Cornish Riviera' ran to Truro before its first passenger stop in the summer, in reality the 'Kings' had to be swapped just before the bridge at Devonport for a lighter locomotive.

Chapter 18
The Zenith

The year 1927 was the Great Western's zenith. It had the most powerful locomotives, the most beautiful trains, the longest non-stop passenger service in Britain and was profitable too. In that glorious year, the Great Western was without question the finest railway in Britain and maybe even the world.

It wasn't just the trains to the West Country that sparkled either. Birmingham's Snow Hill station had been rebuilt in the early part of the century to cope with extra traffic; it provided an elegant, user-friendly and above all, light, counterpoint to the dinginess of the London Midland & Scottish station at New Street. The London trains were timed for 2 hours, 5 minutes longer than the LMS's to New Street but were still competitive and well used. I never saw Snow Hill before it was closed but to look at the pictures makes me yearn to go back in time . . . it just looked so spacious and clean.

Birmingham also saw through trains heading further north to Birkenhead ('The Zulu') and Pwllheli ('The Cambrian Coast Express'), and south west to Bristol via the new direct route. For many Midlanders, Snow Hill was a gateway to the excitement and anticipation of their holidays. By the 1920s it had become as important to the Great Western as Paddington and Bristol Temple Meads.

The holiday traffic, particularly to the South-West, was intense. Rakes of superannuated and old-fashioned coaches were retained by the Great Western in order to soak up demand. It cost the company little to keep them and one thing the company *hated* doing was turning away business. Just as it is today, Saturday was holiday changeover day in Somerset, Devon and Cornwall, and it took a *lot* of planning for the railways to meet the demand.

On Fridays, whole trains formed of nothing but restaurant cars were sent down with their crews and passengers to Newton Abbot to be attached to trains heading back 'up country' the following morning. Every suitable spare tender locomotive available was readied for the following morning's exertions – including the '47xx' 2-8-0s. That evening, sleeping-car trains and specials carrying luggage sent ahead by passengers (known as Passenger Luggage in Advance) left London, Birmingham and other locations on the Great Western network, with many preferring to travel overnight and beat the rush.

On Saturday mornings the pressure was on: from Paddington alone, eight 200-ton-plus trains an hour departed, all heading long distances and stretching capacity to the limit (even in summer, there was less than one departure per hour for the South-West on weekdays). Trains from London and the Midlands took very different routes to get to the West Country but at Taunton they met, the Midlands trains coming via Bristol, and those from the London direction along the Berks & Hants, meeting at Cogload Junction. Some pressure was eased at Taunton by trains heading to Minehead and Barnstaple via beautiful branch lines but there were still far too many trains to be squeezed into the two lines to Exeter St David's. An added complication at Exeter was the Southern Railway train service to and from London, which arrived at the western end of the station and left towards Plymouth and Cornwall at the eastern end, creating a whole set of conflicting moves with westbound traffic. The holiday trains ran if not nose to tail then certainly signal to signal from Exeter to Newton Abbot – at times it would have been quicker for the passengers to walk. At Newton Abbot, although the 'Kings' were generally able to cope with the heavy loads, extra power was needed on many trains and, in the Great Western's odd way of doing things, an extra locomotive could not simply be attached to the front of the train on every occasion – that would be too easy. The train engine – the one which had hauled the train as far as Newton Abbot – was detached and run into a spare siding, while the assisting locomotive backed down onto the train. Then the train engine coupled to its assistant and only then could it move forward.

From the west, a similar amount of trains headed back home, all facing similar constraints in the opposite direction, and added to this were trains from outside the Great Western network too. Knock-on delays could mount quickly and should a locomotive fail or a carriage suffer a hot axlebox they would mount frighteningly. Yet, from what we can tell, there was little backlash from passengers. Delays were expected and accepted, and for those travelling with children, being delayed on the Sea Wall would have only added to the excitement and, in years to come when they looked back at their holidays, to the Great Western's legend.

Of course, the Great Western did all it could to present a positive image. Passengers could buy Great Western biscuits and drink Great Western whisky if they wanted; they could piece together Great Western jigsaws when they got bored, or read one of the company's books about its latest developments – and if they were wealthy enough, they could even stay in a Great Western Railway hotel, of which the company had a chain running from St Ives in Cornwall to Fishguard in Wales, including the Royal Station Hotel at Paddington. The hotels are a separate story in themselves and many are still open today, though not in railway ownership. The Great Western acquired the Tregenna Castle in St Ives for its commanding views even though it was a fair walk from the station, while the famous Manor House Hotel at Moretonhampstead, Devon, even boasted its own 18-hole golf course. These weren't cheap, functional places to stay – they were mini resorts in their own right.

Felix Pole's brilliant publicity was doing its job to perfection: the Great Western appeared to be a modern progressive railway with brilliant equipment, motivated staff and customer service. Looking at the relics in the Great Western Society's museum at Didcot, it's impossible not to be impressed by the sheer sense of confidence the company had at the time. The publicity could only portray part of the reality of the Great Western experience, however, and a journey north from Paddington to Crewe in the 1920s was as good a way as any of revealing how the company really operated.

Leaving Paddington on a train for Birmingham Snow Hill, passengers would have boarded a train formed of modern – probably Churchward – coaches, all with corridor connections at the ends, and most if not all with separate compartments. In second class these compartments were designed to take up to four people on each side, compared with three, the norm on other railways. Most of the time of course, there was enough empty space on the train for three passengers per side to sit in the compartments, but at busy peak periods the Great Western unapologetically crammed them in like a budget airline today. The train would have been hauled by a 'Star' or a 'Saint' – or possibly a 'Castle' though there weren't all that many in service at that point – and given that it was competing with the London Midland & Scottish Railway's London Euston–Birmingham New Street services, the scheduling was fast and competitive.

George Behrend wrote lovingly of the company in *Gone With Regret*, long out of print but the most loving and characterful account of the railway there is. Behrend was something of a gourmet back then (and still was when he visited me in Cornwall in 2006 to interview me about the campaign to save the Cornish sleeper train) so it is no surprise that he paid particular attention to the food on offer on the 'Cornish Riviera' (a similar standard would have been offered on the Birmingham and Wolverhampton services too):

> The dining-car attendants came round fastening long tables taken from the ends of the coaches, and placing them against the compartment doors where they fitted into a special attachment, the other end resting on a single leg. The silverine cutlery, all with the railway's crest, was spread upon white napery. Do not ask why the luncheon fish was invariably a nice piece of fresh turbot; it always was, just as breakfast included finnan haddock for certain, with kippers an alternative that could not be counted upon as they could on certain other companies' lines.
>
> Somehow even the menus were part of Great Western tradition, the company proudly pointing out in 1928 that their table d'hôte luncheon cost 3s. while that of the Canadian Pacific was 7s. 11d. Exactly why they compared their service to the CPR was not stated! For 3s. you got roast

beef and horseradish sauce; potatoes, cauliflower, followed by compote of fruit and custard; cheese and salad; biscuits. But not just any biscuits. They came round in a tin called 'Railway Assortment' containing more variety of Huntley & Palmers than I have seen in one tin since. Of course there was no need to state which railway, for the tin had a picture of a Star and train on the side, and anyway, Huntley & Palmers made Superior Reading Biscuits, whilst the Southern put their catering out to contractors.

Behrend was a world-renowned expert on luxury trains (he wrote extensively for well over half a century on them). If Behrend was impressed it must have been good.

At Birmingham, passengers for Crewe had two options: they could walk the short distance to the LMS station of New Street – more elegant than today but still a dark, gloomy station – or they could change trains at Snow Hill for a local(ish) service to Shrewsbury, which they would take as far as Wellington (Salop).

Leaving Snow Hill, the chances were that the train was still formed of corridor coaches but of an older vintage than the crack expresses. The fussy old clerestory roofs would still have been in evidence at this point, although they were gradually been eased out by more modern designs. On the route to Shrewsbury – then very much a main line rather than the secondary route of today – motive power varied wildly but Churchward's brilliant 'Prairie' tanks were ideal for these tightly scheduled stopping trains. Heading out through the West Midlands, through the magnificent Low Level station at Wolverhampton and then into the Shropshire countryside, there was nothing that wasn't Great Western on the route: the signage, many of the structures, and the colours were all identical to those one might find in Cornwall yet the train was heading rapidly north-west towards the extremities of the Great Western's territory. After passing through the little market town of Shifnal, the train hared through the massive marshalling yards at Hollinswood (around the site of the present Telford Central station, though you'd never guess), through Oakengates Tunnel, probably calling at that station and then into Wellington for the final connection.

Wellington was a bustling junction station with the LMS routes to Stafford and Coalport meeting with the Great Western line to Much Wenlock, the joint line to Shrewsbury and the cross-country route to Crewe via Nantwich – and it was this pretty little railway which gave the Great Western direct access to the London Midland & Scottish Railway's great citadel at Crewe. Wellington station, incidentally, is unusual in being built on consecrated ground, something marked by the crosses on the roof of the main station building to this day.

The Wellington to Nantwich route opened throughout in 1867, serving the pretty Shropshire town of Market Drayton on its way to Nantwich, from where trains used the existing route to Crewe. Even though it looked like a useful route on the map, in truth passenger and freight traffic never amounted to much and the passenger service was just six weekday trains from Crewe to Wellington and five in the opposite direction. Our collective memory suggests that there should have been many more services even on relatively lightly used routes, but of course the reality was quite different.

Even so, it would seem reasonable to expect the Great Western to make a bit of an effort to impress potential passengers at Crewe. The Great Western, however, thought differently. Standing in the platform at Wellington in the 1920s, the elegant Churchward coaches that took passengers to Birmingham might as well have been from a different planet; Great Western policy was to send locomotives and carriages superseded on the main lines to eke out their retirement on less important routes, including that to Crewe. Photographs taken on the route as late as the 1930s show an ancient 'Stella' 2-4-0 (the first of which entered service in 1884) hauling a motley collection of equally antiquated-looking coaches. Most had clerestory roofs – all of which varied in height and some even (though it is difficult to be absolutely certain from the photographs) appear to be four-wheeled coaches, which finally disappeared in the 1930s. Some of the coaches had no corridor connections at the ends, meaning passengers couldn't move along the rest of the train, but all had compartments for passengers that would have differed substantially depending on when the coach was built. There was no sense of uniformity to the interiors or exteriors of the train whatsoever. It was as far removed from the glamour of the 'Cornish Riviera' as it was possible to imagine, but for passengers from Crudgington, Hodnet, Market Drayton, Adderley, Audlem and all the other stations on the pretty route it was a vital link nonetheless.

The line to Nantwich never made the Great Western much money as there simply wasn't the population to do so, but neither did it cost the railway much either. Using locomotives and coaches made redundant from main-line services by more modern equivalents saved the acquisition of new equipment which would have placed the line firmly in the red. The trains weren't modern but they worked well enough for the demands of the Wellington to Crewe line, and that was ultimately what mattered most.

Generally speaking, the timetable remained the same on this sleepy backwater for decades and in the process, the railway percolated into the very fabric of the communities it served. If you spent a day somewhere like Hodnet or Peplow, the overwhelming impression wouldn't have been of trains running but of silence and quiet activity from the station staff and signalmen. There was a most remarkable sense of continuity on these railway byways too. Stationmasters might come and go but generally the staff were the same year in, year out, and so were the passengers. Train crews got to know many of the passengers and their business, and only the passing of the seasons changed things. Market days would provide a boost to traffic, with extra coaches being added to the train, and the needs of the farms which provided much of the goods traffic meant there was a steady if unspectacular flow of goods in and out. In today's profit-maximising culture, the Wellington to Crewe line would never make a case for itself but the Great Western – a consistent profit-maker – always prided itself on providing a service. Providing that the cost of running the service – the staff on trains and stations, fuel and water for the locomotives, and maintenance of the track and rolling stock – more or less balanced the receipts, the Great Western was content.

If the Wellington to Crewe line was a through route that was more like a branch line in the way it ran, that from Newton Abbot to Kingswear was a branch operated more like a main line. It served (and still does) the resorts of Torquay and Paignton that were so popular with tourists, and extended to Kingswear, on the opposite side of the Dart Estuary to the important port of Dartmouth. (The Paignton to Kingswear section is today operated by the Dartmouth Steam Railway & River Boat Company as a heritage railway.) Dartmouth is unique in having a railway ticket office but no station of its own: a railway-owned ferry took passengers across the Dart to the station at Kingswear.

The contrast to the Wellington to Crewe line couldn't be greater: in Summer 1910, there were twenty-three trains in each direction on the Kingswear branch, though some of these only ran as far as Paignton from Newton Abbot. So important was this branch line to the Great Western that in the 1920s and 1930s it upgraded the route to handle the company's heaviest and most prestigious express passenger loco-motives, including the weighty 'Kings' and there were direct trains to London Paddington and many other destinations off the branch. This route was a huge profit-maker for the Great Western, with hundreds of thousands of passengers – perhaps millions – travelling over it every year. Such was the variety of the company's routes.

In 1929, Collett released the first of his most numerous design which would become synonymous with the Great Western's branch lines, the '57xx' series of 0-6-0 pannier tanks. All railways used small tank locomotives for shunting as well as light passenger and freight duties but these almost all had side tanks next to the boiler or rounded saddle tanks which sat on top of the boiler and arched round it like a tea cosy. The Great Western, inevitably, opted for a third way but it wasn't being different for the sake of it. The great weakness of many side-tank locomotives is that gaining access to the inside motion (and all bar a handful of shunting locomotives had this) could be tricky because the tank blocked much of it. With saddle tanks, the motion was invariably easy to access but the tanks themselves were expensive and tricky to manufacture and not all that easy to remove when the boiler needed an overhaul. The Great Western's alternative was to attach long rectangular box tanks to the sides of the boiler, which looked like panniers carried by a donkey. The tanks were easy to manufacture and didn't block access to the inside motion. They were also easy to remove and had lifting rings for this purpose.

The '57xxs' were a development of the '27xx' design going back to 1896, but improvements to the valve settings and higher boiler pressure gave them a turn of speed which critics never give them credit for. O.S. Nock records in *Great Western Steam* the example of a stopping train from Bath to Chippenham which regularly worked up to 60mph on a light load of two or three coaches, and there were plenty more examples of that across the network. Even though they were based on an ancient design and had little in common with the modern outside-cylindered locomotives entering service on principal routes, the little '57xxs' were superb machines and 852 were eventually built by the Great Western and outside contractors, the most numerous design, by far, on the Great Western and probably any other railway in Britain.

Often working alongside 'prairie tanks' of basically Churchward design which Collett continued to build throughout his regime, the little '57xxs' pottered up and down branch lines from Cornwall to Wales looking like the impetuous busybodies they were – and what fantastic little railways the Great Western had! From Gwinear Road to Helston in Cornwall; Totnes to Ashburton in Devon, Wellington to Much Wenlock in Shropshire, Ruabon to Barmouth and many, many others – to today's eyes, those little branch lines are irresistible. Over the years, the Great Western had integrated them – mostly through acquisition – absolutely seamlessly into its empire but the differences in the station buildings, flower arrangements on the platforms, and accents of the staff gave each a character of its own. The staff knew full well that their stations were an important part of the community they served, and although none could be compared with Paddington, the men *knew* their efforts were valued by the management.

Journey times were usually pretty slow but this allowed time for wagons to be added to goods trains, parcels loaded and unloaded, and passengers to chat with the station staff. Providing you weren't in a hurry, all this added to their appeal and, if you were in a hurry, there was no point in worrying because walking or taking a bus was usually even slower. Today the value of many of these shorter and less important routes would be incalculable, providing an alternative to the car in areas effectively bereft of public transport links to the outside world, just as they did until the 1960s.

The 1920s really were something of a golden age for the Great Western's passenger services – it was the only one of the 'Big Four' that can genuinely be said to have had one at all. This is the Great Western we want to remember, and it's achingly poignant. Oh, for a time machine!

Chapter 19
On and Off the Rails

Nineteen Twenty-Eight saw the first cracks appearing in the Great Western's superiority. In May that year, the LNER ran its first non-stop train from London to Edinburgh, the 'Flying Scotsman' and its big 'Pacifics' were being modified to a standard that made them every bit as potent as the 'Kings'. Although no time saving was made on this first non-stop run (due to a long-standing agreement on journey times made with the predecessors of the LMS), its distance of 390 miles far eclipsed the 'Cornish Riviera's' Paddington to Plymouth run.

That year also saw the advent of an important locomotive design that would serve the Great Western well until the end of steam. The 'Halls' were a development of the 'Saints' and followed experiments with No. 2925 *Saint Martin*. This had been rebuilt in 1925 with 6ft-diameter driving wheels (as opposed to the original 6ft 8½in) in a bid to give it greater tractive effort so it could be used on a variety of duties. Its power remained the same but making the driving wheels smaller effectively lowered the gearing – meaning maximum power was available over a lower speed range which made the locomotive more versatile. In the three years since the conversion, *Saint Martin* had shown it could make a good job on everything from fast freights to express trains, so production of eighty similar locomotives was authorised in 1928 and the Works began replacing the express passenger 4-4-0s. As they were designed to perform lesser duties than the 'Castles', they were named after smaller stately homes. There were fears initially that not enough suitable halls could be found in the Great Western region but in the end there were plenty, though when production topped 200 they had to look further afield.

In traffic, the 'Halls' were able and competent machines that the crews took to immediately, though the more spacious and protective cab compared with the 'Saints' might have had something to do with that! Meanwhile, on top-link duties some of the 'Saints' were now being replaced by 'Castles' and withdrawn from service, giving the 'Halls' much of the second-line work.

It would be very easy to glean from the fizzing performance of the Great Western's passenger operations that all in the garden was rosy, but at the time a global depression was affecting industry and, with increasing road competition, in 1928 all four major railways opened negotiations with the railway unions seeking pay cuts. The unions must have recognised the structural challenges facing the rail sector because they negotiated positively to obtain a good but fair deal for their members; it was ultimately agreed that all railway staff from the highest tier of management to the lowliest cleaner would accept a 2.5 per cent pay cut.

With dividends to shareholders remaining at around the 7 per cent level, the Great Western was profitable and safe for investors; so, in a bid to defeat the road competition at source, the company began to offer its own road haulage services to complement the omnibuses it had been running since as early as 1903 (the first was from Helston to The Lizard and many more followed). A small move in this direction had begun in 1925 but by 1927, the Great Western was offering railway-operated lorries from forty-five railheads, usually at rates far below independent competitors. Obviously, the rationale was a case of 'If you can't beat 'em, join 'em.'

For passengers, the railway had gradually increased its bus feeder services too and many of these buses handled local traffic as well as rail passengers. Better still, the Railway Road Powers Act of 1928 gave the Great Western authority to expand its road operation and so it became a joint owner of the Western National Omnibus Company. This new venture would run many bus services across Great Western territory and integrated well with the train timetable.

It wasn't just buses and lorries that the Great Western operated – it had long owned steamers which ran from Weymouth to the Channel

Islands, and from Fishguard to Rosslare, as well as a series of smaller tenders to serve ocean liners at Plymouth. Investment in the Channel Islands services was heavy, with two turbine-powered steamers entering service from 1925, as did a pair of new cargo ships that carried much of the agricultural produce from the islands. An unusual feature of the docks at Weymouth was that a tramway was built from the main line to the docks along the roads; special trains ran on this, a gong sounding to warn motorists and pedestrians of the approaching train. The line still exists today and is nominally open, although it hasn't seen a train for some years now.

This diversity of operations played a large part in retaining the company's profitability but 1928 hadn't been a good year and the dividend fell from 7.5 per cent to 5 per cent, hindered mostly, said the Chairman, Lord Churchill, by falling coal traffic from South Wales.

The following year, 1929, also had its moments. The Great Western introduced its first Pullman services for the Ocean Liner specials and launched the 'Torquay Pullman' but always believed it could offer Pullman standard services of its own (a fee was paid to the Pullman company to run services using its coaches) and these two trains were the only Pullmans which ever ran on the Great Western. That was a positive development, as was an acceleration of the 'Cheltenham Flyer' to give an average speed of 66 ¼mph, but in truth the Great Western didn't really have any reason to try to speed its services. Its focus was in operating a reliable, reasonable and above all profitable operation and the only real benefits of speeding the 'Cheltenham Flyer' were in publicity terms.

Sir Felix Pole resigned on 6 July 1929 to take up the chairmanship of Associated Electrical Industries. Pole had worked his way from the ground floor to the very top non-board job of the Great Western and was largely responsible for the service improvements, investment and technical developments that the railway had introduced in his ten-year-long tenure. He was a brilliant railway manager with achievements aplenty but perhaps his most important was the smooth integration of the independent railways into the company during the grouping process. What could have been a difficult and disjointed procedure ran remarkably smoothly. By the end of the decade, all of those lines had been assimilated into the Great Western without alienating their staff and traditions, something none of the other 'Big Four' companies were ever really able to do. Pole's last year was profitable, with turnover rising £656,509 to reach £36,184,053 for 1928. As they say, if you're going to go out, go out on a high note.

When Sir Felix Pole resigned, his deputy, Assistant General Manager James Milne, stepped up to take his place. Milne had been trained in Swindon Works on the locomotive side and after gaining experience in the drawing office and laboratory, took a degree at Manchester University before transferring to the Traffic Division. Milne took charge of a railway that was well equipped in terms of locomotives and increasingly by modern carriages that were finally replacing the old Dean clerestory stock. It also had well-motivated staff and was profitable – and was also far better prepared than most organisations for the economic turbulence that was beginning to accelerate out of control.

The causes of the Great Depression are invariably attributed to the stock-market crashes of October 1929 but economies around the world were showing the underlying symptoms much before then. Growing protectionism throughout the 1920s had denied key export markets to companies in all of the developed economies, while the fragile nature of some industries – mining and steelmaking in particular – meant they were vulnerable to the slightest perturbations in global markets.

At the time of the 1929 General Election, which resulted in a hung parliament but with the Labour Party having the greatest number of seats, more than a million were unemployed but the real figure was probably much higher. Before the stock-market crashes, and before the start of the Great Depression, a coalition government under the leadership of Ramsay McDonald took steps to create work to alleviate unemployment. The railways were the cornerstone of this plan by virtue of being the biggest engineering concerns of the day, and the government offered to pay interest on loans taken out for capital schemes, effectively guaranteeing them and allowing the railways to borrow for a short period beyond the statutory limits imposed on them by earlier legislation.

The Great Western had a long list of schemes it had wanted to develop, and the vast majority were focussed on improvements to passenger facilities and capacity enhancements on its most constrained routes. The key projects were to complete the redevelopment of Paddington, with longer platforms, better parcels facilities and a new concourse; expansion of Bristol Temple Meads station to provide more platforms for West of England traffic; expansion of Cardiff General station; and most ambitiously, a comprehensive rebuilding and remodelling of Taunton station with accompanying quadrupling of the 7-mile Cogload Junction to Norton Fitzwarren section to provide extra capacity. Other key schemes were the construction of new lines at Westbury and Frome to allow passenger trains to and from the West Country to avoid the speed-restricted stations, upgrades of Wolverhampton Stafford Road and Swindon works, track-doubling in Cornwall, and expansion of marshalling yards at Severn Tunnel Junction and Rogerstone. There were other smaller-scale projects too in what was the biggest network enhancement programme on the Great Western since the construction of the cut-off routes in the early twentieth century.

Work started quickly on the Westbury and Frome avoiding lines, which allowed trains to maintain high speeds, saving a few minutes on journey times and just as importantly clearing space through Westbury station for north–south coal trains, which were far more frequent. The cost of these two projects was £220,000 and they would be commissioned in 1933.

Far more important, however, was the unclogging of Taunton, through which trains from as far north as Aberdeen, and from London and Wales all converged to try and squeeze through double-track railway from Cogload Junction, east of the station, and through the station as far as Norton Fitzwarren, where at least some pressure was eased by trains heading to Minehead and Barnstaple. The station was hopelessly inadequate too, with just the pair of running lines passing under the old broad-gauge-style overall roof. This entire project, which involved a lot of earthmoving, not to mention the expansion and reconstruction of Taunton station and the disruption to traffic, would cost £360,000 – an absolute bargain considering the benefits the project would bring.

At Paddington, platforms were lengthened and a new concourse was created on an area known as The Lawn between the buffer stops and the hotel. This would provide a much greater circulating area for passengers (useful on summer Saturdays) and finally complete the grandeur of this marvellous, elegant station. At Bristol Temple Meads, a host of new platforms were added to the south-eastern side of the station, all with plenty of circulating space, while at Cardiff new connections were added to former Taff Vale and Barry Railway lines, and much needed new station buildings and a stylish frontage were added.

There was one other project of the 1930s which wasn't associated with relief of unemployment but wouldn't have been possible without the funds released for other schemes and that was the extension of Automatic Train Control over the Great Western's principal routes. Although gradual extensions of it had taken place, by 1930 only 372 miles were equipped. In 1930 the board gave the green light for another 1,758 miles of track and 200 locomotives to be equipped with ATC. It would cover the principal routes to Plymouth, Weymouth, Swansea, Wolverhampton via the OWW and Bicester; and also Worcester to Hereford and Newport, Birmingham to Gloucester and Swindon to Gloucester. This improvement scheme would cost £208,000 and given the Great Western's unimpeachable safety record since the early 1900s, might have seemed unnecessary expenditure. Viewed through today's safety-focussed lenses, again, it seems like another good investment.

This was classic Keynesian thinking – invest in bad times to prepare for the upturn – and the Great Western's timing was impeccable because when many of these schemes were coming on-stream, the economy was emerging from recession.

The Great Western *was* seriously affected by the Great Depression, but not nearly as badly as other railways, and the LNER in particular. Traffic fell throughout 1930 as the depression started and then worsened in 1931, with passenger receipts falling by 9.2 per cent year on year, minerals and heavy merchandise by 12.8 per cent, coal by 11.75 per cent, and worst of all, the railway's docks businesses suffering a whopping 17.56 per cent fall as the recession slashed global trade. For the docks in particular, had they been independently owned it is doubtful whether they would have survived the early 1930s as going concerns. Taken as a whole, gross receipts had fallen by around £5 million since 1929 but the actions of the 1920s allowed the Great Western to emerge in a stronger position than it otherwise might have.

For the first couple of years of the 1930s it was a case of holding the fort, with little substantial development. However, one development which wasn't welcome on the Great Western was in 1931 when William Stanier, Collett's principal assistant, defected from Swindon to Crewe. Stanier's loss was a big blow for the Great Western – much of the success of the 'Castles' and 'Kings' can be attributed to him – and also for Swindon, where Stanier undertook many of the community activities traditionally associated with the Great Western's Chief Mechanical Engineers from Joseph Armstrong onwards.

Stanier's move to Crewe wasn't good for the Great Western but looking at the railway network as a whole it was the most significant appointment of the 1930s. The LMS was desperately in need of new equipment and Stanier would soon bring Swindon ideas on boilers, valve settings and much more to bear within its vast territory. For him, being only a year younger than Collett, it was a good move too, as remaining at Swindon would have given him precious little time to make his mark. In time, Stanier would produce some of the finest locomotives ever built, including the legendary 'Duchesses'.

However, there was one development in 1932 that showed the Great Western wasn't entirely content to rest on its laurels. On 6 June 1932, Milne must have decided to show that the Great Western wanted to prove it was still a speedy railway because a special run took place with the 'Cheltenham Flyer' to show just what the company's trains were capable of. No. 5006 *Tregenna Castle*, crewed by Driver Ruddock and Fireman Thorp, was ordered to go all out for a fast run between Swindon and Paddington.

The train left Cheltenham at 14:30 and called at Swindon at 15:48. From there *Tregenna Castle* was pushed up to 64mph within two miles, and by 7.3 miles had reached 81.8mph. The locomotive was only hauling a light train of 186 tons and it tore through Didcot, 24.2 miles from Swindon at 90mph. The train continued at 90mph or above until just past Twyford, and then varied throughout the 80–90mph range until just two miles outside Paddington, where the brakes were slammed on. Driver Ruddock had taken the 'Cheltenham Flyer' from Swindon to Paddington in 56mins 47 secs, an average speed of 71.3mph and a quite remarkable figure for the time.

The Great Western immediately acclaimed this run as giving it the world's fastest train, which was true for the run between Swindon and Paddington in terms of average speeds, but certainly not in terms of maximum speeds. It's interesting that a 'Castle' was chosen rather than a 'King', lending credence to the view that the older design was better suited for really high-speed running than the 'Kings', and there are enough accounts from the 1920s onwards to suggest that except where loads were really heavy, a 'Castle' was usually a better bet.

This run gave the Great Western a much-needed fillip of positive publicity and helped mask the fact that by the standards of the day its locomotives were beginning to look a little outmoded in some of their design features. Nowhere is this more apparent than in the cabs. Although Collett's designs offered better protection than earlier locomotives, there was nothing to stop the crew falling out from the sides between the locomotive and tender, and there were no concessions to ergonomics either. To operate all the controls effectively the driver had to stand, at a time when other railways were trying to make his job easier by placing everything to hand and giving him something more comfortable to sit on than the flip-down wooden seat he had. Another oddity was that the driver was positioned on the right-hand side of the cab and the fireman on the left. This meant the fireman could fire right-handed but it invariably also prevented the driver from seeing the signals as early as he might like. Both men were involved in sighting the signals, though on the main lines the introduction of ATC helped ease the workload.

Tregenna Castle's run on 6 June 1932 was the high water mark for Great Western steam but from then on, developments on other railways would make the Great Western's fleet look distinctly old fashioned.

One of the men who made the modern Great Western died on 19 December 1933. George Jackson Churchward had retired in 1922 but had been a regular visitor to Swindon Works ever since. The Great Western had been his life and retirement must have left a gaping hole in it for him. He regularly visited his old design office and because there was little sign of deviation from his standards, he could bask in the knowledge that his developments and innovations had been carried forward to a new generation.

Always keen to keep an eye on the railway, in December 1933 Churchward had spotted a loose rail-joint on the line near his company-owned house at Swindon and having reported it, was keeping an eye on its condition, which was getting worse with every train that passed over it. But his hearing was fading and on this foggy morning he was unaware that the 10:20 Paddington to Fishguard was running along the line. It struck and killed him instantly but the crew of the locomotive, 'Castle' No. 4085 *Berkeley Castle,* probably didn't even realise they had hit anyone in the fog. A freight train heading in the opposite direction spotted Churchward's body but although medical assistance was sought, it only confirmed the inevitable. George Jackson Churchward was dead, aged seventy-seven. He was buried at Christ Church, Old Town, Swindon.

In an odd kind of way, it was an appropriate way for Churchward to pass on. He was a bachelor with no wife or children, and must have been quite a lonely man, like the old boys who pop into their offices ostensibly to see how things are going but really for a bit of company.

His death would have been instant and unforeseen. It was a cruel irony that Churchward's death echoed that of young Joseph Armstrong in 1888, and that it was one of his own locomotives that killed him.

In one of those uncanny times of symmetry, as Churchward died the ultimate replacements for the steam locomotive were beginning to enter service on the Great Western — the pioneering diesel railcars.

Chapter 20
Dawn of the Diesels

Alternatives to the steam locomotive had long been sought. Steam locomotives were comparatively inefficient and needed a lot of maintenance and servicing, resulting in any railway of size needing a vast number of locomotives to cover its duties.

By 1933, the diesel engine was a proven if slightly immature alternative. The best engines of the day weren't all that powerful and certainly couldn't replace the likes of the 'Halls' and 'Castles'; private locomotive builders, however, were beginning to apply the technology to small shunting locomotives for use in goods yards. The diesels' ability to operate twenty-four hours a day, only being interrupted by refuelling and with little need for servicing made them a vast improvement on the army of steam shunting locomotives.

Diesel engines were now also thoroughly proved in buses and the Great Western started talks with Hardy Motors of Southall, which was based just next to the Paddington to Bristol main line at Park Royal, London. The plan was to combine a 130-horsepower diesel engine on a rail-borne chassis with a streamlined body on top. At 63ft long, it was slightly longer than the Great Western's standard passenger coaches. It would seat sixty-nine passengers and had a luggage compartment, and was intended for local services between Paddington, Slough, Reading and Didcot, running at a maximum speed of 60mph. It was delivered to Southall depot, London, on 24 November 1933 at a cost of £3,249.

This spectacular-looking vehicle was as revolutionary – perhaps more so – than the 'Saints' because in its fundamentals, Hardy Motors and the Great Western had built the first modern diesel passenger train in Britain. It entered service on 4 December 1933. The Great Western didn't treat this new arrival with kid gloves either, running it on sixteen trains a day in addition to the normal steam service. For a prototype, it ran remarkably well, carrying more than 136,000 passengers and running more than 60,000 miles in its first year of service.

The success of the first diesel railcar, appropriately known as Railcar No. 1, prompted the Great Western to order three more but this time for high-speed cross-country 'businessmen's' services between Birmingham, Gloucester, Newport and Cardiff, which had limited demand and were then running expensively with steam traction. Three of these railcars were built, and entered service in July 1934. They had two engines as opposed to the prototype's one, and a higher maximum speed of between 70mph and 80mph depending on conditions. They were an immediate hit with passengers, even though a supplementary fare of 2s 6d was charged on top of the standard third-class rate. Accommodation on the railcars was all third class, but of a superior nature to the locomotive-hauled equivalents. Tickets issued on these trains were limited to the number of seats, guaranteeing every passenger a seat. The accommodation included a modern buffet counter, which proved an instant hit.

The interiors had removable tables between each pair of seats, and their ends and framing were of weathered oak. The luggage racks were of chromium-plated steel netting, golden-brown Rexine lined the walls, and the floors were covered with green linoleum. It was a stylish modern design inside and out, which encapsulated the streamlined, clean designs of the period.

Inevitably the Great Western published a book about these new trains, called *The Streamline Way* and heralded them as 'a new era in rail travel'. For once the hyperbole was not exaggerated. These four railcars offered a compelling and glamorous insight into the future of rail travel and at the end of 1934, orders for another three were placed, followed by a further ten in January 1935.

The Great Western was also thinking ambitiously when it came to another area – it was taking to the skies. It had started a joint venture with Imperial Airways to operate a scheduled air service between Cardiff, Haldon near Teignmouth and Roborough, near Plymouth. A six-seater Westland Wessex aeroplane was painted chocolate and cream, and given similar interior decor to a first-class coach and services began on 12 April 1933. Single fares were £3 and returns £5, and the journey from Cardiff General station to Plymouth North Road took 1hr 55mins – much quicker than the almost four hours by rail. The service was soon extended to Castle Bromwich aerodrome near Birmingham in order to serve Birmingham Snow Hill. The experiment wasn't successful – and neither was it likely to be given the limited capacity of civil aircraft at the time – but it proved that the Great Western was keen to explore new ways of building business and, of course, defeating any potential competition before it could even get off the ground.

Although the Great Western was behind the times in terms of advances in steam technology by the mid 1930s, it was very much ahead of all bar the Southern Railway (which was pursuing an extensive electrification programme) in introducing steam's successors. It was just in time for the Great Western's centenary, a unique celebration.

For any company to reach its centenary is an achievement of note. For a railway company to do so is even more remarkable, given the amalgamations and restructuring the industry had been through. The Great Western had, at times against the odds, survived the trauma of successive recessions in the nineteenth century, made a successful transition from the broad gauge, modernised spectacularly and burnished its reputation to a sheen.

There was a big celebration – it's not every day you get to mark a hundredth birthday, after all – and it was marked with two formal gatherings, one in Bristol on the anniversary, 31 August 1935, which heralded the start of a new fast London to Bristol service called 'The Bristolian', and another in London on 30 October. There, the Prince of Wales, the Duke of Windsor (later Edward VIII before he abdicated), said:

I have a personal association with the Great Western Railway because it serves the West of England. Your tracks pass through the counties of

Somerset, Devon, and Cornwall, where, as Duke of Cornwall, I have many tenants dependent on your services. You carry their produce from the West Country to their chief market and, which is as important, you bring them holidaymakers and tourists who in the summer season rejoice to be able to visit some of the most beautiful parts of the British Isles.

So it is not only as a traveller but as a landowner and indeed a customer of the line, that I have the pleasure of accepting your hospitality tonight. I wish, therefore, to pay my tribute to all that the Great Western Railway has done for the West Country during the century of its existence. Speed, comfort, convenience, flexibility, have all been keynotes of your administration. It can never be said that the Great Western Railway has not moved with the times. It is a fact that your company was the first railway company to establish, a few years ago, a regular daily air service. You have held the balance fairly between competing interests. You have discharged your duty to the public with loyalty. You are a venerable, honourable institution in our native land.

Many of the Prince's sentiments held true, but as to the company moving with the times, there were ominous signs that wasn't quite the case. On the locomotive front, the only main line design which deviated an inch from the Churchward principles was the '56xx' series of 0-6-2 tank engines designed for service in the South Wales valleys, which entered service from 1924 (and this was a development of a Rhymney Railway design), while the new '48xx' 0-4-2 tanks were designed for branch lines and owed more to Dean and Armstrong than anything in the twentieth century. The '48xxs' (later renumbered in the '14xx' series) were delightful little locomotives that seemed to sprint away from stations with a load of one or two coaches – they're a favourite of mine – but they looked old fashioned even when they were built.

Of the bigger locomotives, 'Halls', 'Castles' and slightly altered versions of the '28xx' and '43xxs' continued to be built, and the advent of the 'Granges' in 1936 finally completed Churchward's standard locomotive line-up of the early 1900s as a 4-6-0 with small 5ft 8in driving wheels. When Stanier was building truly modern mixed-traffic

4-6-os with easy-to-maintain outside-valve gear, when the LNER was breaking speed records and the Southern extending the third rails of electrification, the 'Granges' went rather against the mould. That said, they weren't merely admired by engine crews like the 'Kings', or respected like the 'Halls' – the 'Granges' were *adored*. Despite having some outmoded features, account after account of them pays tribute to their power, acceleration and tenacity with heavy loads. Most of all though, men paid tribute to an indefinable 'friendliness' that meant the 'Granges' seemed to want to work with their crews even when conditions were tough. Even though they should have been almost identical to 'Halls' to operate, they would cope with an inexperienced fireman's efforts and not punish him by running out of steam at the drop of a hat, and drivers knew they could thrash a 'Grange' to the limit and it would keep time on all but the very fastest schedules. When the last was scrapped in 1965 they were genuinely and deservedly mourned.

In 1936, Collett also designed the outside-framed 'Dukedogs' by combining parts of the 'Duke' and 'Bulldog' 4-4-os for use on the Cambrian Coast Line in Wales. The outside-framed 'Dukedogs' inadvertently highlighted one of Collett's more admirable traits according to John Daniels on his www.greatwestern.org.uk website. He could not stand pomposity, and especially not from certain directors who had suggested that locomotives should bear their names. The 'Dukedogs' looked archaic and Collett decided these 'new' locomotives should be given the names of those directors who were so keen to have a locomotive named after them. When those directors arrived at Paddington to see the first they were stunned, having been expecting to see something rather more modern. The nameplates were later fitted to 'Castles' but Collett had made his point. The 'Dukedogs' may have looked archaic but they were a cost-effective solution that Collett supplemented in 1938 with his lightweight 'Manor' 4-6-os.

The departure of Stanier in 1932 and the sudden death in January 1934 of the long-serving Chairman Viscount Churchill meant that for the first time since the 1860s, the Great Western lacked a leader of substance. The other three 'Big Four' railways were making bold innovations in rolling stock and services, yet the Great Western – irrespective of any accelerations in services – seemed content to rest on its laurels.

If proof was needed that the Great Western wasn't on top form, it introduced a new train called 'The Bristolian' which departed London at 10:00 – too late for the core market of businessmen to have a more-or-less full day in Bristol. The LMS would make a similar mistake later in the decade when it launched a streamlined service from London to Glasgow, but for the Great Western, normally so attuned to its customers' needs, this was an aberration.

There were bright spots – new alignment tools installed in Swindon Works in the 1930s enabled the Great Western to build and overhaul locomotives with incredible precision. It was said that Swindon Works scrapped components when they reached tolerances that other railways struggled to build to and this reflects the fact that the focus was very much in making the existing locomotive stud as efficient to operate as possible by extending overhaul intervals.

In terms of speeds and services, in 1936 despite apparently standing still, the company still operated more trains at an average speed of 58mph or above than the other railways. A new set of coaches for the 'Cornish Riviera' was built in 1935 (known as the 'Centenary' stock) which were bigger than anything bar Churchward's 'Dreadnought' stock, and standards in other trains were improving too. The relative position of the Great Western compared with other railways changed completely in operational terms in 1937. The LNER's crack stream-lined trains headed by 'The Coronation' and hauled by the streamlined 'A4s' started in 1937 and put the Great Western's speed records firmly in the shade. (The Great Western made a desultory attempt to streamline a 'King' and a 'Castle' but this amounted to a few fairings and a hemispherical smoke box door that hampered maintenance and servicing and made little if any difference to services.) The following year, 1938, saw any hope of the Great Western recapturing its reputation for speed end for good when on 3 July 1938, the iconic 'A4' 4468 *Mallard* set an all-time speed record for steam traction of 126mph, which still stands to this day.

By the late 1930s however, speed was something of a sideshow because road competition was making inroads into railway business for all of the 'Big Four', which by then were fighting a long-running campaign for a level playing-field against road operators.

Railway companies have long claimed that road haulage and bus companies compete unfairly against them as they do not pay the full costs of the roads they run on, nor of the ancillary services such as police which keep them running smoothly, and in the 1930s this situation was exacerbated by the railways' common carrier status. Cutting rates was subject to approval by the Railway Rates Tribunal, and effectively rendering fair competition impossible because gaining approval was a lengthy process by which time the load would have long gone.

A view was emerging that the railways existed to provide a service but the politicians didn't seem to grasp the simple concept that if a service is important it has to be funded. By fixing goods rates, government after government were really asking the railways to provide a service but without providing either subsidy or flexibility to allow them to do so. The low taxes enjoyed by road hauliers, the fact that they weren't liable for the upkeep of the roads, were under no obligation to accept all and any traffic, could charge what they like and could keep their rates secret, just made things worse. In the words of one old GWR man, 'We had to fight the roads with one hand tied behind our back.'

As Chancellor of the Exchequer, Winston Churchill had said in 1928: 'It is the duty of the state to hold the balance even between road and rail.' It was this statement that prompted the railways to issue a booklet called *Fair Play for the Railways*. A long-running campaign seeking a 'square deal' – fair and even competition – had been running throughout the decade and in the late 1930s, shortly after the 1938 Munich Crisis, it seemed to be gaining momentum. Progress had been made up to the point of examination by the Minister of Transport with more than a hint of settlement which would have relaxed statutory rates control in favour of transport co-ordination. The worsening political situation leading up the Second World War meant this was shelved.

This question was the start of a debate which has run ever since: what level of service should the railways provide, and who should pay for it.

In the third volume of *The History of the Great Western Railway*, the author, O.S. Nock, relates how the fundamental arguments of the 'Square Deal' campaign went completely over the heads of passengers who when delayed, unsurprisingly believed *they* should be getting a square deal, not the railways. The debate rumbles on today, with additional concerns about the environment and the effects of road congestion thrown in, but more than seventy years on there is still no sign of a consensus emerging.

In a bid to evade rising coal prices, the Great Western investigated the merits of electrifying the railway between Taunton and Penzance because it offered a way of increasing speeds on the steeply graded routes west of Newton Abbot and cutting the considerable expense of hauling coal all the way from Wales to the far South West. Studies showed that although electrification would be hugely expensive, in time significant operational savings would result. The LNER investigated the possibilities too and reached an identical conclusion, but whereas that railway pushed forward plans to electrify its key main lines, the Great Western decided the efficiency gains would never pay for themselves. In the late 1930s this was true but those savings would have been far greater a decade later. It was a missed opportunity but nobody could possibly have predicted just how much Britain would suffer in the years after 3 September 1939.

Chapter 21
Total War

The start of the Second World War had been expected for months and the government had been expanding military production ever since the Munich Crisis of 1938. The rapid developments in aviation technology throughout the 1930s had combined with the German Luftwaffe's bombing of Guernica in the Spanish Civil War to whip up near hysteria about the apparent devastation that fast bomber aircraft would unleash in a major war.

It was widely expected that within hours of the war's declaration the Germans would target Britain's major towns and cities in a bid to destroy key military, political and logistics sites and undermine civilian morale. Because both the war and this attack had been anticipated, remarkably comprehensive plans had been drawn up to operate the railways. On 1 September 1939, as the Germans invaded Poland, the Minister for Transport, Euan Wallace, took control of Britain's railways under the Emergency Powers (Defence) Act of 1939. This legislation gave the government complete control over the railways and their property for the duration of the war and would be used to the full.

Even before war was declared, plans to evacuate children from Britain's major cities to reduce their vulnerability to air attack were implemented. The Great Western was mostly responsible for those children from London, as the area west of Reading as far as Penzance was – with exceptions such as Plymouth, Cardiff and Bristol – considered relatively safe. The GWR also helped evacuate children from Birmingham and Merseyside.

The order to evacuate the children was given on 31 August and the first evacuation specials departed the following morning at 08:30. Most children were sent to Ealing Broadway station, which connected the Great Western Main Line with London Transport's District and Circle

Lines. Children were taken to their schools, issued with tickets and then taken to Ealing Broadway and other stations around London fifteen minutes before their train's departure time, along with children from other schools being sent to the same area.

In a remarkable feat of organisation replicated all over the country, coaches, locomotives and train crews were drawn from all over the GWR network to run these specials. The plan was to run twelve-coach trains carrying 800 passengers, and between 08:30 and 17:30 for four days, the evacuation trains would run at nine-minute intervals, depending on how many children needed to be evacuated. On 1 September, fifty-eight trains carried 44,032 children, while on 4 September, the last day of the evacuation, twenty-eight trains carried 17,796.

To cope with these extra trains, scheduled services were restricted heavily and the evacuation specials ran non-stop to their destination except where locomotives and crews needed changing. The trains themselves ran at express speeds, mainly using the GWR's plentiful fleet of express and mixed-traffic 4-6-0s, though on some shorter-distance runs 'large prairie' tank locomotives were used. In total, the Great Western ran 163 trains from London alone and carried 112,994 children. Add to that the numbers from Birmingham and Merseyside, and then the hundreds of thousands of children the other railways carried and the magnitude of this extraordinary feat is clear. It had taken a lot of planning and caused an incalculable amount of distress to parents and children, but at least when the Luftwaffe began bombing London and other cities, most of the children would be safe.

Because few expected this conflict to be over quickly, no attempt was made to continue passenger services as normal. The limited timetable imposed by the evacuations was retained until 24 September, when an emergency timetable was imposed. The cuts were drastic and a maximum average speed of 45mph was imposed on all express services, with sleeping and restaurant cars eliminated altogether. The increases in journey times were dramatic. Penzance had a fastest journey time of 6hrs 30 mins in October 1938, but a year later this had stretched to 8hrs 35mins and most journeys took an hour longer than that. Adding to the delays in the early weeks of the war was the decision to route all daytime passenger trains to the West of England via Bristol in order to serve as many destinations with as few trains as possible. The public were asked whether their journeys were really necessary but with an average journey time of more than nine hours, it would have to be to prompt anyone to travel from London to Penzance.

It soon became apparent that the much-feared air attacks were not happening as expected, so restaurant cars were reinstated on some trains from 16 October. It was difficult to see how their cessation would have helped the war effort even with rationing: with vast numbers of people travelling all over the country, providing adequate sustenance on the extended journeys was vital.

Travel still wasn't pleasant, particularly at night where despite the provision of blackout curtains on coach windows, light still leaked out, making trains more visible to any enemy aircraft looking for a target. Until black surrounds were painted on the window, only an eerie dim light was provided. On the locomotives, those with proper windows on their cabs had them plated over, while tarpaulins were in theory meant to be stretched between locomotive and tender to reduce the visibility of the firebox glare. It was fine for locomotives fitted with high-sided tenders but rendered effective operation impossible for those with small 3,500-gallon tenders and the tarpaulins were soon abandoned.

The Great Western moved its headquarters from Paddington to four large country houses at Aldermaston, Cholsey, Padworth and Thatcham, and another two at Midgham, to continue operations should London be bombed, while key structures such as signalboxes at key junctions were fitted with blast walls to limit the spread of damage. In anticipation of large-scale disruption, track and signalling materials were stockpiled at important locations to speed repairs.

Swindon Works soon found itself building Stanier's rugged and powerful '8F' heavy freight locomotives, which were selected as the standard type to be built during the war by virtue of their relative ease of construction and maintenance, reliability and proven performance, and it also prepared one hundred 'Dean Goods' locomotives – some of which had seen service overseas in the Great War – for use abroad. Their lightweight and gutsy performance would allow them to work on more lightly laid railways than the Stanier design.

There things rested for a while, the Germans recovering from their invasion of Poland and the Allies building strength in France – then the Western Front collapsed. Much of the British Expeditionary Force was cocooned in a shrinking perimeter around Dunkirk. The Great Western's steamers were called on to assist in the evacuation, which began on 23 May 1940. The *St Andrew* and *St David* of the Fishguard to Ireland service had been converted into hospital ships, as was the *St Julien* which was used to reach the Channel Islands in peacetime. The *St Helier* and *Roebuck* were converted to transports. All of these boats drew shallow draughts and that made them perfect for getting to the heart of Dunkirk's harbour.

One tale of *St Andrew* that Nock recounts is worth retelling here because it vividly illustrates the difficulties many of the vessels involved in the Dunkirk evacuation faced in addition to the perils of being machine-gunned and bombed. The boat had been ordered to find a berth from where it would take on board seriously wounded service-men. It was asked to move to be nearer some ambulances on the harbour but when it got there, the ambulances had been bombed and only dead bodies were found there. The ship set sail again to another part of the heavily bombed harbour where there were casualties waiting to be sent home. Amidst another heavy air-raid, the crew improvised a gangway to help the wounded board before finally, in darkness and without navigational aids, making her way through the harbour entrance, which was crowded with ships and wreckage, and covered in a greasy black smokescreen. After exceptional seamanship, Captain Reed and his crew safely reached Dover without any loss of life.

St Helier made seven trips to Dunkirk and the last was to evacuate more than 2,000 men in Operation Dynamo's last gasp on 2 June 1940. More than 338,000 soldiers had been saved from capture by the German army and although almost no equipment was saved, these men formed the core of the armies that would fight through the war. Once the troops arrived from Dunkirk, the burden of moving them from the ports fell on the Southern Railway, which stretched itself to the limit dispersing the soldiers to bases and hospitals around the country. All in all, the railways played a small but significant part in the success of this vital operation.

With the Dunkirk veterans back home, passenger traffic soared, with servicemen on leave adding to the thousands who still wanted to take a summer break but although a few bombs in the right place could have wreaked havoc in any number of railway locations in the southern half of England, the Luftwaffe's strategy was to defeat the Royal Air Force in what became known as the Battle of Britain (a story superbly told in *The Most Dangerous Enemy* by Stephen Bungay). It wasn't until the Luftwaffe started bombing London from September 1940 (and in the process losing the Battle of Britain) that the capital's railways started taking damage.

There were countless acts of bravery by railwaymen and women volunteering in casualty clearing stations, as Air Raid Precautions wardens and other roles but one Great Western employee won a George Cross for his bravery during an air raid on Birkenhead Docks on 26 September 1940.

A shunter called Norman Tunna was on duty that night and like the other staff had been busy trying to extinguish fires caused by incendiary bombs. They had been largely successful until a bomb fell on an ammunition train carrying bombs, which was just ready to leave.

A fire sprang out, and Tunna raced to try and extinguish it. First he tried water from the locomotive and then a stirrup pump, but one of the problems of incendiary bombs was that they were quite difficult to put out, so the water had little effect and the bombs in the wagon were getting dangerously hot. Tunna levered apart the bombs that the incendiary was trapped between using his shunter's pole and then, in an act that might well have resulted in his own immolation, picked up the incendiary with his bare hands and hurled it as far away from the bomb-laden wagons as possible. The danger wasn't over yet though, as the British bombs in the wagons were approaching 'cooking off' point where they would explode. Tunna and the locomotive crews resurrected the stirrup pump and sprayed them with water to cool them and gradually the danger receded.

Tunna is largely forgotten today, but his bravery saved a large part of Birkenhead docks from utter oblivion. He certainly deserved his George Cross, as did the GWR recipients of two British Empire Medals and a George Medal, for their bravery in Birkenhead that night.

The danger of invasion gradually receded and the railways predictably found themselves at the core of the war effort, moving men and supplies all over the country. This was only possible because of the multiplicity of routes built in the chaos of the railway manias – there was rarely only one railway that served key towns and cities – and it meant that when one route was closed for maintenance or by enemy action there was usually another way to get men and materials to where they were needed.

As in the Great War, railwaymen were put under a lot of strain, with delays and long shifts adding to the worry about families. In 1940, the level of this strain became apparent in a dreadful accident at Norton Fitzwarren.

On 4 November 1940 the 21:50 overnight train from London to Penzance left Paddington behind a 'King', No. 6028 *King George VI* under the stewardship of Driver P.W. Stacey and Fireman W. Seabridge. It was formed of thirteen coaches and was carrying a whopping 900 passengers, many doubtless resting where they could in the corridors of the coaches because the compartments would have been jammed full. The train had been routed via Bath and Bristol and like many others was running late, in this case, 68 minutes, by the time it reached Taunton. Its arrival at Taunton coincided with that of the 00:50 Paddington to Penzance newspaper train, which was running slightly early and was booked to pass through the station.

With the passenger train running late, the signalman at Taunton decided to let the newspaper train continue through the station on the main line, and send the 21:50 express forward on the relief line, which ran as far as Norton Fitzwarren (this was the stretch of track quadrupled in the 1930s under unemployment relief schemes). Doing this was good operational sense – a few minutes' more delay to the passenger train would make little difference now and the newspaper train should overtake it before Norton Fitzwarren.

The express departed Taunton at 03:44, 14 minutes after it arrived, and a minute later the newspaper train hared through the station at around 45–50mph. Driver Stacey however, thought he was running on the main line and accelerated his train rapidly to try and make up some of the delay. He would have driven this route many times before in all sorts of conditions and would have been used to being unexpectedly switched from the main line to the relief. The blackout conditions may not have helped but Stacey was reading the wrong signals – those for the main line on the right-hand side of his train rather than for the relief, which were on the left-hand side of his 'King'. His fireman was busy shovelling coal into the 'King's' huge firebox to maintain steam pressure and must have assumed Stacey knew what he was doing.

Approaching Norton Fitzwarren station, the signals on the relief line were at danger because Stacey couldn't access the double-track main line beyond there until the newspaper train was safely past. Automatic Train Control was sounded once, and Stacey acknowledged it but didn't brake, still believing he was on the main line. As he got closer to Norton Fitzwarren's danger signal – which he couldn't pass – he saw the newspaper train begin to overtake him on the main line and suddenly realised he wasn't on the track he thought – and what an awful moment this must have been.

His evidence to the inquiry was harrowing:

As this train passed me on my right-hand side, I immediately shut my regulator and applied the brake, being under the impression that we were getting nearer the verging point and I saw this train and the station on my right-hand side which brought to my mind that I was on the Down Relief. At the time I turned to my mate [his fireman] and told him that we were on the Down Relief, and with that the train derailed at the catch point.

Catch points are a last-resort safety measure at critical junctions which de-rail a runaway train rather than allowing it to career onto the main line – and that is what happened to the 21:50 express from Paddington. *King George VI* rolled over on the soft ground, but the two leading coaches passed it on its right-hand side and came to rest parallel to each other diagonally across the Up and Down lines. The third coach 'telescoped' – crushed along its length – against the tender, the fourth was thrown out to the right, the fifth telescoped for about half its length into the third coach, and the sixth was derailed and damaged at the leading end. The other seven coaches remained on the rails and upright.

Twenty-six people died in the crash, as well as Fireman Seabridge. Another victim worked for the Great Western, while thirteen were naval personnel. A further fifty-six passengers were injured and taken to hospital while others suffered shock. A naval Surgeon Commander on the train gave what help he could, and very soon military and railway assistance was on the scene. It was the worst accident the Great Western had suffered in decades.

It could so easily have been even worse: had the newspaper train been running even a few seconds later it would have ploughed into the debris at high speed, drastically raising the death toll. As it was its guard felt something hit his rear coach.

Driver Stacey survived and admitted his error to the subsequent investigation. This found that there were no other reasons for the accident to have taken place. But the investigator, Lieutenant Colonel A.H.L. Mount, also acknowledged that Stacey was under huge stress: his house had been bombed, with regular raids taking place on London at the time, and he was worried about his family. Mount was remarkably humane in his judgement of Stacey:

> The issue is largely psychological; Driver Stacey was fit and did not lack
> rest, but I feel that his breakdown may be partly attributed to operating
> conditions in the blackout, and to the general strain (for example, his
> house at Acton had been recently damaged), which Railway Servants, in

common with other members of the community, are undergoing at the present time.

Mount also recommended that the signals for the Down Main line be placed in their usual position on the left, which might have prompted Stacey to realise he was actually on the relief, but the impression from the report is that it was regarded as a rare and inexplicable aberration from a normally highly competent driver. Stacey would have to live with the consequences of that mistake on his conscience for the rest of his life.

Summer 1941 saw the retirement of Charles Collett as Chief Mechanical Engineer at the age of seventy. His contribution to the Great Western was immense, and in the 'Castles', 'Kings' and 'Halls' he had maintained the level of locomotive excellence established by Churchward. His lead in improving the productivity and precision at the railway's key engineering centres of Swindon, Wolverhampton and Caerphilly had also proven well judged, particularly given the demands of the war. Against that must be set his refusal to deviate from Churchward's standards when a different approach might have been appropriate. The 'Kings', as good as they were, might well have been even better had Collett looked afresh at Pole's power challenge, while in the 1930s, it was Stanier on the LMS who showed what could be done by developing Swindon principles. Collett was something of a withdrawn man – perhaps shy would be a better description – and he certainly never had anything approaching the rapport with the design staff that Churchward had. Collett's reign certainly wasn't inspired in the way Churchward's was, but he provided the Great Western with locomotives and carriages of a standard that took the LMS and LNER until the late 1930s to equal and surpass.

Collett was succeeded by Frederick William Hawksworth, a Swindonian raised in the Great Western's traditions. Born in January 1882, he was fifty-nine when he reached the top job so he wouldn't have long to make an impact before he retired, and the war prevented him from having much freedom. In his official portrait, Hawksworth appears rather stern (as did most of the CMEs, it must be said) with his left arm folded firmly on the desk and his writing hand rather forcefully posed on an open page. He was more open to new ideas than Collett, but it would be a little while before he could implement them.

With the entry of the United States into the war from December 1941 and the inevitability that its army and air force would use Britain as a springboard for an invasion of Europe, more capacity enhancements were pushed forward. More passing loops where freight trains could be overtaken by faster trains were installed, and the Didcot, Newbury & Southampton route took on considerable strategic importance, and was closed to passengers entirely from 4 August 1942 until 8 March 1943 for line doubling to take place. It had been rather lightly used before the war, but now it was a north–south connection which bypassed virtually all the other busy main lines.

Some of the most important movements were of troop trains, and in his book *Firing Days*, Harold Gasson recounted a remarkable tale of how he and his driver set out to prove to American soldiers that their antiquated 'Duke' No. 3283 *Comet* could really run. The soldiers were making fun of the locomotive – hardly surprising given its appearance – and had upset Gasson and his mate.

After taking the troop train from Didcot East Junction to Newbury (it had started in Birkenhead, where the troops presumably disembarked from a ship) Gasson asked the signalman to phone ahead and get his counterparts further down the line to place the single line tokens in special racks for Gasson to pick up at speed, wearing a thick leather glove for protection. He wrote:

Through Litchfield we were on a falling gradient of 1-in-106, and we went through like the 'Bristolian'. The token which I threw onto the post went round and round like a spinning top and when I picked up the token for the Whitchurch section the speed was such that it flew back, hitting the tender with such a thump that it knocked out a great lump of paint.

At Sutton Scotney the troops departed, having stopped their card games in order to bet on whether Gasson would miss a token exchange. One Sergeant was a former railwayman in the States and had won heavily by backing Gasson all the way. As a gesture of thanks, he gave the enginemen a carton of 500 cigarettes.

The war effort was all consuming. Newbury Racecourse – famous for its race-day specials in happier times – was turned into a supply depot by the United States army and Gasson mentions passing the winning post opposite the grandstand in the cab of a steam locomotive! *Firing Days* is a superb account of non-express Great Western running during the war, which comes highly recommended.

Women were extensively employed on a range of duties – far more so than in the Great War – and did good work. In a bid to reduce delays caused by loading and unloading luggage at stations, many were employed as travelling porters, helping to transfer luggage at their stations, and then boarding a train to help load and unload at each of the stations the train called at. These women made a huge difference to the punctuality of trains yet the importance of their contribution is only just coming to be recognised today.

Other women worked in signalboxes or as guards, and many as engine cleaners. It was made clear from the outset that their appointments were for the duration of the war only, but even so they were largely treated as equals by the men, and were allowed to join the National Union of Railwaymen. Some of the jobs could prove tricky for women unused to moving heavy weights – some of the levers in signalboxes were extremely stiff to pull backwards and release – but most not only accepted the work; they flourished in their roles.

It wasn't just women – some Italian prisoners of war were put to work on the railways, particularly after the deposing of Mussolini in 1943 – and inevitably they got the hard, physical work of cleaning locomotives, shovelling coal and ash and more besides. Some, however, were former railwaymen and when they came into contact with the Great Western men, that common bond which seems to tie railway workers the world over broke down the barriers. Difficult circumstances can be a great leveller.

Swindon Works, of course, was used to the full, building components for guns, heavy bombs and much else but perhaps its most interesting jobs were the construction of fifty superstructures for midget submarines, and landing craft for the amphibious landings that began from 1943, first in Sicily, then Italy and finally in 1944, in Normandy. All of this was in addition to the railway work that the site still had to perform.

Hawksworth finally made his mark on locomotive design in 1944, with the introduction of a modified version of the 'Halls', inevitably known as 'Modified Halls'. He departed from old tradition by simplifying the frame arrangement at the front end, and abandoning the complex cylinder and smoke box castings in favour of separate cylinders. At a stroke it removed one of the great structural weaknesses of Churchward and Collett's locomotives and made manufacture simpler. He was also planning a big new 'Pacific' to supplement and possibly replace the 'Kings', and a new type of express passenger 4-6-0 to sit somewhere between a 'Hall' and a 'Castle' in terms of power and capability.

The war might have been nearing its climax as far as the Allies were concerned but the Germans' V1 flying bombs resulted in a second blitz on London and the South. Unlike the manned bombers, it was completely unpredictable as to when and where these weapons landed. At this time, restrictions on running extra trains in the aftermath of D-Day led to a dangerous situation at Paddington, when the station had to be closed because of overcrowding as people tried to get away to safer areas. It was a similar scene at Waterloo and Euston.

The Great Western called up engine crews and marshalled trains of empty coaches at Old Oak Common to disperse the crowds but the government refused to relax the restrictions and as the crowds mounted, so did the devastation a flying bomb would cause. Eventually Sir James Milne threatened to contact the highest levels of government to get permission to do what was so obviously needed, and finally the Ministry of War Transport relented. It could have been so much worse.

The Second World War showed Britain's railways at their very best. Freed from the constraints of road competition (petrol rationing eliminated much of it almost by default), all of the railway companies had performed prodigious feats in moving traffic of far greater intensity and importance than anything in peacetime. It had come at a huge price, however. Maintenance of track and structures had been deferred because of material shortages, and any repairs which took place to bomb-damaged buildings were temporary and hasty. Locomotives and rolling stock earmarked for replacement had eked out another few years of existence, and the staff, like everyone else, were exhausted.

Matters were made worse still by the government's financial arrangements, which paid the railways a fixed fee for all of their services. Any surplus made beyond that from revenue was to go directly to the Treasury. Given the amount of military traffic running on the railways, this effectively amounted to the railways and their shareholders subsidising the government. Under normal circumstances, the railways would have expected to see their revenues increase dramatically by virtue of the extra traffic, but the capping arrangement imposed by Whitehall evaded this and couldn't begin to fund the repairs needed by the end of the war. By 1945, even if sufficient funds and manpower had been available, O.S. Nock estimated that there was a fifteen-month maintenance backlog for track, a two-year backlog in locomotive construction, and a three-year backlog for carriages. The railways were worn out and the government was refusing to play fairly.

The Great Western suffered casualties in the war too, and of the 15,000 members of staff serving in the forces or full-time civil defence, 444 were killed or injured, 155 were reported missing, and 271 were prisoners of war. Casualties amongst GWR staff while on company service amounted to 68 killed and 241 injured, while 88 employees were killed and 255 injured while off duty.

*

The election of Clement Attlee's Labour government in 1945 muddied the waters further because an extensive programme of nationalisation was planned which included the railways, waterways, and long-distance road haulage services. Unlike the 1923 Grouping, however, nationalisation was quite popular amongst staff, who felt the railways had worked well under central control.

The management disagreed, which was unsurprising as the Great Western was still a profitable company which could pay its shareholders a worthwhile dividend (5 per cent in 1946), and plans to develop its operations continued despite the likelihood of state control being introduced.

On the locomotive front, Hawksworth introduced his 'County' 4-6-os. They were two-cylinder locomotives with a boiler based on that used on the Stanier '8F' 2-8-os of which some were built in Swindon during the war. With a tractive effort of 32,580lbs they were theoretically more powerful than a 'Castle' but this was another misleading case of relying on tractive effort to judge power. The 'Counties' were intended for fast express work on steeply graded routes which the 'Castles' sometimes struggled with because their four-cylinder layout didn't provide enough torque at low speeds. With a boiler pressed to 280psi, above even the 250psi of the 'Kings', the great strength of the 'Counties' was in hill climbing. Here, the boiler pressure meant the driver could maintain full throttle and let steam pressure drop quite a way when climbing a hill, knowing that there ought to be time to build it up again on the way down. This technique is known as 'mortgaging' the boiler pressure and it allowed the 'Counties' to maintain time on routes such as that between Newton Abbot and Penzance. What the 'Counties' couldn't and weren't designed to do was to maintain high speeds with heavy loads for long periods of time: for that, the 'Castles' and 'Kings' were unsurpassed on the Great Western.

Some services were accelerated from 1946 after wartime restrictions were removed; then, because the best Welsh steam coal was earmarked for export in a bid to restore Britain's balance of payments, a whole host of steam locomotives were converted to oil firing. This was a similar rationale on the Great Western as electrification – to reduce the lengthy coal hauls to Devon and Cornwall from Wales – but it fell apart even though the Minister of Transport had ordered 1,217 locomotives nationwide to be converted to oil firing. There wasn't enough foreign currency to import the oil! It was a crazy decision, though in fairness, the oil-fired locomotives performed extremely well.

In November 1946, the Transport Act was introduced, making provision for bringing the railways into public ownership. At its second reading, the Chancellor of the Exchequer, Hugh Dalton, attempted to justify the nationalisation by saying: 'This railway system of ours is a very poor bag of assets. The permanent way is badly worn. The rolling stock is in a state of great dilapidation. The railways are a disgrace to the country. The railway stations and their equipment are a disgrace to the country.'

That dilapidated rolling stock included those designs as brilliant as Gresley's 'A4's, Stanier's 'Duchesses', 'Black Fives' and '8Fs', and the 'Castles' and 'Kings' of the Great Western. The railways weren't a disgrace; they were just worn out because the government had reneged on its obligation to pay them properly for their war service. Dalton's statement was irresponsible and inaccurate – and sadly, has been echoed by successive generations of politicians since who wouldn't know a train if it crashed into their front rooms. The die for nationalisation was cast and the date was set for 1 January 1948. There was just time for Hawksworth and the Great Western to re-establish the 'Castle' production line once more, and to usher in the jet age to the rails.

The 'Castles' were, by 1946 when production resumed, an old design but still a good one for its operational remit and hadn't really been improved on by any other railway company. Hawksworth believed that by increasing the level of superheating he could increase their power and efficiency, but except in small details they were identical to *Caerphilly Castle* of 1923. I have criticised Collett's reluctance to depart from old standards but in the case of the last

'Castles' it was difficult to argue against further construction because there was no guarantee Hawksworth could design anything better. Certainly, Stanier had tried and failed on the LMS with his 'Jubilees'. The last 'Castle' built by the Great Western was No. 7007 *Ogmore Castle*, in July 1946.

At the same time, Hawksworth hoped to make a quantum leap in traction power by using a jet engine in a railway locomotive. Gas turbines can produce a lot of power from a very small package and Hawksworth wanted to build on experience gained by the Swiss in this pioneering technology.

Hawksworth ordered a pair of gas turbine locomotives, one from Brown-Boveri in Switzerland and the other from Metropolitan-Vickers in Britain. Both locomotives were gas-turbine electrics, whereby the jet engine drove a generator which supplied current to electric traction motors on the axles. The ultimate aim, had the Great Western remained private, was probably to develop a gas-turbine locomotive fuelled by pulverised British coal, but this was soon put to rest by the nationalised British Railways.

Given what was known about jet engines at the time, using it in a locomotive seemed to make a lot of sense. Experience since, however, has shown that trains powered by gas turbines need constant power outputs to work efficiently. The typical cycle of railway operation with alternating demands for high and low power doesn't suit them at all, and they are very inefficient as a result.

The decision to explore gas-turbine propulsion made a lot of sense in technological terms but there was another element to it, and that was to secure power and influence in the forthcoming British Railways for the Great Western. All of the railways were pursuing high-technology projects in the last three years of their independent existence. The LNER was electrifying the Manchester to Sheffield via Woodhead line; the LMS had ordered a pair of main line diesel locomotives; the Great Western planned gas turbines, and the Southern trumped the lot by ordering a new main line diesel, continuing its electrification programme, and developing a radical new steam locomotive called

Leader. In isolation, all of these were worthy of investigation but with nationalisation virtually guaranteed by way of the Labour Party's hefty Parliamentary majority, wouldn't the 'Big Four' have been better off trying to trim costs and maximise profitability for their shareholders? This technological jostling would certainly prove useful to the embryonic British Railways in gaining insight into which technologies were most suitable but it all cost money and that was in short supply immediately after the war.

Chapter 22
The Last Years

In 1947, the Great Western's last year of independent existence, it operated 3,737 route miles of railway, 3,857 steam locomotives, 8,368 coaches, 87,403 wagons, sixteen docks, five hotels, owned 3,831 houses and employed 113,601 staff. The year would also see Princess Elizabeth and Philip of Mountbatten announce their engagement and fulfil their marriage vows in Westminster Abbey. Tommy Lawton became the first £20,000 footballer in a move from Chelsea to Notts County, and the coal industry was nationalised. At the start of the year though, most Britons couldn't have cared less about this, because they were freezing cold.

The winter of 1946–7 was the coldest on record and by the end of January, Plymouth in Devon had received almost a foot of snow in less than twenty-four hours and on higher ground it was deeper still. On the Devon banks, the snow was drifting and it soon brought the Great Western Main Line to a standstill. At the top of Hemerdon Summit, 6½ miles east of Plymouth, the line was blocked. It took until 14:44 for the 08:45 Plymouth to Paddington to be released from the snow; at Newton Abbot the snow was 2ft deep and blocking points, and difficulties mounted across the country. The Great Western wasn't alone – other railways and roads were blocked, telegraph wires sagged under the strain of ice, and transport slowed to a crawl.

The cold weather sent demand for coal through the roof and the hard-pressed mines weren't able to cope. Even if they had been, it was questionable whether the railways could move the coal quickly enough or unload it. There was a national shortage of wagons, with 200,000 waiting repairs, and some mines even had to close because there were so few available. Power generation started to stutter through lack of supplies and factories were forced to close due to lack of electricity and coal. The railways had to trim services too, with sixty local weekday trains cancelled on the Great Western alone. Services that did run were extended to try and fill the gaps but bit by bit, services got back to normal. So began the last year of the Great Western.

The thaw was followed by gales which blew part of the roof off Didcot station and even ripped signals clean out of the ground – this was then followed by a lengthy drought in the summer which buckled rails, forcing many repairs or the slowing of trains to a crawl over the affected stretches of track.

This was not a vintage year for the Great Western on any level, but despite all of this the Great Western's staff gave their very best to the last. In the very final issue of *Great Western Magazine*, Sir James Milne wrote: 'Every possible effort will be made to make the new administration a success, and I know that, in the duties entrusted to you, you will worthily uphold the traditions which have so long been associated with the name of our great company.'

Those efforts would not include Sir James, however. He had been approached to chair the Railway Executive, the body which would oversee policy on the new nationalised railway but he refused the post, choosing instead to retire at the age of sixty-four.

The last rites of the Great Western were held on 31 December 1947. Paddington station was as brilliant as ever but there was no grand formal farewell. As the clock ticked towards the departure of the 23:50 to Plymouth, a few railway staff and enthusiasts gathered at the ends of the platforms to mark the occasion. The guard waved his handlamp and blew his whistle, and No. 5037 *Monmouth Castle* pulled away from Brunel's old cathedral with crisp exhaust and quiet assurance, in the way only a Great Western locomotive could. Even before it reached Reading, *Monmouth Castle* would no longer be a Great Western locomotive – it would belong to British Railways. After 112 years of existence, the Great Western Railway was extinguished, though still profitable and with its reputation intact.

The last Annual General Meeting was held on 5 March 1948 at the Great Western Royal Hotel, Paddington. With no resolutions to put before the shareholders, all that needed to be announced were the details of the final payout, and the meeting lasted just twenty minutes. Shareholders received a final dividend of 7.25 per cent, a rate few companies could manage today, and when a proposal was put by some shareholders offering the directors compensation for loss of office, the directors declined to a man – the only directors of a 'Big Four' railway to do so. Even in the very last act of the Great Western Railway, its servants put others first.

*

The magnitude of the change to Britain's railways imposed on 1 January 1948 was vast; it had a greater effect than the grouping of 1923, and probably even than privatisation in the mid 1990s. The grand old traditions of the Great Western and those more recently won by the LMS, LNER and Southern were replaced by a gaping uncertainty about what would happen next.

Initially, little changed; most of the former Great Western was renamed as British Railways Western Region, although a few rumples in the regional boundaries were ironed out, such as the GWR shed at Crewe Gresty Lane, which was transferred to the London Midland Region. The locomotives, carriages and wagons were still all Great Western. Most retained their old identity, save for a few tender locomotives which had the Great Western insignia replaced with 'British Railways' on their tenders, and the staff still wore their old uniforms. For the first year or so, there was little to suggest the Great Western wasn't still in existence. Better still for the opponents of nationalisation, in a pure act of defiance, No. 7007 *Ogmore Castle* was renamed *Great Western* in January 1948. A further batch of 'Castles' had been planned and would be built under British Railways auspices, as would 'Modified Halls' and a couple of other designs. In a sense, it was business as usual.

But things did change. The Chief Mechanical Engineer was Robert A. Riddles, a graduate from the LMS who had designed the successful

'Austerity' freight locomotives during the war. He wanted British Railways to replace many of the Victorian and pre-Grouping anachronisms that were still running on the rails in 1948, with a new range of standard locomotives and, once funds were available, electrify Britain's key routes. One of his first acts was to hold a comparative series of trials known as the Locomotive Exchanges that would evaluate the best of the 'Big Four' designs and from which it was said the best features would be taken and applied to his new range of locomotives.

The Locomotive Exchanges were much more a public- and staff-relations exercise than a considered engineering study. The Western Region submitted a 'King', 'Hall' and '28xx' for the trials but the extra width and height of them limited the routes on which they could run, meaning they could never get a fair shout. In any case, it was generally accepted that the lessons which could be learned from the single feature that really stood out on the Great Western designs – their excellent boilers – had already been taken on board, applied and developed by Stanier, Fairburn and Ivatt of the LMS. This was hardly surprising, given that Stanier had been instrumental in the design of the 'Castles' and 'Kings' while at Swindon.

The Great Western designs put up reasonable performances but the results of the tests could have been anticipated without too much difficulty. The 'Duchesses' of the London Midland Region were judged to be the most powerful passenger locomotives and the 'A4s' of the former LNER the most efficient; in the mixed-traffic contest the 'West Country' of the Southern Region (which was really an express passenger design and had only been classified mixed traffic to allow its construction in wartime) was the most powerful, but the latest models of the 'Black Five' were more versatile and efficient; and in the freight stakes, the best all-round design was the Stanier '8F' of the London Midland Region. None of this was at all surprising to observers at the time, although there were wide variations in performances between locomotives of the same design on various runs. It didn't help that nobody in Swindon or Paddington seemed particularly bothered about ensuring the Western Region gave of its best.

What would have been more interesting was a comparison of the second-line passenger locomotives – the 'Castles' of the Western, the 'Jubilees' of the London Midland, the 'V2s' of the LNER and a 'Lord Nelson' from the Southern because there was no obvious winner. Despite being the oldest of the four, there was a good chance that a 'Castle' (perhaps No. 7007 *Great Western*!) would have been the best all-round design of its type in Britain. Sadly this never happened.

Most Great Western designs showed a long ancestry but in 1949, the last original Great Western Railway locomotives were built, the '15xx' series of pannier tanks. They made a startling break with tradition by having outside cylinders with Walschaerts valve gear and no running plate. They were the first really modern steam shunting engines Swindon had built, and their short, stocky appearance was backed by a hefty amount of power. They were based around London and Newport and were a frequent sight at Paddington after hauling in rakes of empty coaches. Their power and acceleration meant they could take the coaches into the station quickly and remove them for servicing without blocking the main line for any longer than necessary.

More visible changes to the Western Region's locomotive stud came with the first applications of British Railways' first liveries. The initial plan was for top-link passenger locomotives such as the 'Kings' to be painted blue, second-line passenger locomotives such as the 'Castles' in apple green, mixed-traffic engines in lined black, and freight engines in plain black. The blue scheme looked impressive and suited the locomotives well but on a 'Castle', the apple green looked rather anaemic. In the end, it was decided to paint all passenger locomotives a dark Brunswick Green instead. The dark-coloured liveries looked smart when they were clean but it's difficult to avoid wondering whether the final choice of liveries was decided at Swindon because most of the steam locomotives in service away from the Western Region looked rather drab. Only the former Great Western locomotives could really carry off the Brunswick Green or black liveries convincingly because their copper-capped chimneys, brass safety-valve bonnets and cast numberplates offset the dark tones so nicely. There were exceptions on other regions – the 'Black Fives' and '8Fs' on the London Midland region suited black but they had always been painted this colour in any case – it's fair to say, however, that the Western Region's locomotives carried the nationalised railway's new identity better than any others.

Other than the changes in livery and the addition of smoke box numberplates to aid identification, it was largely business as usual in the early 1950s. The final 'Castle', No. 7037 *Swindon,* was built in August 1950, bringing to a close a lengthy and proud chapter of locomotive history, while pannier tanks of the '94xx' series continued to be built until 1956.

The advent of the British Railways standard steam locomotives did ruffle feathers at Swindon, however: in a speech on 20 May 1953, the Western Region's Chief Regional Officer, K.W.C. Grans, gave a speech at a mayoral lunch. 'Standardisation is now a fetish on British Railways,' he said, 'I believe it may mean standardisation of brains. When you get this it is the end of progress.' Grans added that he would welcome competition to produce new locomotives and stock, arguing that standardisation might prevent new blood coming into the industry. His plea was ignored, and British Railways built 999 steam locomotives in the 1950s until 1960, most of them having horribly short working lives.

British Railways gave the regions a surprising degree of autonomy over their own affairs and once the shock of nationalisation had worn off, Swindon Works once again came to the fore – first by tweaking the 'Kings', 'Castles', 'Counties' and 'Manors' to extract maximum performance from them and then by doing the same to other regions' designs. It was helped immeasurably by the commissioning of a comprehensive static testing plant in the last years of the Great Western, which allowed locomotives to be tested at full stretch on a rolling road. This allowed very precise observations to be made about what was happening on and in a locomotive at any moment, and provided a way of testing modifications in a controlled environment.

What Swindon Works did, under the aegis of Sam Ell, was to

optimise the draughting of a whole range of locomotives. The comprehensive testing plant allowed Ell's team to find that elusive sweet spot where back-pressure of exhaust steam is minimised in the cylinders while still providing enough updraft through the chimney to draw the fire through the boiler tubes. The results revamped a large proportion of the Western Region's steam locomotive fleet in striking fashion. By tweaking the draughting (and on the 'Kings' and 'Castles' fitting double blastpipes and chimneys later on) and introducing a higher degree of superheating to give the steam as much energy as possible, the 'Kings' were more powerful and could sustain their efforts for longer. The 'Castles' became even more free-running and gained a useful extra margin of strength; the 'Counties' sometimes indifferent steaming was revolutionised, and the 'Manors' – a fleet of lightweight 4-6-0s designed by Collett in the late 1930s to run on routes barred to the other 4-6-0s because of weight restrictions – were turned into machines that almost matched bigger locomotives for power. The limit on the 'Kings', 'Castles' and 'Counties' was not now so much the locomotives: it was whether the fireman could shovel the coal in fast enough to maintain the higher outputs they were capable of.

The Swindon modifications were applied to other fleets too, such as the ex-LNER 'V2' 2-6-2s, which had been struggling for steam ever since spark-arresting baffle plates were fitted inside the smokeboxes to reduce the hot embers thrown out of the chimneys, and the ex-LMS 'Flying Pig' 2-6-0s. Again, the performance of these alien locomotives was transformed out of all recognition. It was all just in time for the steam railway's remarkable Indian Summer from the mid 1950s to the early 1960s.

In the mid 1950s, a casual observer on the Sea Wall at Dawlish could be forgiven for not noticing the nationalised railway at all. The engines were a slightly different shade of green perhaps, and the new range of British Railways standard coaches was becoming increasingly common but at a glance, it was pure Great Western. In 1956, the confusion became even greater because British Railways gave the regions more autonomy, and that stretched to the colours of the coaches.

Immediately, the Southern Region reverted to green from the standard BR livery of crimson and cream, the London Midland Region opted for all-over maroon, and the Western Region chocolate and cream. Only the former LNER lines couldn't revert to its pre-grouping varnished teak colours, not least because many of the coaches entering service had metal-panelled bodies.

It was as if the clock had been turned back twenty years and the increasing affordability of photography meant the old Great Western patch was thoroughly snapped, and a fair amount in colour too. There always seems to be a propensity to look back at a time a generation or so before one's own as a kind of golden age, but the 1920s, 1930s and 1950s seem to have stuck in the minds of successive generations as special periods.

It was certainly special for Nick Deacon, now a railway journalist who was a child in the 1950s:

My father hated family shopping in Reading and more often than not he evaded it in favour of a couple of hours at Reading General watching trains go by. I was about three or four at the time and I can still remember sitting on his knee on Platform 4 watching the passage of a fully functioning railway which at the time was essentially still the Great Western and from this sprang my lifelong interest in that legendary company.

A present of an Ian Allan Western Region *ABC* book for my eighth birthday in 1957 springboarded me into a more structured trainspotting 'career'. A schoolfriend had also acquired an *ABC* at the same time, and together this bond of shared interest would see us travel to many parts of the country over the next decade or so, always with the Great Western as the taproot of our interest.

Reading General was always our base and the Bristol end of Platform 5 was THE prime location for trainspotters. The station staff were remarkably tolerant and as long as common sense was seen to prevail (which invariably it did) they left us very much to our own devices.

At the London end of the station if one was ingratiating enough and lucky with the crew of the station's East End pilot locomotive, it was possible to grab an all too brief cab ride from one side of the station and back again. As long as you kept your head out of sight of the signalman in the East Main signalbox you were okay. Those lucky enough to get a cab ride dined out on the experience for weeks!

And so we watched the old Great Western at work. Week after week and season by season the pantheon of passing trains roamed before us. It was a world undisturbed by the implications of the 1955 Modernisation Plan and its clouds that would eventually darken our world. Our ignorance was bliss and for a time unshaken.

The expresses would flash by with their evocative names – we were spoiled for choice. We even had the privilege of enjoying Cardiff Canton shed's magnificently turned out 'Britannias' (a British Railways 4-6-2 of around the same power as a 'Castle') and 'Kings' on the Welsh expresses. 'Kings' to my mind always evoked that fabled land of the West Country and of beaches bathed forever in summer sunshine, so 'Kings' were all about Dawlish and Teignmouth, whereas 'Castles' were more of a roving breed – forever in my mind at least, linked with the gentility of places like Hereford, Worcester, Oxford or Shrewsbury, or at the muckier end of the scale, Birmingham and Wolverhampton. The 'Counties' we regarded as slightly odd, always seeming to creep by with a secretive air about them. We later discovered that they were always associated with the services west of the Tamar; an area even further beyond our comprehension, which helped nurture them as 'rarer species' in much the same way as the 'Manors' used on the Welsh services.

For children such as the young Nick Deacon, British Railways' Western Region was the provider of endless and free entertainment, and when friends came back from holidays in the South-West, he was envious.

I always envied the lucky few of my acquaintances who were able to take a holiday in one of the old recycled Great Western coaches which had been converted into holiday accommodation in the 1930s. These were still dotted around the extremities of the system and always had a strong West Country connection. Situated in sidings at places such as Bampton, Blue Anchor, Fowey, Luxulyan, Marazion and St Agnes, these coaches are now remembered by the children who stayed in them as being the holiday itself rather than a mere base for travelling further afield. It seemed straight from the pages of Enid Blyton – that English dottiness which embraces all the hardships of camping as 'fun' and could never get enough of Punch & Judy and donkey rides.

When the diesels arrived, although the railwaymen knew they meant that steam's number was up, for the trainspotting children on Reading General, they were just another attraction, as Nick remembers:

At this time, the new diesel-hydraulic locomotives were being turned out in increasing numbers and were beginning to displace steam from the top line services. We spotters accepted their appearance and diligently added their numbers to our *ABCs* as well. It was almost as if we expected that the new arrivals would merely complement the existing steam locomotives and exist cheek by jowl with 'proper' engines. If we had thought about it and done some research we would have been horrified.

The spectacle of the railway of the 1950s – with the very best of the 'Big Four' designs doing what they were intended for, and British Railway's handsome new standard locomotives entering service – does tend to disguise the fact that operating profits had turned firmly into losses by then. Much of the decline can be blamed on road competition and increasing, though far from universal, private car ownership but the railway itself must shoulder some of the blame. It was expensive to run and maintain and unable, it seemed, to react swiftly and head-off the competition. To make matters worse, a strike called by ASLEF to harmonise pay and conditions nationally caused huge disruption and drove business off the rails for good, and for a settlement worth about the price of a packet of cigarettes. This was the point where the government really began to lose confidence in the railways.

With losses becoming a significant concern, British Railways went to the Treasury seeking funding for a silver bullet which would eradicate the losses and set the railway fair for future. It was time for the Modernisation Plan.

In my previous book *The Duchesses* I described the Modernisation Plan as a £1.24 billion all-or-nothing gamble to revitalise British Railways and this was as true for the Western Region as it was for the former LMS and LNER routes. Chief Mechanical Engineer Robert Riddle's ambition to gradually replace steam locomotives with electrics and a few diesels was abandoned while his steam locomotive construction programme was still underway, with a new plan to replace steam with diesel as soon as possible.

The rationale was that, because diesels needed less day-to-day servicing than their steam equivalents, British Railways would need fewer of them and that the higher purchase costs would be outweighed by savings in servicing and maintenance. This made a number of high-risk assumptions, the biggest being that the new diesel locomotives would be more reliable than their steam counterparts, and that passengers and freight customers would be attracted back to the rails by this. Advocates of dieselisation also proclaimed loudly that diesels were faster and more powerful than steam locomotives, meaning journeys could be accelerated too.

Sadly the latter view was wrong from the start. The sort of locomotives British Railways wished to impose on the regions were big and heavy, and not that powerful. The best their engines could manage was around 2,000 horsepower, and this was whittled down by losses incurred by the generators, traction motors and other onboard equipment to around 1,500hp for the locomotive to haul a train with. This was no better than a 'Duchess', a 'King' or any of the former LNER 'Pacifics' and when the steam locomotives worked really hard, they could better it for short periods. In terms of power and speed, there were no gains at all to be had from the initial diesels, and levels of reliability and attractiveness were complete unknowns. The Western Region looked closely at the locomotives on offer and realised that even if it bought them, it would still need to double-head trains over the Devon banks and couldn't offer any worthwhile service improvements elsewhere. It decided to look elsewhere for inspiration.

In West Germany, the state-owned railway, Deutsche Bundesbahn, was introducing a range of light but powerful diesel locomotives with marked success. These locomotives used much higher-revving engines than British and American equivalents, coupled to lighter hydraulic transmissions that offered greater torque than was possible with diesel-electric locomotives at the time. The diesel engines themselves weren't as powerful as the slow-revving British designs but they were much smaller and lighter; that meant two could be fitted in the space of just one of the engines used in the most powerful British diesels. The Western Region believed this combination of power and torque with light weight would solve the problems presented by British Railways' choice of diesel locomotives.

In great secrecy, the Western Region developed its proposals and in summer 1955 placed orders for five 2,000hp and five 1,000hp diesel-hydraulics. From the start, these locomotives were compromised by the British Transport Commission's insistence on using conventional heavyweight bodyshells rather than the stressed skin the Western Region wanted and, for the 2,000hp design, three-axle bogies rather than the two axles used in German practice. This meant that the first diesel-hydraulics would be heavy and underpowered for their weight – the opposite of the Western Region's intentions. When the first was built by the North British Locomotive Company in Glasgow, the fears were realised – the new locomotives could pull heavy loads but they couldn't do so very fast. Most of these were named after naval ships, giving these and later diesel-hydraulics their nickname of 'Warships'.

The Western Region then obtained a license to build a derivative of the successful German 'V200' design at Swindon Works. It needed to be shrunk to fit the British loading gauge but it was a much purer execution of the original concept and the first entered service in 1958.

Initial experiences with all the diesel-hydraulics were mixed. The Swindon-built locomotives could perform well but they were unreliable, unproven and weren't able to replace top-line steam in the way the Western Region had intended. Above all, they were still not powerful enough to offer any meaningful acceleration of services.

Not daunted, however, the Western Region called for a lower-powered design of around 1,740hp, the 'Hymeks', which entered service from 1961 and would replace the mixed traffic steam fleet; then came a 2,700hp design which would finally allow the 'Kings' to be superseded – these also entered service in 1961. The latter design had an imposing and elegant bodyshell and all seventy-four were given names starting with the prefix 'Western'. It was yet more Western defiance, though the region at least had the good sense not to give one of its flagship diesel-hydraulics *that* great name!

The diesel-hydraulic fleet was too unreliable; there were problems galore and it wasn't unknown to see many lined up at Swindon Works needing attention. The steam locomotives the Western Region was so keen to replace had to hold the fort, and for a while it looked as if they would work alongside the new arrivals for some time to come.

But quantity eventually has a quality all of its own and as the numbers of diesel locomotives in service increased, it became possible to withdraw steam locomotives from service. In addition, a range of self-propelled diesel passenger trains called Diesel Multiple Units (DMUs), based on the Great Western's diesel railcar concept, were flooding into traffic and displacing steam on branch line and local services. Bit by bit the steam railway was starting to die.

The first sign that the end of the steam railway was really nigh came on 18 March 1960, when the last British Railways steam locomotive was built, appropriately at Swindon Works. No. 92220 *Evening Star* was one of Robert Riddle's British Railways standard '9F' 2-10-0 freight locomotives (probably the finest freight locomotives ever built in Britain). All had been painted in the unlined black before *Evening Star* but Swindon marked the occasion by finishing No. 92220 in express passenger lined green complete with copper-capped chimney. At the final whistle, Swindon had found a way of making British Railways' last steam locomotive its own.

The oddity of *Evening Star*'s construction was that even before it was built, widespread withdrawals of steam locomotives were taking place. Withdrawals of lesser locomotives began in the 1950s but the first major shockwave came in 1962 when the 'Kings' were withdrawn over a period of just eleven months as they were losing their principal duties from London to Birmingham and the South-West to the 'Western' diesels. The first, No. 6006 *King George I,* was withdrawn in February that year. Others followed at intervals throughout 1962 until December, when the last three were abruptly taken out of service. However, one, No. 6018 *King Henry VI,* was sent from storage at Old Oak Common to Swindon for repair in March 1963 in order to work a 'farewell special' for the Stephenson Locomotive Society. It spent a week running on local passenger trains from 19 April around Birmingham before its final fling on 28 April. That day it took a train full of enthusiasts from Birmingham to Swindon Works running a long way round via Southall and Didcot, returning via Didcot, Oxford and Leamington. Shortly afterwards, the locomotive was sent to Swindon where it languished until September, when it was unceremoniously scrapped. Nick Deacon was a horrified observer in the early 1960s:

My first clear intimation that steam was on the wane was a Cornish holiday in summer 1961. Expecting steam to be fully in charge, I was shocked by the numbers of small diesel hydraulics which seemed to be everywhere, and on the main line services, the 'Warships' seemed to hold sway on the expresses. By the time of next year's holiday, steam had been virtually eliminated west of the Tamar . . . it was almost a relief to return to Reading where steam was still in abundance!

A greater shock in early 1962 was the withdrawal of the first 'King', No. 6006. This really did send shivers down our collective spines. What was to follow? We would soon find out.

At the end of December 1962 occurred the first great culling of Western steam locomotives. Class after class was being decimated. First the 'Kings' were eliminated; serious inroads were made into the ranks of 'Castles' and 'Halls' and the legions of pannier tanks and freight locomotive winnowed as if before a combine harvester.

The slaughter accelerated through 1963 but at the back end of the year a small miracle occurred when Swindon suspended its diesel building programme in favour of catching up with the growing number of diesel failures. More importantly for us trainspotters, Swindon also resumed servicing of steam locomotives. Withdrawn steam engines were even patched up and returned to service, such was the shortage of available locomotives of any type.

As 1963 turned to 1964 our local shed, Reading, lost more and more of its traditional allocation of steam locomotives. Gone were the pannier tanks blasting up the incline from the lower level goods yards, the '61xxs' busying themselves on the local passenger turns: the motley collection of 'Halls,' 'Granges' and others were running out too.

I witnessed the closure of Reading shed on 2 January 1965 on a biting frosty day which took the breath away. Our local favourite, No. 4962 *Ragley Hall*, looked forlorn, stripped of her numberplates and in appalling external condition. As I left the shed for the last time, a 'Grange' rattled by on an infrastructure train as if to emphasise the passing of steam. The crisp exhaust beat echoed across the shed buildings from the main line and her exhaust hung in the still air as she headed towards the station.

Although steam locomotives hung on in the Oxford area for another year, for me the pallbearers had already collected the body. For me, it was the end of Great Western steam.

The Western Region was determined to be the first to eliminate steam completely and accelerated withdrawals. From a total of 152 'Castles' in service in 1961, there were 97 left by the end of 1962, 49 by the end of 1963 and just 12 at the end of 1964. For other types, extinction came sooner. The last of the 'Counties' – the most recent Great Western passenger design – went in July 1964 and by then most of the Churchward locomotives had been sent for scrap too.

The death of the steam railway was accelerated by a process of route closures initiated to eliminate loss-making operations. Even before Dr Richard Beeching was charged with slashing railway expenditure, the Western Region was taking its own axe to unprofitable services. The oddity was that when railways lost their passenger services, they often remained open for goods traffic. Invariably this was only a stay of execution because routes now had to justify their existence with even less traffic and, constantly in the background, the road haulage industry was nibbling away at customer after customer.

Where lines didn't close, stations certainly did. Whole stretches of main line were swept clear of unprofitable stations; a pruning exercise which had no consideration for the effect that lopping off branches and reducing facilities would have on the whole tree. Just in Devon and Cornwall, the closure process was intense: the Plymouth to Launceston line closed in 1962 as well as the remaining freight services on the Totnes to Ashburton branch, the Churston to Brixham, Chacewater to Newquay, and Brent to Kingsbridge branches in 1963, while the Helston branch, which lost its passenger service in 1962, succumbed completely in 1964. Twelve stations on the main line between Exeter and Penzance were closed between 1957 and 1964. That scale of closure was just on the Western Region lines in Devon and Cornwall but it was repeated all over the country on a similar and in some cases, much greater scale. Even lines to busy resorts, such as the St Erth to St Ives and Liskeard to Looe branches were slated for closure; both, in the end, were reprieved (it was said that Barbara Castle, Labour Transport Minister in the mid 1960s, travelled on both of them for her holidays and would be inconvenienced by their closure).

It was as if Britain's railway managers had suddenly joined some cult that made them want to commit commercial suicide and it didn't help that fares were credited to the purchase station only – a seaside town might receive hundreds of thousands of passengers a year but it probably wasn't big enough to generate that sort of business in its own ticket office. Under the new rules it would still have to close.

The writing was firmly on the wall for Great Western steam but in 1964, a number of 'Castles' were given a final chance to show what they could do on a special railtour from Paddington to Plymouth returning via Bristol to mark the sixtieth anniversary of *City of Truro*'s 100-mph run. By now, the only top-link turn for the 'Castles' was the Paddington to Worcester 'Cathedrals Express' and in the run-up to the railtour, which would attempt to replicate *City of Truro*'s feat, the 'Castles' in best condition were sent to Worcester shed for fettling up.

Anticipation was keen at Paddington on the morning of 9 May. No. 4079 *Pendennis Castle*, the locomotive that so outshone the much larger 'A1s' in 1925, handled the first leg from Paddington to Plymouth. In a station largely populated by diesels, it looked magnificent, having been polished to a deep sheen. The target was to reach Plymouth in 3hrs 30mins and initially the run went well, with *Pendennis Castle* reaching 96mph near Lavington. The crew and the passengers must have really enjoyed the performance so far and were anticipating even greater things later on but shortly after reaching 96mph, No. 4079's firebars melted under the intense heat of the fire and fell into the ashpan, with firebars and hot coals spilling onto the tracks. There was no way the locomotive could continue much further. *Pendennis Castle* limped in to Westbury where it was replaced by 'Modified Hall' No. 6999 *Capel Dewi Hall* as far as Taunton. There, No. 7025 *Sudeley Castle* was attached and completed the run to Plymouth, arriving just 45 minutes late.

At 16:00, No. 7029 *Clun Castle* backed on to the return 'Great Western' for its turn to Bristol, and hammered up Hemerdon and over the Devon banks to Newton Abbot, then along the Sea Wall and to Exeter, where it arrived on time. Heartbeats on the train started to speed up and fingers were twitching in anticipation of a magical run: if 100mph was likely to be reached anywhere, it would be on the descent from Wellington Bank where *City of Truro* hit or at least approached that mark sixty years before. Speed rose rapidly from Exeter, the double-chimney 'Castle' demonstrating the sprinting acceleration for which the design is renowned. Topping Whiteball at an exhilarating 67mph, *Clun Castle* nosed down and gathered speed: 90mph, 94mph . . . and then Driver Roach eased off. The Western Region civil engineer had imposed an 80mph speed restriction through Wellington, which had to be obeyed. Once clear of the restriction, however, Roach opened *Clun Castle* out again and this time hit 96mph before Norton Fitzwarren and the approach to Cogload Junction again compelled them to slow to 35mph for another speed restriction. Between Cogload and Bristol *Clun Castle* sparkled, with speed consistently in the 80s and occasionally 90s. The second leg of the 'Great Western' arrived in Bristol Temple Meads 9mins 45 secs early, to a rousing reception from those onboard and those at the station who had received word of its progress. The final 'Castle', No. 5054 *Earl of Ducie*, also ran well from Bristol to London but couldn't manage 100mph despite the efforts of its crew. It was perhaps the last great achievement of the 'Castles' in front-line service.

The spectacular run on 9 May really heralded the last gasp of Great Western steam. A deadline of September 1965 was set for the elimination of steam locomotives on the main line, including the use of 'Castles', 'Halls' and 'Granges'. A few trains continued to be steam hauled after that but the last tender locomotives – most of the few remaining 'Granges', 'Manors', 'Halls' and 'Castles' – were withdrawn in December 1965. Some pannier tanks would remain on the books of Western Region sheds for another year but to all intents and purposes, it was almost over. What is thought to be the last scheduled service by a Great Western steam locomotive was on 1 January 1966 on the 17:00 Gloucester to Cheltenham, which was hauled by No. 7029 *Clun Castle*. Although withdrawn and subsequently privately owned, it still worked occasional freight turns between Banbury and Birmingham but, by then, that route had been handed over to the London Midland Region.

There was one final cruel twist of fate for the Great Western. Birmingham Snow Hill and the line to Wolverhampton Low Level were transferred to the London Midland Region in 1963; before long, the ambitious plans to rebuild (many would say wreck) and electrify New Street station made the region's management question whether Birmingham needed two major stations, given the forecast decline in traffic. The decision was made for expresses to stop serving Snow Hill in March 1967. The last through-trains from Paddington were a pair of railtours organised by the famous railway book publisher Ian Allan – the 'Birkenhead Flyer' and 'The Zulu'. The first ran on 4 March, hauled by No. 4079 *Pendennis Castle*, and the second a day later hauled by No. 7029 *Clun Castle*. Snow Hill lingered on, served by a few local trains, until 4 March 1972 when it closed for good. Wolverhampton Low level closed to passengers at the same time.

It was a sorry end for the Great Western's Midlands outposts but by then the spirit of the Great Western had undergone a remarkable resurrection, thanks to four schoolboys standing on a footbridge at Southall, London, in the early 1960s.

Chapter 23
Western Rebirth

Although British Railways was hell-bent on ridding itself of steam in the 1960s, it was also conscious that many of its locomotives could be considered artefacts and should be saved for future generations. In addition to the challenge of deciding what should be saved, the British Transport Commission in charge of the process also had to find homes for anything it did save and that was tricky because, aside from the Bluebell and Middleton railways, which were now running as heritage lines, there were few sites away from the main line railway which were suitable.

Seventy-one locomotives had been selected, but only ten were of Great Western origin. No. 3440 *City of Truro* had been acquired by the LNER after its withdrawal in 1931, for display in the York Railway Museum. A 'Dean Goods', No. 2516, had been saved, and 'Star' No. 4003 *Lode Star*, 'Castle' No. 4073 *Caerphilly Castle*, and No. 6000 *King George V* were all to be part of the National Collection. Space was found too for a '28xx', No. 2818, and one of the final generation of conventional pannier tanks, No. 9400.

Caerphilly Castle was sent to Swindon for cosmetic overhaul and then to the Science Museum but today, volunteers at STEAM, Swindon, believe the overhaul was far from cosmetic. Conscious that *Caerphilly Castle* might be the last chance to demonstrate their workmanship, did Swindon Works undertake a full overhaul of the first 'Castle'? Given the rundown of steam, it might just have been possible because, to a casual eye at least, a cylinder under overhaul could have come from any number of locomotives. The story goes that one could fill No. 4073's boiler with water, light a fire and steam off with a machine overhauled to the most exacting standards of Swindon Works. What a tantalising prospect that is but, with a number of other 'Castles' operational or under overhaul today, it will not happen soon, if ever, as checking *Caerphilly*'s condition would partially destroy the very workmanship that has been preserved.

There were some glaring gaps in the preservation list, however. In an act of wanton vandalism, Churchward had scrapped the original *North* Star and *Lord of the Isles* in the early years of the twentieth century, ostensibly to make space in Swindon Works; and equally unforgivably, the last 'Saints' were withdrawn in June 1953, all scrapped at Swindon. In the early 1960s, it looked as if designs of such significance such as the '43xxs', 'Halls' and '57xx' pannier tanks would disappear without trace, as could many other equally loved but less-glamorous mixed-traffic and tank locomotives. Four particular teenage trainspotters in Southall, London, were outraged by these gaps in the preservation list. Jon Barlow, Angus Davis, Mike Peart and Graham Perry were old enough in 1961 to realise that the railway they knew and adored was being taken away without anyone really having a say in the matter – and they were young enough to believe they could do something to save some of it.

'No "14xx", no "Hall", no "Manor",' Angus wrote years later, 'I was distraught and angry – the world that was my bedrock was to be destroyed. Others must feel the same way. I cycled alongside the grim Great West Road to Isleworth Grammar the next morning. The first person I saw was Jon Barlow. As we chained our bikes up in the racks, I told him, "We have to have a meeting and try and save a '14'." Mike Peart arrived and I told him the same.'

The four young men decided they would try to save one of the charismatic little '14xx' 0-4-2 tank engines, which had been used extensively on push–pull services across the former Great Western network; John Barlow wrote a letter to the main enthusiast publication at the time, *The Railway Magazine*, inviting subscriptions to help acquire one of these locomotives.

It might seem odd today that they opted to try and save one of the smallest designs of Great Western locomotive but in 1961, nobody had bought anything larger than a tank engine for preservation – it simply wasn't conceivable then that enough money could be raised to buy a tender locomotive – nor was there any certainty that a home could be found for one.

Barlow's letter appeared in the August 1961 edition of *The Railway Magazine* and struck an immediate chord with readers, who replied to the appeal with one offering £10 towards the '14xx', a fair amount at the first time of asking. The four lads were joined by a friend, Frank Dumbleton, who spent term-times at boarding school; they then formed a committee to begin organising and formalising the appeal. Frank Dumbleton recalls that first meeting:

It was decided that a committee meeting was needed to draft a quick reply to the respondents before they lost interest. Jon and Angus were the only founder members able to make a meeting the next day, so I volunteered to go along. It was held at Jon's house, and I suggested that we might describe the letter in *The Railway Magazine* as our first tentative step to preserving the locomotive.

'Tentative' was approved as being a good summary of where we were, so the business of the meeting was concluded in just a few minutes. Jon's parents were out, and as his father was a hi-fi buff we decided to try out his equipment. A Sandy Nelson recording of *Big Noise from Winnetka* took Angus's fancy, and we played this over and over again. Jon's parents were also keen winemakers, and Angus raced around the house with a stick, accompanying Sandy Nelson's percussion rhythm by hammering on the demijohns full of fermenting liquid that stood in various locations. That was my introduction to the serious business of railway preservation.

The four teenagers might have been serious about saving a '14xx' but they were still teenagers!

The response to their initial letter proved the group were far from alone in feeling angry and upset about the mass extinction of the steam locomotive: men and women all over Britain felt the same but most didn't believe there was anything they could do to change the situation.

Yet there's a magic time in the teenage years where everything seems possible, and in the absence of anyone telling these four young men that they couldn't buy a steam locomotive, they went ahead and rallied support anyway.

They changed the name of their group to the Great Western Preservation Society to broaden its appeal and the society held its inaugural public meeting on 4 May 1962 at Southall Community Centre, London. It had been dreamt up in a flash of inspired anger and outrage but by the end of the first public meeting, there were enough older and more experienced people offering their support for the Great Western Preservation Society to move forward and raise the money to buy its first locomotive.

The original group had been given a welcome lift earlier in 1962 with the arrival of one of the final outside-framed 'Dukedogs', No. 9017, at the Bluebell Railway, Sussex; then, at the start of 1963, businessman Alan Pegler made the remarkable acquisition of No. 4472 *Flying Scotsman* – the first express passenger locomotive to be acquired by a private individual. Throughout 1962 and 1963–4, the Great Western Preservation Society raised funds to buy a '14xx', getting ever-nearer its target and in March 1964, No. 1466 was acquired by the society for £750. It was to be based at the organisation's Totnes base, where plans were being developed to operate the Totnes to Ashburton line as a heritage railway.

That month, Frank Dumbleton, Angus Davis, and the society's treasurer, Graham Perry, were driven from London to Totnes by the chairman Ken Williams in his Ford Anglia. The society's south-west representative, Peter Lemar, hosted the party for lunch at his home in Torquay and suggested that perhaps they could steam No. 1466 that afternoon. The proposition was too good to resist and although none of them knew how to drive a full-size steam locomotive, Lemar reckoned he had a fairly good idea.

So they travelled the short distance from Torquay to Totnes, where No. 1466 was stabled on a private siding, lit a fire and raised steam and, when they blew the whistle for the first time, people flocked to see what was happening. An old sheet that Frank Dumbleton had brought with him for cleaning rags was stretched between some gateposts to straddle the track, the brakes were released, regulator opened and, as No. 1466 broke the impromptu 'ribbon', the Great Western Preservation Society was in business.

The steaming of the little '14xx' generated a new wave of interest in the society and in June 1964, it was able to acquire a second locomotive, the little 0-6-0 saddle tank No. 1363 – the last saddle tank ever built at Swindon Works. It was just in time – while British Railways was ridding itself of steam with indecent haste, those four angry schoolboys had created an organisation that continues to preserve and conserve the very essence of the Great Western to this day.

The early success of the Great Western Preservation Society – though it soon dropped the 'Preservation' from its title – helped to inspire others to preserve steam railways; just as the last fires were being dropped on the Western Region, a whole host of other such preservation schemes were being prepared. These were made possible because, when railways were closed, there was usually a window of opportunity for a preservation society to establish itself before the tracks were lifted, signalling decommissioned and the route abandoned – and that was how some of the most highly regarded heritage railways today began.

Following Alan Pegler's example, private individuals began to acquire steam locomotives too. Patrick Whitehouse, railway author and presenter of the popular *Railway Roundabout* television series, bought No. 7029 *Clun Castle* in 1966; No. 4079 *Pendennis Castle* was bought in 1964 by Mike Higson and then sold to the Hon. John Gretton and the industrialist William McAlpine – and railway enthusiast's railway enthusiast. In private ownership, these two locomotives performed the last rites at Birmingham Snow Hill in 1967.

By then, British Rail (now so-named, having lost its 'ways' in an attempt to appear more modern) regarded these privately owned steam locomotives as something of a pain and banned them from its routes, with the exception of No. 4472 *Flying Scotsman*, whose owner Alan

Pegler had inserted a clause in the purchase agreement with British Railways in 1963 which guaranteed access to the main line network. The 'steam ban' wasn't watertight though. The Great Western Society had rented Taplow's goods shed from 1965 and this became the epicentre of the organisation's activities in the London area. The locomotives shuttled up and down the goods yard in full sight of the diesel-hauled passenger trains – not on the main line but next to it – until the Western Region's General Manager, Stanley Raymond, saw 'prairie tank' No. 6106 in the goods yard. He was travelling with the man who made that arrangement possible, London Divisional Manager David Pattison, and, turning round to his junior said, 'Funny, I thought we had scrapped all those.'

Pattison realised that Raymond wasn't impressed and arranged a deal with the Great Western Society to relocate its locomotives and carriages to the old Great Western engine shed at Didcot, which was largely invisible from the station. It was a case of 'out of sight, out of mind' as far as British Rail was concerned.

So, on 4 November 1967, with British Rail's steam ban in full force, No. 6106 ran light engine from Taplow to Kensington Olympia and collected two Pullman cars that had been part of Winston Churchill's funeral train, *Isle of Thanet* and *Lydia*. On the way back, three more coaches were collected from Taplow, and the train continued to Didcot. Next, No. 6106 went on to Oxford to collect a pair of ex-LNER sleeping cars used by General Eisenhower in the Second World War.

A month later, on 2 December, the Great Western Society (GWS) decided to move its rolling stock from Totnes to Didcot as well, because the Dart Valley Railway (the original name for today's South Devon Railway) was aiming at a commercial operation with limited enthusiast involvement. Pattison – and he must have been risking the wrath of his superiors – agreed that the society could run a train and, on 2 December No. 6998 *Burton Agnes Hall* hauled the tiny No. 1466 (in light steam to keep its cylinders lubricated) and three coaches from Totnes to Didcot. It was one of the longest journeys the little '14xx' ever undertook.

At Didcot, the GWS shared space with *Pendennis Castle* – which they were seldom allowed to see, let alone touch – and British Rail locomotives that also stabled there. The initial plan was that Didcot would be used as the maintenance base, with trains running on the nearby Cholsey & Wallingford branch line. British Rail's own steam operations finally finished on 11 August 1968 – yet two days before, No. 6000 *King George V* had been released from Swindon to sidings at the cidermaker Bulmers, which had leased the locomotive with a view to it hauling its promotional 'cider train'. In September 1968, the GWS ran a single-coach train all day up and down the Wallingford branch. Huge crowds turned up for a chance to travel behind a Great Western locomotive but many were disappointed – there simply weren't enough seats and few wanted to travel in the vintage bus that was laid on alongside it.

The event never happened again. British Rail banned the society from operating on its metals, and restricted it to Didcot engine shed. The decision forced the GWS to focus its attention on the shed itself, and it began to open the shed to visitors. On open days, it ran shuttle trains up and down a siding but because the tracks officially belonged to British Rail, it needed one of the national railway's locomotive inspectors on the footplate to supervise.

There was one other significant chink in the BR steam ban. London Transport had acquired thirteen '57xx' pannier tanks to haul engineering trains to and from its depot in Neasden when the power was switched off, and in 1969 word got out that one was to pass through Paddington, which it did. So, steam was banned on British Rail unless it suited it. However, No. 7754 was the last ex-GWR locomotive at work in industrial service; originally purchased by the National Coal Board, it was based at Mountain Ash Colliery, and it remained working until 1975.

It wasn't just the Great Western Society that was trying to preserve the old company's memory. Following Tom Rolt's success in continuing operations at the narrow gauge Talyllyn Railway and then Alan Pegler's equally important *reopening* of the Ffestiniog Railway in the 1950s (another Welsh narrow gauge line), the Middleton Railway in Leeds just about beat the Bluebell Railway in Sussex in opening a standard gauge heritage railway in 1960. In 1968 the owners of *Clun Castle* and LMS 'Jubilee' 5593 *Kolaphur* took a lease on a large part of the ex-GWR shed at Tyseley, Birmingham, and started establishing an inspiring collection which remains there today. A year later in 1969, the Dart Valley Railway began public operations on the Totnes to Ashburton line in Devon (though aspirations to run all the way to Ashburton were crushed in 1971 by the A38 dual carriageway, which restricted operations to between Totnes and Buckfastleigh); and in 1970, the Severn Valley Railway started running its first passenger trains between Bridgnorth and Hampton Loade in Shropshire.

These early heritage railways bought many of their locomotives straight out of service from BR, but once steam had finished there was an abundant second source of dozens of Great Western locomotives, thanks to a scrapyard owner in South Wales. The tale of Dai Woodham and his Barry Scrapyard has been told many times because Woodham's actions in the late 1960s provided the bedrock on which the locomotive fleets of virtually all of our heritage railways are built. Woodham acquired hundreds of redundant steam locomotives from British Railways in the 1960s but, rather than scrap them as soon as they arrived, he stored them in the open. There were plenty of carriages and wagons arriving at his yard which were easier to scrap than the locomotives, so his workers cut them up first: the locomotives could be left to rot until the supply of easy work ran out.

Barry Scrapyard became a kind of elephant's graveyard for steam locomotives, and word got round quickly amongst enthusiasts and preservation societies. Suddenly it was possible – for a price – to acquire a locomotive from Barry and many required very little work to get them running again. It was a treasure trove, with a host of locomotives from pannier, 'prairie', 2-8-0 and 2-8-2 tank engines to 'Manors', 'Halls', a '43xx' and one of its '93xx' sisters, as well as 'Castles' and even a pair of 'Kings'. Over time, almost all of these were bought and the vast majority have been restored. Sadly, two of the three major missing gaps in Great Western preservation, the 'Granges' and 'Counties,' never made it to Barry.

The Great Western Society got another boost in 1971 when No. 1466 was selected to be mocked-up as an armoured locomotive for scenes in the film *Young Winston* – and filming would involve breaking the steam ban too. The locomotive was sent to the line between Coelbren Junction and Craig-y-Nos in Wales and remained there while filming took place for two months.

No. 1466 may have evaded the steam ban on a technicality but steam was still barred from passenger trains. However, in 1971 after extensive negotiations, Peter Prior of Bulmers finally won approval to use *King George V* on the main line. All in all, British Rail's vaunted steam ban had barely lasted three years before it collapsed.

The 'King' was in working order when it moved from Swindon to Hereford in 1968 and had been steamed regularly since then. When Inspector Norman Tovey ran the rule over the locomotive, he could find nothing to fault and in preparation for its return to public service, the locomotive undertook a secret trial run from Hereford to Newport on 15 September 1971 to ensure that it was still up to running long distances on the main line. Finally, on 2 October 1971, it hauled the 'Return to Steam' special from Hereford to Tyseley via Newport and Didcot. The reaction of the general public was electrifying. Crowds gathered everywhere the locomotive could be seen all along the route. Many were former Great Western railwaymen and for them, seeing the old company's most famous locomotive was almost too much. It's not an exaggeration to say that tears of joy were shed all the way from Hereford along the train's route by enthusiasts and wellwishers overjoyed to see 'KGV' back on track.

Two days later, the 'King' returned under steam from Birmingham Moor Street to Kensington Olympia and then, on 7 October 1971, returned to its Hereford base with the final leg of the specials from London. These trains were an absolute triumph for railway preservation and an eye-opener for British Rail. Britain's love affair with the steam locomotive, far from having been diminished with the advent of more modern trains, was actually enhanced. Steam was no longer the sole preserve of the hundreds of thousands of rail enthusiasts – by running on the main line, it was accessible to everyone. *King George V* prompted British Rail to re-examine its attitude to steam and bit by bit, it opened up its network once more to locomotives able to pass reasonably stringent railworthiness conditions.

With a secure and large base, other locomotives acquired by GWS members were moved to Didcot, as well as rolling stock. The society had always intended that the collection wouldn't be just locomotives and it was fortunate that former Great Western coaches and wagons had run on the national network until the end of steam, allowing it to save them in working order. British Rail abandoned Didcot shed in the 1970s, retaining ownership of the site but allowing the GWS and John Gretton to coexist together as tenants. It wasn't a particularly good arrangement as neither group could do all they wanted but eventually, Gretton moved *Pendennis Castle* to Market Overton in Rutland.

Then the floodgates opened – after British Rail closed the Taunton to Minehead line in 1971 as well as the Paignton to Kingswear line in 1972, the West Somerset Railway took up the baton for the former, beginning operations in 1976; the Dart Valley Railway bought the latter and ran its first solo services almost immediately, in 1972. Great Western preservation was becoming established and these two railways as well as the Dart Valley Railway, alongside the GWS, formed the vanguard of a dizzying array of heritage railways based on former Great Western routes. Bit by bit, the Severn Valley Railway extended south towards the former junction station of Bewdley, Worcs, while in Wales, on the former Ruabon to Barmouth line, Llangollen station was reopened in 1975 which formed the basis of today's Llangollen Railway.

One of the ironies of steam preservation was that by 1977 the last of the diesel-hydraulics had been withdrawn – the very ones which the Western Region had rushed into service to replace steam. Throughout their careers the diesel-hydraulics had never proved as reliable or cheap to maintain as their diesel-electric counterparts. Although they were every bit as capable when they did work, as the 1970s progressed, British Rail regarded them as expensive luxuries that were becoming increasingly redundant with the spread into service of air-conditioned and electrically heated coaches which the hydraulics couldn't provide a power supply for. There was another departure too – the Australian company Hammersley Iron Propriety Ltd had bought *Pendennis* Castle for entertaining its staff and the locomotive departed Britain's shores later that year after a final farewell railtour. In 1978 it was possible to see Great Western steam locomotives on the main line and at a host of heritage railways, but the few diesel hydraulics that survived were restricted to heritage railways. The steam ban of the 1960s had now turned into a ban for preserved diesels!

Throughout the early 1980s, railway preservation blossomed, with more schemes starting and existing railways establishing themselves as vital and popular attractions in their own right. In addition, as the amateurs who acquired locomotives from Barry Scrapyard gained experience, they became more and more professional, every year restoring engines to working order which barely a decade before had been regarded as no-hopers. By the mid 1980s, it was possible to see Great-Western-based heritage railways and projects from Cornwall through Devon to Somerset, Gloucestershire, the Forest of Dean, the West Midlands and Shropshire to Wales. There was one oddity in Wales too – the Vale of Rheidol Railway remained in British Rail ownership until 1989, complete with steam locomotives! The last standard gauge trains might have run in 1968, but BR ran its last steam trains more than twenty years later, and the three Swindon-built steam locomotives even carried the company's Rail Blue livery and double-arrow logos.

Things were looking up on the main line railway too after the demise of the diesel-hydraulics. The Western Region was the first to receive the new 125mph High Speed Trains in the late 1970s, and these superb trains – to my mind without doubt the finest ever to run in Britain in any period – helped transform the railway. For a while in the 1970s and 1980s, British Rail operated more trains at 100mph or faster than anywhere in the world, and there are credible tales of Western Region drivers taking full advantage of Brunel's 'billiard table' to work the new trains up to speeds of more than 140mph with no problems and no risk to passengers. Although freight was continually being lost to roads, the advent of the High Speed Trains gave the railway a fillip. I remember my first ride on one as a child, and it was like a massive leap into the future. The trains looked streamlined and ultra-modern – they still do – and the sound of the turbochargers spooling up as the trains departed was like a million banshees screaming for release. The High Speed Trains were noisy but they were also comfortable and stylish – Churchward would have loved them. Better still, towards the middle of the decade, there was the possibility of a fantastic party.

Chapter 24
Stabbed in the Back

Nineteen eighty-five was supposed to be a year of celebration to mark 150 years since the Act of Parliament which set the Great Western Railway on its way. British Rail was heavily involved, sanctioning an impressive series of steam-hauled charter trains over Western Region metals using many of the locomotives restored to main line condition. It even agreed to a special steam-hauled freight train using '28xx' No. 2857 from its base on the Severn Valley Railway to Newport, Wales as a finale to the celebrations. An exhibition train would tour the old Great Western, showing artefacts and films to visitors, while *City of Truro* and the broad gauge replica of *North Star* were also to return to steam, the former returning to the main line, the latter obviously being extremely restricted to a short demonstration track.

Before the celebrations started, *Steam Railway* magazine took full advantage of the hubris around the anniversary to perpetrate a hoax that still gives some Great Western enthusiasts the shudders: it showed a photograph in its April issue of *City of Truro* painted in British Railways black, a livery it never carried. Digital manipulation of images wasn't possible then and the prank was in fact arranged with the Severn Valley Railway's Chief Engineer, Alun Rees, for one side of the engine to actually be painted black before the final coats of (authentic) green.

Reactions were extreme: readers by the score wrote in and their letters were published in the following issue. Many were 'aghast', 'astonished' or 'appalled', one reader wrote to say that he was 'recovering from shock' after seeing the picture, another said it 'was more than flesh and blood can stand'. The anger was tangible – it may have been a coat of paint, but defacing a Great Western icon in this way really did upset people and showing, if proof were needed, that thirty-seven years after nationalisation, passions for the Great Western still ran strong. All was revealed soon enough and most in the end appreciated the April Fool's joke. It would be a rare moment of levity that year.

The curtain raiser to the Great Western 150 celebrations was the 'Great Western Limited' railtour from Bristol to Plymouth, double-headed by No. 6000 *King George V* and No. 7819 *Hinton Manor*. It didn't go to plan, however. At Taunton, just 46 miles into the journey, the 'King' suffered a hot axle bearing on its tender and had to be removed from the train. The smaller 'Manor' took it forward with assistance from a diesel but it suffered an almost identical failure and had to come off the train at Exeter. The 'Great Western Limited' arrived in Plymouth behind a pair of Class 37 diesels. It wasn't a good start. Alun Rees, who was travelling with *Hinton Manor* had brought a spare bearing just in case of a failure and with help was able to repair the locomotive overnight. In the meantime, No. 4930 *Hagley Hall,* another Severn Valley Railway-based locomotive, was sent to Plymouth overnight, and the pair successfully returned the train, as planned, to Bristol the following day.

Then, on 15 May, the British Railways Board's engineering sub-sidiary British Rail Engineering Limited (BREL) dropped the mother of all bombshells. Swindon Works was to close by May 1986 with all 2,300 staff made redundant. The timing couldn't have been crueller.

Unsurprisingly staff at the works immediately withdrew their cooperation with the GWR 150 celebrations, which would have seen a display of relics and locomotives taking centre stage at the Great Western's heart, and also stopped examinations of *King George V*'s tender wheelset. The disgruntled staff also refused to allow volunteers to inspect it. David Rees of the National Union of Railwaymen spoke for many when he said: 'We have nothing to celebrate here. If it wasn't for this works there wouldn't have been a GWR; there is no way GWR 150 can go ahead here.' In the circumstances, it was hard to argue with his position.

The announcement was cynical, badly timed and heartbreaking.

The railway works had created Swindon and provided employment for generations. The craftsmanship of the men and women who worked there was incredibly highly regarded even at the time. Their skill and dedication was in no doubt and they knew that cuts were likely, but were not prepared for complete closure. (Ironically, in his seminal book *Gone With Regret*, George Behrend had suggested as far back as 1962 that Swindon Works would close, so this distinguished gentleman was one of the few who wasn't surprised.)

A fightback began, with Thamesdown Borough Council allocating £42,000 to oppose the closure of the works – and a petition had scored 14,000 signatures by the beginning of August. It was all to no avail. *Steam Railway*'s cover for August 1985 summed up the fury the announcement generated. Inscribed on a gravestone on a specially commissioned cover were the words: 'Here lies Great Western 150 killed by British Rail's disregard for the skill of the men of Swindon and the G.W. tradition. May God forgive them for there are many who never will.'

Many of the other Great Western 150 celebrations took place but the impending closure of Swindon Works was always in the background. Niggling problems and failures affected a number of other main line railtours, but amongst the bright spots was the return to the main line of *City of Truro* on 3 September, while No. 2857 hauled its main line freight train on 9 September.

As the closure of Swindon Works neared in March 1986, the outlook was bleak for many of the workers, particularly those over forty-five years old who faced redundancy and uncertainty. The finely honed skills they had simply weren't required in the new high-tech Swindon, and with so many jobs needing to be found, older men found themselves callously discriminated against by new employers who wanted younger and cheaper staff.

Andrew Bowley, aged twenty-one, had just finished as an apprentice and spoke to the BBC shortly after the announcement of the closure:

My family have been involved with the railway for the last four or five generations. My father started as an apprentice with the GWR and he reckoned working on the railway inside the works was a secure future.

To a certain extent I have got used to the idea of the works' closure. For a person my age it's totally different from those my dad's age . . . older men have no chance in life to get a job. I feel sorry for them – it's like they've been stamped on and they're just being tossed onto the scrapheap . . . it's a total waste really.

As the flag was lowered on 27 March 1986, the 1,000 or so men remaining pocketed their redundancy cheques – an average of £7,000 each – and walked out, almost as if it was another working day. Some lingered, unable to believe the axe had fallen, while others went to the pub to reflect on an uncertain future.

Viewed dispassionately, there was little doubt that at the time, BREL had far too much capacity for the work the modern railway required. The high levels of servicing demanded by the steam and early diesel locomotives were no longer required, and the new coaches and diesel multiple units that entered service from the early 1970s also required less attention. The railway of 1985 used fewer trains more intensively than even a decade before and this process was going to continue through to the present day. At least one of its major facilities had to go and the axe fell on Swindon; then, over time, as rolling-stock orders dried up through the 1980s and 1990s, trainbuilding stopped at all bar one of the other works too. Doncaster, Crewe, Eastleigh . . . all are now, at most, overhaul centres, with only Derby building new trains.

Perhaps the most telling reason for BREL selecting Swindon for closure was that at the time, the town was reputed to be the fastest growing in Europe, and the 120-acre site on which the works stood, worth a whopping £16 million.

Chapter 25
Western Legacy

For many years, the Great Western's formidable legacy was ignored by British Rail. Although it was ignored, however, the GWR was never entirely forgotten; like a half-remembered poem, it was always there as a kind of background noise, and one which must have been maddeningly difficult to tune out by those who wanted to disregard it.

But if the 'big railway' seemed content to forget its roots, the heritage railway movement certainly didn't – it grew and grew and grew. Richard Croucher, Frank Dumbleton and the other young men who formed the Great Western Society could have had no idea of how much of the Great Western Railway would be preserved, and of the remarkable variety of railways there are today.

My nearest heritage railway is the Bodmin & Wenford Railway in Cornwall. Starting at Bodmin General, a picture-postcard Great Western branch-line terminus, it runs in a 'Y' shape outwards to Bodmin Parkway on the Cornish Main Line in one direction, and towards Boscarne Junction in the other. Steeply graded and tightly curved, the railway's collection of GWR locomotives have no choice other than to emit that beautiful crisp Swindon 'bark' as they get their trains moving.

In Devon, the two lines once owned by the Dart Valley Railway, the Totnes to Buckfastleigh and Paignton to Kingswear routes, are now under separate ownership. The former has become the South Devon Railway, a wonderfully restored branch line with *Tiny*, the only surviving original broad gauge locomotive in existence, at its Buckfastleigh museum. The Kingswear line, by contrast, is operated by the Dartmouth Steam Railway & River Boat Company which runs a more conventionally commercial service. Some purists deride it for its pursuit of profit, but it is a beautiful route that combines with a boat trip to Dartmouth and is deservedly popular.

The West Somerset Railway, at 21 miles, is now Britain's longest standard gauge heritage railway and showcases a classic GWR secondary route to an important resort. It has even taken full advantage of GWR standardisation to adapt a 'prairie' tank into a small 2-6-0 tender locomotive, which was envisaged but never built. No. 9351 might not be a genuine GWR design but it is pure Great Western nonetheless. Near London, there is a Great Western Society base at Southall and, on the old Birmingham route, is the Chinnor & Princes Risborough Railway, a fairly recent arrival but one which is blossoming.

At Didcot, the GWS headquarters has developed into a fabulous attraction which offers a slice of everything from the broad gauge to branch lines and the glamour of the expresses – as well as, of course, its atmospheric engine shed and coaling stage. Accessed from Didcot Parkway station, it's a huge site that is even building new engines – a recreated 'Saint', No. 2999 *Lady of Legend*, a 'County' 4-6-0, and a steam railmotor.

At Swindon, little remains of the original works today but alongside the sympathetically developed McArthur Glen retail outlet is the STEAM museum, which tells the story of the GWR accessibly and without pathos – here you can also see some of the most significant locomotives and artefacts at close quarters. If you visit Swindon, there's also the Swindon & Cricklade Railway offering a slice of branch-line nostalgia.

The Gloucestershire Warwickshire Railway runs from Toddington to Cheltenham Racecourse on a genuine piece of GWR main line. It might be single track today but this was the route that the South-West to Birmingham expresses ran on. The railway is extending northwards towards Honeybourne and, it is hoped, a main line connection. The Forest of Dean Railway at Norchard, meanwhile, comes achingly close to recreating the sleepy and rustic nature of the routes in that often overlooked region, while near Birmingham, Tyseley Locomotive Works holds open days to showcase its collection and restoration projects, and is the base for Vintage Trains, which runs steam locomotives on the main line.

The Severn Valley Railway extended from Bewdley to Kidderminster in the 1980s, giving it a total length of 16 miles, and since then has transformed disused railway land into a spectacular terminus station based on authentic GWR plans. Sadly the original timber-framed main line station was demolished and replaced with a typically utilitarian structure – but many are fooled into thinking the SVR station is original! The SVR is amongst the most popular steam railways in Britain, thanks to its beautiful scenery, pretty stations and authentic atmosphere. Nearby is the Telford Steam Railway, which hopes ultimately to run to the tourist honeypot in Ironbridge.

In Wales, you can still travel on the Welshpool & Llanfair Light Railway; the Vale of Rheidol was sold in 1989 and runs today, and part of the Corris Railway is being preserved too – a fantastic hat-trick of the GWR's narrow gauge operations. Standard gauge preservation is well represented in Wales by the Llangollen Railway which now runs west to Carrog with plans to go further to Corwen, as well as the Gwili, Pontypool & Blaenavon, and Barry Island railways – all well worth a visit and all completely different.

You can even travel on the main line at speed behind a Great Western Railway locomotive. Both the 'Shakespeare Express' from Birmingham to Stratford-upon-Avon and 'Torbay Express' from Bristol to Kingswear run regularly through the summer. To stand at an open window on the 'Torbay Express' as it flies along the Sea Wall behind a 'King' or a 'Castle' is a magical experience.

Great Western Railway preservation continues to develop and expand long after the sceptics thought it would run out of steam. The latest railway to approach operations is the Helston Railway, which has laid a quarter of a mile of track at Trevarno Gardens, Cornwall, and plans to reopen the railway to Truthall Halt and, ultimately, to the outskirts of Helston itself. Who'd have thought that when the railway closed in 1964?

Sixty-two years after the company was nationalised, there is still enough preserved to able to say that wherever you are in the company's former territory, you won't be far from a preservation centre of some sort – visit them, travel on the trains and spend money in their shops and cafes, because doing so helps secure the Great Western Railway for future generations. It is by far the best way of all to get a sense of what this remarkable company was about.

While the heritage railways have long understood and valued the Great Western Railway, it took the shock of privatisation for the name to reassert itself on the main line. When passenger operations were sold to the highest bidders in the mid 1990s, the long-distance express trains from Paddington were operated by a company called Great Western Trains and today, all services from Paddington (bar those to Heathrow Airport) and the vast majority through the West Country as far as Devon and Cornwall are run by its successor, First Great Western. (At privatisation, commuter and regional services were split up over Great Western territory between – take a deep breath – South Wales and West, Thames Trains, Chiltern Railways and Central Trains.)

The early years of privatisation weren't kind – accidents at Southall and Ladbroke Grove caused by drivers passing signals at danger, undermined confidence in railway safety. Provision of services was patchy too, with First Great Western coming under heavy and sustained fire for delays and cancellations. The situation has vastly improved, with regional and inter-city services in the West Country operated by First Great Western, and Chiltern continuing its highly competent stewardship over the former GWR lines from Birmingham Snow Hill and Moor Street, though that company runs into the former Great Central Railway terminus of London Marylebone. In the Midlands and Wales, the former GWR routes are by and large operated by London Midland and Arriva Trains Wales.

The move to integrate local and long-distance passenger services in the West Country led to the creation of the 'Greater Western' franchise, and when the Strategic Rail Authority (SRA) – the body then responsible for awarding franchises – opened bidding in June 2005 there was a shock in store. It asked bidders to present 'costed options' for the 'Night Riviera's withdrawal, arguing that the train was uneconomic to run, poorly used and, as people could fly instead, it should be axed. Rail industry contacts investigated whether the claimed loss of £1 million per year was true, and none could find any evidence to back up the SRA's assertion. Furthermore, personal experience suggested the train was often very busy – particularly when flights were cancelled due to bad weather at Newquay Airport.

In the weeks after the announcement, the Save Our Sleeper campaign was formed which I chaired with local rail activist Stuart Walker, who himself is now chairman of the project to restore part of the Helston branch line. Other local services were under threat too, so Stuart focussed his attention on fighting those cuts, leaving the majority of the Save Our Sleeper campaign to myself, ably assisted by the campaign's website designer Rory Hill (a student from Jersey studying in Falmouth), my then colleagues at *International Railway Journal* – and of course, the train's crew, who were busy rallying support from the start.

We talked to the local media, explaining that not only were the SRA's claims of the sleeper's economics unclear and quite probably inaccurate, but that the service itself was difficult to find information on and even for those who did, frustratingly difficult to book. In 2005, the 'Night Riviera' was to all intents and purposes a secret service for the vast majority of rail users, but the campaign helped change that. Even with the difficulties of booking and obtaining information about the train, however, businesses still depended on the connections and time savings it offered; people from the South-West and beyond still used it to see family and friends, and tourists still valued the fact that they could bypass the crowds and spend an extra day in the region.

Petitions started on the train by its crews, and online by Save Our Sleeper proved the point and soon attracted interest, helped by frequent updates on local radio and in the regional press, updating listeners and readers with progress. As the campaign gathered momentum, more and more people from all walks of life offered their support. The Mount Prospect Hotel in Penzance offered its facilities for public meetings; the poet Murray Lachlan Young reworked W.H. Auden's 'Night Mail' for BBC Radio 4's *Today* programme; former governor of the Bank of England, Lord Eddie George, weighed in with unimpeachable authority on the train's economic benefits; the explorer Robin Hanbury-Tenison worked his contacts among the Devon and Cornwall's great and good for all his worth, and the region's MPs lobbied for the train, which they all used regularly to get to and from Parliament.

Most importantly of all though, almost 8,000 people put their names to petitions and did whatever they could to show their support. Many travelled on the train in order to prove that it was well used and perhaps to take what might be their last journeys on it. More still wrote letters to MPs, newspapers and the railway itself and almost all told as many people as they could that this wonderful vital service was under threat. A delegation that included four of Cornwall's five MPs, Eddie George, Robin Hanbury-Tenison, the hotelier Olga Polizzi, two sleeper stewardesses Marion and Linda, time-served railwayman Tim Naylor and myself presented the petition to 10 Downing Street on a day which saw the campaign lead most of the local news in the South-West, and win precious national coverage too from a surprisingly sympathetic media.

The Eden Project's founder, Tim Smit, let us have the run of the place for a day to hold another public meeting in November 2005 and, in a show of transport integration that shamed the government's efforts, the local bus company Truronian offered free travel for people to Eden from St Austell station. The journalist Christian Wolmar waived his usual fee in order to visit Cornwall and host the meeting, bringing his own bow wave of publicity right when the final decision on the Great Western franchise was being prepared.

Barely six months after the campaign began, in December 2005 it was announced that the 'Night Riviera' would survive after all. Thanks to thousands of people contributing their time, energy and expertise, this much-loved service — the umbilical cord linking Cornwall with the outside world — was saved. At the time, we claimed Save Our Sleeper was the biggest rail campaign since the one that saved the Fort William sleeper in the 1990s. Certainly, it was one of the most concentrated and intense ever. Only later was I told by a highly placed rail industry contact just how high the stakes were: if Save Our Sleeper had failed, the way would have been clear for a whole swathe of rail service cuts across the South-West and beyond. As he said, if we couldn't win with the support we had, what chance would campaigns to save other important but less glamorous services stand?

Now, five years on, the 'Night Riviera' is busier than it has been in years and the real limitation now is the cost and difficulty of acquiring extra sleeping cars to cope with demand: far from making a loss, the train is now *profitable* in financial as well as social terms. First Great Western has upgraded the coaches, addressed the booking issues and promoted the service with the importance it deserves. The hope is that at the next franchise renewal there will be no question of cutting it again.

The legendary men of the Great Western – Brunel, Gooch, Saunders, Churchward, Inglis and Pole – would doubtless have been impressed by the affection in which the 'Night Riviera' is held, and probably by some of the technology deployed on the railways today too. None, however, would have approved of the profligacy of the railway system since 1948. They would never have countenanced the wastage of the modernisation plan, the constant reorganisation and political interference, or the insane duplication of management and monitoring functions of the privatised railway that adds so much to its cost. Neither, one suspects, would they have been impressed with the idea of the railway relying on external companies for its rolling stock. That wasn't the Great Western way.

It is impossible to escape the legacy of those great men when you take a train from Paddington. Today the station is in superb condition and in my view, retains an airiness and spaciousness unmatched anywhere in London. Bristol Temple Meads is still magnificent, the tunnels under the River Severn and Box Hill as dramatic as ever, and the Royal Albert Bridge at Saltash seems set to far outlast the upstart road bridge next to it. The importance of the London to Bristol section together with the structures alongside has been recognised with their application to designate them as a World Heritage Site; the 'Cornish Riviera' still departs Paddington, and its overnight counterpart the 'Night Riviera' is still the umbilical cord connecting Cornwall with the outside world, enabling people to get into London before breakfast for meetings, leisure or to travel still further. You can still catch a train from Paddington to Fishguard, and you can still enjoy the unique switchbacks on the Looe branch. In many ways, the railway today is recognisably that of the 1920s.

It would be wrong to suggest that the old Great Western routes are a timewarp, however. There are now overhead electric wires powering trains from Paddington to Heathrow Airport, which might just be extended all the way to Plymouth and even Penzance in years to come. The sleepers are concrete or steel and the trains run at up to 125mph yet the original route Brunel laid out from Bristol to London has needed very few improvements to allow these speeds; in fact, the only thing preventing much faster trains from London to Bristol is the signalling system, and that too might be improved towards the end of the decade. There is much to look forward to.

The Great Western Railway remains astoundingly popular amongst generations who never saw or travelled on its original incarnation. At the Great Western Society's main 175th anniversary celebrations on 1–9 May 2010, a queue formed at 09:30 that ran from the main entrance, down the steps into the connecting subway at Didcot Parkway station, all the way along that, out of the booking office and along the main road outside – and didn't diminish until lunchtime. Thousands and thousands of people, many of whom wouldn't even begin to consider themselves as railway enthusiasts, came to Didcot from all four corners of the country to pay tribute to the remarkable old company and the fruits of the efforts started by those four schoolboys. It was one of the most astonishing sights in railway preservation I have ever witnessed.

Despite the passage of time though, something of the Great Western's spirit still remains on the twenty-first century railway because if you go to Paddington late at night, something magical happens. Throughout the campaign to save the 'Night Riviera', many of us felt there was something intangible but important about the train that simply didn't exist anywhere else in the world. We couldn't put our fingers on it then, but spending eighteen months writing a book about the GWR has helped give it some sort of form. As Paddington calms down from the evening rush hour and breathes again, it's as if the ghosts of the men who shaped the Great Western Railway descend from the transepts of Brunel's great trainshed. That almost imperceptible background hum which has never quite disappeared from the railway can finally be deciphered as passengers wait to catch the 'Night Riviera' to Devon and Cornwall.

The 'Night Riviera' stands in Platform 1 just as it always did, with one of the four Class 57 diesel locomotives dedicated to its use (named, appropriately, after castles in Devon and Cornwall) thrumming at its head just before the quarter to midnight departure. When the stewards and stewardesses greet you with a friendly smile, then show you to your berth and take your breakfast order, and when they serve you a drink in the lounge car, it is uncannily close to that romantic vision of the Great Western Railway George Behrend conjured up so many years ago. It's amplified by watching from your bed as the 'Night Riviera' floats dreamily along the sea wall, bustles over the Devon Banks, and threads through Plymouth and over the Royal Albert Bridge into Cornwall. It is a train – if ever one can be said to have one – with heart and soul: the men and women who crew this much-loved service unconsciously maintain and uphold the Great Western's traditions and standards night in, night out. Their ethos, their demeanour, their pride in a job well done – the knowledge that their expertise and dedication is valued from the railway boardrooms of Paddington to the bedrooms of the Mk 3 sleeping coaches they crew – exemplify that indefinable and inde-fatigable Great Western spirit. Just like the Great Western Railway, the 'Night Riviera's' passengers trust the railway to deliver its promises, the railway trusts its staff to perform their duties with dedication and conscience, and the staff trust the company to treat them fairly. Charles Saunders would be proud to call them all his own.

Acknowledgements

As always there were numerous people who helped in the research and preparation of this book. First and foremost I must thank the railway historian and writer Nick Deacon who has assisted tirelessly with the massive research task this book has involved, been a sounding board throughout, and checked the copy again and again for inaccuracies and inconsistency.

I am indebted, on so many levels, to the Chairman of the Great Western Society, Richard Croucher, Frank Dumbleton and everyone else at Didcot who helped reveal their remarkable story and that of GWR preservation as a whole. On a slightly different aspect of preservation, Dave Fuszard and the men and women of the 6024 Preservation Society took time out to show me how hard it is to care for a 'King' on the main line – but the acceleration through Newton Abbot on the return journey of the 'Torbay Express' is the reward: their locomotive is like a finely tuned sports car, just as it should be.

Thanks also must go to First Great Western's excellent public affairs team; Elaine Arthurs of STEAM, Swindon; Andrew Fowler for his invaluable suggestions; Brian Stephenson for access to his wonderful photographic archive; Mike Wild of Hornby Magazine; Gary Boyd-Hope and Nick Brodrick of *Steam Railway*; and Tim Naylor for his in-depth knowledge of the railways of Devon and Cornwall.

My wife Jenny and my little daughter Emeline have been marvellous throughout the book's production, tolerating disruption and research material scattered all over the house with good humour and no little amusement.

Finally, I must thank my publisher at Aurum Press, Graham Coster, whose support and encouragement have been fundamental in producing this book, the third we have worked on together, and my editor, Helen

Williams, who has burnished the copy to a sheen worthy of the Great Western railway itself.

Inevitably it has been impossible to include every aspect of the GWR in this volume, or to go into as much detail as one might like, but if you have any comments about the book, please contact me via my website at www.andrewroden.com.

Further Reading

More books have been written about the Great Western Railway than any other railway, and possibly any other type of company at all, something the extensive literature search rather dauntingly confirmed. A full bibliography would take many pages to cover and still only scratch the surface of the available material, so here is a selection of titles and resources which I found especially important and which add further depth to this history.

The first books on any list for further reading about the GWR must be E.T. MacDermot's peerless and fantastically detailed two-volume *History of the Great Western Railway*. Originally published in 1927 and revised by C.R. Clinker in 1964 (Ian Allan Publishing), then followed by a third volume by O.S. Nock in 1967 (Ian Allan), they are not always easy reads and are not easy to find these days but are essential reading for any serious student of the GWR.

A more readable history of the period, *History of the Great Western Railway: 1923–1948,* was written by Peter Semmens from 1985 (George Allen & Unwin), offering a slightly different take to Nock's equivalent, while Alan S. Peck's *The Great Western at Swindon Works,* (Heathfield Railway Publications 2009 and previously published by Ian Allan) is a remarkable operational, engineering and above all social history of how the Great Western Railway transformed Swindon. All are well worth seeking out for more detail on their topics than there is space for here.

George Behrend's *Gone With Regret* (Jersey Artists, 1964) is an incomparably evocative and personal account of the GWR that is a vital companion to this volume – if you can find a copy because it seems terribly rare.

The Great Western Railway: 150 Glorious Years by Patrick Whitehouse and David St John Thomas (David & Charles 1985) and their follow-up volume *Great Days of the GWR* (David & Charles, 1991) offer a warm-hearted take on what made the Great Western great and shine a light on aspects of the railway there simply wasn't enough space to include. There are many accounts of footplate work on the GWR too but some which have proved particularly useful were Harold Gasson's *Firing Days, Footplate Days and Nostalgic Days* (OPC), Derek Brock's *Small Coal and Smoke Rings* (John Murray, 1983), Peter Johnson's *Through the Links at Crewe* (Xpress Publishing), and *Laira Fireman* by Philip E Rundle MBE (Irwell Press, 2009).

On matters of detail, *Brunel's Broad Gauge Railway*, Christopher Awdry (OPC, 1992), *Brunel – An Engineering Biography* (Adrian Vaughan, Ian Allan Publishing, 2006), *The Diaries of Sir Daniel Gooch* (Nonsuch Publishing, 2006), *The Grand Experiment* by Stuart Hylton (Ian Allan, 2007) and *Fire and Steam* (Christian Wolmar, Atlantic Books, 2007) are good sources for the nineteenth century. *Brunel: The Man Who Built The World* (Steven Brindle, Weidenfeld & Nicolson, 2005) and *The Great Western in South Devon* (Keith Beck & John Copsey, Wild Swan, 1990) are also particularly good sources.

On the technical front there must be hundreds of books but those which proved particularly useful for the more general overview in this book include *The GWR Stars, Castles & Kings* (O.S. Nock, David & Charles, 1980), *GWR Steam* (O.S. Nock, David & Charles, 1972), W.A. Tuplin's *Great Western Steam (George Allen & Unwin, 1958) and Great Western Saints and Sinners* (George Allen & Unwin, 1971), *Great Western 4-6-0's at Work* (Michael Rutherford, Promotional Reprint Company, 1995), *A History of the Great Western AEC Diesel Railcars* (Colin Judge, Noodle Books, 2008), *The Western's Hydraulics* (J.K. Lewis, Book Law, 1977), and *The Locomotive Exchanges* (Cecil J. Allen, Ian Allan, 1949). There are many, many more on just about every aspect of the Great Western's rolling stock fleet imaginable. One mustn't forget the structures either, and Adrian Vaughan's *A Pictorial Record of Great Western Architecture* (OPC, 1977) is complemented beautifully by Chris Leigh's *GWR Country Stations* (Ian Allan, 1981).

Just about all of Adrian Vaughan's books provide an entertaining and thought-provoking read, but in particular I enjoyed *Railwaymen, Politics & Money* (John Murray, 1997), *Signalman's Nightmare* (John Murray, 1987) and *Grime & Glor: Tales of the GWR 1892–1947* (John Murray, 1985).

The sheer range of railway periodicals has allowed a far greater range of coverage than might otherwise have been possible, and *Backtrack, British Railways Illustrated*, *Great Western Railway Journal*, *Heritage Railway, Steam Days, Steam Railway, Steam World, and The Railway Magazine* have all been referred to.

When it comes to online resources, there is much material on Wikipedia (www.wikipedia.org) but John Daniels' superb www.greatwestern.org.uk contains a wealth of detailed technical information about locomotives, as well as many more illustrations than there is space for in this book. It is well worth a visit.

Finally, for those seeking a glimpse of Swindon Works in its last days, the BBC's *Requiem for a Railway* television series is heartbreaking and poignant, and can now be viewed online at http://www.bbc.co.uk/wiltshire/content/articles/2008/05/21/requiem_for_a_railway_swindon_films_80s_feature.shtml. Again, all three programmes are well worth checking out.

Appendix

There are dozens of heritage railways and museums dedicated to preserving aspects of the Great Western Railway. One, the Helston Railway, is presently under construction, but others are well established and visiting any, some or even all of them helps further their sterling efforts. Details of regular main line trains that often use Great Western locomotives are also included. Details of opening times, operating days and fares can be found on their websites.

Birmingham
Tyseley Locomotive Works
http://www.tyseleylocoworks.co.uk/tlw_ods/index.html

Cornwall
Bodmin & Wenford Railway
www.bodminandwenfordrailway.co.uk
Helston Railway
www.helstonrailway.co.uk
Lappa Valley Railway
www.lappavalley.co.uk

Devon
Dartmouth Steam Railway & Riverboat Company
www.paignton-steamrailway.co.uk
Devon Railway Centre
www.devonrailwaycentre.co.uk
Plym Valley Railway
www.plymrail.co.uk

South Devon Railway
www.southdevonrailway.co.uk

Tiverton Museum of Mid Devon Life
http://www.tivertonmuseum.org.uk/

Gloucestershire

Coleford Great Western Railway Museum
www.colefordgwr.150m.com

Dean Forest Railway
www.deanforestrailway.co.uk

Gloucestershire and Warwickshire Railway
www.gwsr.com

London

Southall Railway Centre
www.gwrpg.co.uk

Oxon

Chinnor & Princes Risborough Railway
www.chinnorrailway.co.uk

Cholsey & Wallingford Railway
www.cholsey-wallingford-railway.com

Great Western Society – Didcot Railway Centre
www.didcotrailwaycentre.org.uk

Shropshire

Cambrian Heritage Railway
www.cambrianrailwayssociety.co.uk

Severn Valley Railway
www.svr.co.uk

Telford Steam Railway
www.telfordsteamrailway.co.uk

Somerset
East Somerset Railway
www.eastsomersetrailway.com
West Somerset Railway
www.west-somerset-railway.co.uk

Wiltshire
STEAM – The Museum of the Great Western Railway
www.swindon.gov.uk/Steam
Swindon and Cricklade Railway
www.swindon-cricklade-railway.org

Yorkshire
National Railway Museum, York
www.nrm.org.uk

Wales
Barry Island Railway
www.valeofglamorganrailway.co.uk
Corris Railway
www.corris.co.uk
Gwili Railway
www.gwili-railway.co.uk
Llangollen Railway
www.llangollen-railway.co.uk
Pontypool & Blaenavon Railway
http://www.pontypool-and-blaenavon.co.uk/
Welshpool & Llanfair Light Railway
www.wllr.org.uk
Vale of Rheidol Railway
www.rheidolrailway.co.uk

Main Line tours
While a number of tours operate through the year using GWR

locomotives, two operations run repeatedly through the year, offering steam-hauled trains to attractive destinations. They are the 'Torbay Express' from Bristol to Kingswear and return (www.torbayexpress.co.uk) and the 'Shakespeare Express' from Birmingham Snow Hill to Stratford-upon-Avon and return (www.vintagetrains.co.uk). In addition, Vintage Trains operates a range of less-frequent trains that may use GWR locomotives.

Index